K

GW00994516

SMALL BOAT ON THE LOWER RHINE

SMALL BOAT ON THE
LOWER RHINE

BY

ROGER PILKINGTON

Illustrated by David Knight

MACMILLAN
ST MARTIN'S PRESS

First published 1970 by
MACMILLAN AND CO LTD
London and Basingstoke
Associated companies in New York Toronto
Dublin Melbourne Johannesburg and Madras

Library of Congress catalog card no. 71–125603

SBN (boards) 333 11534 1

Printed in Great Britain by
ROBERT MACLEHOSE AND CO LTD
The University Press Glasgow

This volume is dedicated to all those who have travelled
aboard the *Thames Commodore* on the lower and middle
reaches of the Rhine: John, Cynthia and Semantha Silvester-
Horne; Hugh Pilkington, Brian Dodds, Fred and Lisa
Doerflinger, Mike and Pam Ashby, Richard Jaboor, Christine
Craig, Jan Pilkington-Miksa, Joanna Ide, and Bill Gardam;
and especially to the ship's mate, my wife Miriam.

                                    Far away
Rolls the swift Rhine beneath the mooned ray;
But to my listening ear and dreaming eye
Murmur the pines, the blue wave ripples by;
Through the deep Rheingau's vine-enamour'd vale
I see dark shapes careering down the gale: —
Or hear the Lurlei's moaning syren call, —
Or walk with song by Roland's shattered hall.
                                    Bulwer-Lytton

MAPS

The Hook of Holland to Mainz   *pages* x-xi
The River Lahn   94
The Rhine Gorge   168

A2

FOREWORD

FOUNDED in the melting of the last glaciation, extended by the Romans, improved by medieval engineers, enlarged by men of renaissance imagination and now mechanized with modern machinery, Europe's waterways provide a useful means of transport for coal and timber, gravel and grain and wine. But they also offer a magnificent network of trails for the waterborne explorer, a new dimension for any who are wondering whether it is really worth while becoming a third-party fatality pay-out on some hideous monoxide-shrouded motorway. These waters are the happy hunting ground of French family barges, Dutch privateers and immense German Europa-ships, and also of the *Thames Commodore*, a red-ensigned little ship of considerable determination and resourcefulness which has thrust her bow into most of the creeks and inland harbours from the Baltic to the Mediterranean shore.

If these waterways large and small are the arteries and veins of European trade, then certainly the aorta is the great River Rhine. To many the name of the Rhine evokes memories far removed from barges. Those surviving older men who recall November 1918 will think of it as the line beyond which the broken remnants of the German army were to remove themselves within a month after four years of bitter and senseless slaughter had at last come to a stop, a wholesale killing which now seems almost incredible in its pig-headed folly. Others will remember the Rhine as the demilitarised limit which Hitler crossed when he first decided to test the determination of France and Britain, and got away with it unmolested. To some the mere mention of the name evokes memories of the Nibelungen and the treasure hoard flung into the Rhine itself, or of Rhine-maidens golden-haired and Germanic, alluring but not always slim – for operatic singers are often somewhat full-busted, and it is of Wagner that the musician inevitably thinks when the Rhine is mentioned, although Schumann

xiii

had a more intimate connection with it. Did he not fling himself
into its waters?

Then there is that very special danger to mariners, the lovely
girl of the Lorelei who would sit upon the cliff top and comb her
gorgeous tresses to distract the helmsman and take his eye off the
rather tricky current which still demands his full attention where
the stream turns a sharp bend at the foot of her one-time perch. To
myself she has always been a symbol of the fact that, without
navigation and a certain degree of hazard added to the mists of
medieval romance which hang over the slopes of the gorge between
Bingen and Koblenz, the Rhine might be much as any other river.
In fact the Rhine is unique.

A woman (and I regret to say that she was a teacher) once told
me that she had been on a package trip to Boppard or some such
place, and she thought the river pleasant except that it was
'completely spoiled by all those horrid black barges'. I had to leave
the room for fear of doing her some injury, because for myself the
sheer liveness of the Rhine consists very largely in the pulsing and
throbbing of the ships which career down the fairway as little as a
boat's length apart – ships of Switzerland and France, Belgium and
the Netherlands, Poland and the D.D.R., Luxembourg and the
Bundesrepublik, and just occasionally one flying the flag of
Austria, Norway or Denmark, or (rarer still) the red duster on a
grimy coaster of Britain's merchant marine.

To many, the Rhine evokes only the famous defile below Bingen,
a half-day's steamer run past vineyard villages and below the ruins
of a score of ruined robber nests glowering down from their crags.
Yet that is only one section of the river. The lower reaches are
flanked by age-old Dutch towns where the bells of the carillon
towers float tinkling down through the often rather bleak air, as
they have done for centuries. The long stretch from Duisburg to
Düsseldorf is overhung with smoke, white and orange, black and
purple, and the night is aglow with the glare of coke-ovens and
refinery vents. Further upstream the same water has passed by
scenes of Roman elegance and washed the quayside close to the
shrine in which the three kings of the Nativity are said to be
contained. A few hours further ahead Beethoven's house lies

hidden behind the modern blocks of Bonn. Then comes Godesburg with its memories of a fateful meeting in 1938, and at Remagen the stumps of the bridge are still in the stream, the bridge which speeded the end of Germany's darkest age.

Caesar's Rhine bridge at Urmitz has gone, and so has that of Charlemagne's engineer Einhard at Mainz. Yet even in that great emperor's day the girls were already binding the vines on the shaly slopes, and where the water ran most swiftly a fishing boat would lie at anchor with a spread of nets, as it still does more than one thousand years later. Other scenes have changed. The French have built vast locks, though at the foot of one of them they have kept a tongue of land reserved as a sanctuary for warblers. The Swiss reaches of navigation pass close by Geigy and Sandoz and Ciba, those world-famous pharmaceutical giants, but a few hours further on toward its source the river ceases to bear ships and the Rhine, steely-grey and rippling over the shallows, belongs only to canoeists and waterfowl, and to the fish which revel in a fast-flowing river as yet unstained by the spoil of factory effluents.

That, then, is the variegated river which we are about to ascend. As for our faithful and efficient ship, she is the same stout *Thames Commodore* as before, built on the London River. She has two strong diesels, and on the Rhine she will certainly need them. She also has every reasonable comfort but very little chrome and ostentation, for she is a busy craft with no time to dally at a rally. Her crew is variable. I have run parts of the Rhine single-handed, but for most of the five hundred navigable miles my wife Miriam has been at her post as mate, steering much of the river.

As this book is the result of a number of voyages, so the crew must appear large indeed, for most of the ship's own friends accompany her for only a week or two. On the Rhine itself they have a comparatively easy time, for there are no hand-worked locks to be opened and closed, and not everyone aboard is necessarily allowed to steer in waters which flow fast and not always smoothly but which are invariably ploughed by a stream of heavy-laden ships such as would hardly feel the impact of a head-on collision with our own if the Lorelei or a water-sprite should send us off our precisely regulated course.

Strictly, this voyage should start at the Hook of Holland, 1,031 kilometres below the town bridge of Konstanz. But I have never entered the river from the sea, and that is why we shall take up the tale a little further inland, at km 1,006.3, where the Oude Maas or old course of the Meuse comes swinging in from Zeeland and the channels which have brought us from the Thames and Tower Bridge. Three long blasts and one short as laid down in the regulations, and the *Thames Commodore* cuts round the junction light to follow in the wake of a dozen big ocean-ships steaming up the fairway toward Rotterdam. We are on the Rhine, starting our long haul upstream toward the foothills of the Alps.

St Aubin, Jersey, 1970   ROGER PILKINGTON

I

*The Rhine in disguise – the Leiden emigrants – Grotius in
the Loevenstein – the waterway to Cleves – Brienen lock –
the fate of Johanna Sebus – the knight of the swan – Helyas
and Lohengrin – King Henry and Anne of Cleves*

THE point where the Rhine reaches the sea is extremely hard to
define. The only watercourse to issue through the Dutch
sands still bearing the name Rijn is in fact a rather miserable sort
of canal running from Leiden to end in an ordinary regulating
sluice. Above Leiden this same old Rhine, or Oude Rijn, is a
pleasant waterway of little shipyards and flowerpot manufactories,
of nursery gardens and butchers and bakers, a river which I have
navigated so many times that it is more familiar to me than some
of the reaches of the Thames, but it is as different as can be from
the Rhine of Wagner and Schumann, of Lorelei and Mouse
Tower. Indeed, if the Rijn flows at all it is not easy to say in which
direction, so I should perhaps add that by 'above Leiden' I mean
'further inland than Leiden', for it is a curious fact that everything
to do with rivers and the sea seems to be reversed in Holland.
Except on the mighty main arms of the Rhine itself – masquerading,

of course, under quite other names – the flow of current may be from mouth to source, the rivers may be lower than the sea, dry weather can bring floods and wet weather a drought. The Oude Rijn is no exception. It is as likely to flow eastwards as westwards.

Still further inland this stream becomes static, reed-bound, weed-clogged, a home for domestic ducks and a receptacle for garden rubbish, motor-tyres and the all too prevalent floating objects which indicate to the visitor that the Dutch are no more universally Roman Catholic in their outlook and habits than they were in the fearful closing decades of the sixteenth century, when they desperately fought themselves free for ever of the unspeakable cruelties of the Spanish Inquisition. In Leiden itself the last dog and cat had been eaten, the leaves and bark stripped from the trees to provide food, and the brave mayor stood up before the city hall and quelled the talk of surrender by offering to cut off one of his arms with his own sword to provide a meal for any who would rather give in than starve.

Long before it reaches Leiden this so-called river which once was indeed at least a part of the course of the proud Rhine itself becomes so turgid, torpid and soupy that navigation is impossible. I know this, because the mere fact that a lock-keeper said so was enough to make our original and obstinate old *Commodore* try to force a passage. We had at length to pole her round to get her out again, and then dismantle the cooling system to remove some of the bouillabaisse from her tubes.

But this is not the Rhine up which her successor is now going to take us. Our Rhine, whatever its local name, will be that splendid, fast-flowing river which rises as one of St Gotthard's twin nymphs (the other being the Rhône), washes one side of Liechtenstein, nips through a mile or two of Austria, pours into the Bodensee, cascades down the famous fall of Schaffhausen, and then becomes a busy artery of the trade of Switzerland, France, Germany and Holland before it reaches the North Sea. And even then it will be mainly the German Rhine of which I shall write – partly because I have touched on the Dutch reaches in other books, but more for the simple reason that below the Germany–Netherlands frontier the river is dull. Apart from its shipping, that is, for there is no place in the world quite like Rotterdam for sheer romance of ships of every kind.

And Rotterdam is a good starting point. Every summer, English and American visitors in hundreds will board the magnificent cruise-liners *Helvetia* and *Nederland* or their sisters and speed up the stream in ships which already look huge enough in the wide expanses of the docks but appear unbelievably large four hundred miles further inland. One morning when we were moored just above the bridge of Chalampé at the foot of the Vosges the *Nederland* came sweeping down from Switzerland, and if at that moment the steersman of the bridge-deck quickly took off his cap I am sure it was to prevent it from being knocked from his head by the concrete of the roadway above.

Rotterdam's miles of waterfront are lashed by the unceasing waves flung against it by the wash of tugs and ferry-boats, cargo-liners and Rhine pushers, and about once a year by the *Thames Commodore* herself. She likes to start the spring with a night at the hospitable yacht club 'de Maas', right at the centre of things and only a mile or two above the quay where the canal from Leiden and Delft reaches the tideway at the point where, three and a half centuries earlier, the English emigrants watched as their belongings were hoisted over the side of the horse-drawn canal boats on which they had travelled with their friends from Leiden, and were swung aboard the *Speedwell*. That night there was a party, with music and dance. Next morning there were tears as the faithful John Robinson, their pastor, knelt on the quayside to utter the farewell prayer over those who were sailing away under Elder Brewster. Nearly half the party were teenagers. Others, like Degory Priest the society hatter from London's smartest quarter, were newly married. He was only one of those who left his wife behind and sailed away to die in the first cruel winter of Plymouth Bay, Massachusetts.

The Pilgrim Fathers – yes, but they were not the puritanical greybeards of the history books. Pilgrims in search of freedom to worship, certainly. Fathers in the sense that from them was to spring most of the finer values which survive in the United States to this day. Puritans, definitely, in that they liked their Bible *pure* and uncluttered by vestments and casuistry. But narrow, dull, a collection of wet blankets they never were. After a year they still had some gin left, and their casks of beer did good service for a while in keeping the terrible scurvy at bay.

Rotterdam was all but destroyed in one vicious air raid of the Second World War. A memorial on the waterfront shows a young man trying to hold up the heavens which are collapsing upon him. Most of the older buildings have vanished, blown apart by bombs or pulled down by town planners, but the new city has many delights. There is the Euromast with its view over the quay where the coastal ships of the Scandinavian trade lie waiting for a berth. Further back is the Lijnbaan, one of Europe's first shopping centres for pedestrians only, its birches hung with baskets of geraniums and the bright parrots sitting on perches and indulging in a few pert remarks in Dutch for the benefit of the children who come to stare at them – for there is little a parrot cannot do if it puts its mind to it. But to the boatman Rotterdam is first and foremost the busiest port in the world, a place of floating grain-elevators, of giant cranes, of dredgers creaking and of the big ships hooting in the dark as they signal to the tugs which are swinging them to berth.

'There is a cheerfulness about the operations of commerce – a life – a bustle – an action which always exhilarates the spirits at first glance. Afterwards they fatigue us; we get too soon behind the scenes and find the base and troublous passions which move the puppets and conduct the drama.' That was what the author of *Pelham* had to say about Rotterdam; and in case he was right we had better flick off the lines and shoot out between the pierheads to move on upstream.

Aboard a well-found ship like the *Thames Commodore* one does not so easily become obsessed with the base and troublous passions which, for all I know, may indeed be found in the shipyards and unloading docks along the flat reaches of the Dutch River Rhine. Or, more correctly, along the Nieuwe Maas, the Noord, the Merwede and the Waal, these being the successive names under which the river masquerades as we head up for Germany two easy days' cruising away. The scenery is dull, the towns above Dordrecht somewhat uninteresting, and yet the stream has a curious fascina-

tion which is not entirely derived from the enormous quantity of
shipping racing down the channel or hugging the inside of each
long slow bend on its patient haul to the frontier. The strange lure
comes in part from the shore, the line of which is broken by the
groynes of Belgian and Norwegian basalt, smoothly rounded ribs
which help to induce the silt to deposit itself at the edges of the
river but also break the shore itself into a series of hundreds of
little bays or backwaters in many of which something is going on.
It may be children bathing, a dog barking at the wash lapping on
the stones, or perhaps an eel boat lying in a position which
experience has shown to be a favourite with the long, living
delicatessen, bound for the Sargasso Sea. There may be a beach
where the black and white Frisians stand knee-deep as though
wondering whether the whales had hit on something good when
they decided to return from the land to the water, or perhaps a
Dutch family has camped there with everything spread out for a
picnic. Through the glasses one can even see what they are eating,
but the glance must only be a quick one or the Rhine (Merwede,
Waal, and so forth) will have twisted our stem to one side and put
us on a course which might cause concern to the coaster galloping
down river toward us.

In the days of the Grand Tour by water, every traveller spent a
night at Gorinchem (or Gorkum). Once we did the same, for we
arrived on a Saturday and found ourselves in an area where the
canal authority was sabbatarian enough to keep all the locks closed
through the weekend. We saw more than enough of Gorkum, and
I cannot recall that there was anything about the place worth
setting down, but at least we cannot move upstream without
noticing on the opposite shore the neat hats on the turrets of an
extremely mellowed and faded brick castle which from the river is
only visible down to the waist because it actually stands in a moat
behind the bank. On this occasion we are not thinking so much of
the protestant preachers once imprisoned there as of the great
Hugo Grotius, the man who perhaps made our own voyage
possible by declaring that basic principle of the freedom of the
seas, and who first enunciated the doctrine which was eventually
to become the charter of the Rhine itself. It was in 1650 that this

founder of international law declared in his *De Jure Belli ac Pacis* that navigation of rivers as well as of the sea was free for ships of all nations, and over the centuries it was the Rhine above all other rivers for which this principle was to be vital, if only because of the number of states which bordered upon it.

Grotius was imprisoned in the Loevenstein, but the fact that he was known to be a scholar made his captors soften enough to allow him to be constantly supplied with books. This gave his devoted wife the chance to rescue him. She was smuggled into the castle in a crate of books, changed clothes with him and took her husband's

6

erway

place while he was similarly conveyed out of the Loevenstein. It is pleasant to know that her enterprise brought her no punishment but only praise for her loyalty to her Hugo.

An easy morning to Zalt-bommel, and a run of a few more hours after lunch has brought us already to Tiel, a place of shippers and fishers with a pleasant carillon tinkling out above the light mist of evening. Next morning we shall be in Nijmegen, having seen little but tow-trains, cows, gravel-pits and small brick-and-tile works strewn along the banks. Nijmegen sits on a hill, an improbable thing for a Dutch town to do. It has a bleak and rather dirty

harbour in which aged bargemen live on aged boats, talking to
their aged wives and dogs, and waiting for a quiet death. Up on the
hill the town swarms with people shopping in the familiar large
stores – C and A, V and D, P and C. We have been to Nijmegen
before, for it has the only reasonable harbour for some distance,
but it is not a place of much interest. Its memory is connected
mainly with the desperate and ill-conceived British attempt to
seize Batavia (the area between the Waal and Lek branches of the
Rhine). Arnhem with its bridge over the Lek became a tragic
name to many a British family, and that town as well as Nijmegen
was wrecked in the fury of the fighting. Both are curiously proud
of their role, and Nijmegen even has its own particular Queen-
Elizabeth-slept-here type of speciality. I have never inquired where
one may eat in Nijmegen without being referred to one particular
hotel.

'You must go there. General Montgomery stayed there, you see.'
I have never been in it yet.

On a more recent voyage my wife and I were alone and we
decided to shop, eat our lunch, and move upstream for another
hour or two before stopping for the night. Several times on our
way down the Rhine we had noticed on the left bank just below the
frontier an intriguing waterway curving away between fields and
copses of willow, but we had never had time to explore it. The
channel we knew to be the Spoy Canal which led to Cleves (Kleve),
and we let the *Thames Commodore* sidle out of the current in the
Bijlandsche Kanaal (which is what the Rhine is called at this
point) and steer toward the city.

Apart from a couple of thoughtful anglers standing up to their
ankles at the confluence, the Spoy Canal was at first deserted. A
fishing punt lay empty, floating dreamily between two stakes by
the willows, and on our starboard hand a high floodbank was
crossed every hundred yards or so by a cattle fence which climbed
from the water to disappear over the top and drop down to a ditch.
After a while we came upon two brown-and-white calves taking a
drink. Whether they were Dutch or German I do not know, for
just beyond them was a small landing stage with a notice asking
mariners to halt and present themselves to the customs of the

Bundesrepublik. On a post there was even a bell-push for service, but it seemed to be disconnected. We drew alongside in the pleasant sunshine of this July afternoon and made fast. Then climbing over the bank we crossed a stile and set off up a track between the fields.

The path led to a farm, and beside it stood a green wooden hut such as customs men inhabit. We knocked and entered. A young man in the green of the Bundesrepublik was sitting back in an armchair, his feet on the desk. He was absorbed in a novel and I had an uneasy feeling that we had come in at a moment of impending crisis for the heroine.

The officer sat up, looked us up and down as though we had emerged from a flying saucer.

'Where have you come from?'

'A ship. On the canal.'

'A ship! But no ship is expected.'

I explained that we had a way of being unexpected. We were English I added, for experience over the years had taught me that to a foreigner this fact was enough to account for the most extraordinary eccentricities and was also taken as a sign that one was probably mad but not dangerously so.

'*Ach so!*' English – that accounted for our shorts, too. The officer stood up and said he could not see a ship. No doubt it was very small.

Yes, a small boat by Rhine standards, I said. All the same, it had made the voyage from London with the skipper and mate who now stood before him, and if he were to look out of the window and across the fields he might just see a small object protruding beyond the top of the bank. That was the tip of our mast. If he wished, he might come aboard.

The officer was obviously tempted, torn between setting foot upon the ship of the eccentrics and the more immediate matter of discovering what was to happen to the heroine. Literature won, and declining even to stamp our passports he waved us on our way, adding that we need not bother to come up to the hut again on our return down the canal.

The Cleves Navigation starts as an old arm of the Rhine, a

section of river cut off when the course was improved and straightened. It curves this way and that as though not absolutely certain that it is on the right course for the city, and after a while the banks open out to meadows gay with such summer flowers as the cows have not grazed to the ground. As it happened to be a Saturday afternoon when we passed that way there were families encamped along the shore, grandparents snoozing in the sun and youngsters splashing out into the shallows to scream with delight as our wash ran in past the channel markers and broke upon their legs. It was a happy, rural scene, and the cows and peewits and coots seemed to enjoy the sight of a strange ship as much as the children. So did the passengers upon the little cable-ferry for which we dutifully blew off a warning – the Dückenward–Schneckenschanz ferry, our map told us, and it was hard to believe that a crossing with such a name could exist outside a fairy tale.

Further ahead we came to a broad sheet of water where the old arm of the Rhine was dammed off at its inner end. Round to the right was the entrance to a lock, beyond which an extremely narrow and rather Dutch canal cut ran straight as an arrow into Cleves, some three miles ahead. We could have passed through, but as the lock was to be closed on the following day we should not have been able to return, so we elected to drop the anchor in the broad and stay there. At least that was the reason we gave ourselves, but I think that both of us knew that quite by chance we had come upon one of those moorings which insists that one must stay there.

I cannot really say why the open water at the foot of Brienen lock should be so lovely a place, for the catalogue of exhibits would not run to much more than a sheet of still and embanked water mirroring the reddening glow of evening, a few cows on the flood bank, a pontoon beside which float the small craft of a local club, a dusting of farms and cottages along the cut behind the lockhouse, and a tight clump of trees on the inner dike. Indeed, few people have ever heard of the place, and outside the Spoy Canal I never met a German yachtsman or inland navigator who could even guess where Brienen lock was situated. Yet it has an irresistible peace about it, and it is one of those places where the real world of bustle and activity seems to be an illusion, or at least as far away as the moon. We sat on deck, then bathed again and again in the clear warm water before rowing ashore in the last of the daylight in the hope of finding something to eat, only to discover what must be the only inn in Germany which could not provide so much as a sausage.

The inn behind the lock was for some reason the choice of firemen. Apart from ourselves every customer who came in was a fireman in uniform, and they were as surprised to see us as we were to see them. On the wall behind the bar was a monument plaque very much like a tombstone, with an inscription in fine seriffed letters which began with the words *Hic fuit domus*. . . . One of the firemen explained to me that this was a strange language which had apparently been spoken by the local people. It might be Celtic, he suggested. It had defeated all attempts at understanding until some great academician of Cleves (and here he moved his hands in arcs to indicate the vast size of the brain of the man of learning) had deciphered it and composed the translation printed below the stone.

The stone had once stood in another house, now vanished, which had been presented to the widowed mother of a girl to whom a monument still stands upon the inner dike, not far from the lock. There upon the bank is a hedge surrounding what appears to be a sacred grove, the kind of place in which long ago birds and beasts and humans would have been hanged in bunches of seven to delight Freyr. However, the grove is not very ancient, and when at the following dawn I rowed over and climbed the gate to inspect its central monument I found the column to have an inscription in French, because it was first composed at the time when Napoleon had extended his empire over Brienen. A later translation had been added on the reverse side in prickly German gothic lettering.

It was a sad story that the inscriptions told, of how once a girl had lived in the house on that spot, a brave teenager named Johanna Sebus. She had been only seventeen years old when, in the year 1809, the Rhine rose in one of its periodic floods. Close by the old lock at Brienen the bank slipped, and the water streamed over the land to carry away cattle and byres, houses and families. Johanna first plunged in to swim through the water and bring her own mother to safety. Then she saw a woman with her children in imminent danger of being swept away by the torrent, and as they screamed for help she made to dive into the flood once again. The Deichgraf, a sort of local commander in the battle against the floods, tried to stop her.

'No, Hännchen. It is much too dangerous.'

'When it is a matter of saving life, then one has got to take risks,' the girl answered. And so she plunged in, but the bank broke beneath her and she was not seen again until a sheep-dog dug up her body three months afterwards.

The French commissar gallantly had the monument erected to the memory of this brave girl, and her action so caught the public imagination that Goethe wrote a poem about her – admittedly not one of his best.

The flood of 1809 was caused by a very severe winter. The snow lay deep, the streams and marshes were frozen solid. So also was the Rhine, but when the thaw began the massive blocks of ice ground and pounded at the dikes and broke them. Even in Cleves, which stands on a rise, many of the houses were under water to the first floor, whereas in the low-lying land nearer the river the farms were covered to their roofs, the families perched on the ridge until the structure finally collapsed.

Such disasters were rare. Yet according to local tales there was another hazard to add to that of a severe winter, for along the lower Rhine floods were also sometimes caused by the giants. Usually good natured, whenever a bank was in danger of slipping these oversized individuals would come striding along in their punt-sized wooden clogs and trample the clay firm, but if anyone was foolish enough to laugh at them or play tricks upon them then they would go off and shovel a sack full of sand, to tip it in the Rhine and dam the entire river. Then the water would rise and overflow the banks, and whole hamlets might be washed away.

Looking down from the bank and along the course up which we had come I suddenly realised again that the peaceful water had once been a dangerous and capricious stream. And might it not have been just there, at the nearest point of the original bank to the city of Cleves, that there once came into view the mysterious craft propelled not by two hundred diesel horses but by a single swan which held the tow-line round its neck? It came, as Wagner reminds us, in answer to the urgent call for help which the beautiful young Widow Elsa gave by raising to her lips the rosary from which dangled a tiny bell of silver, and in its stern sat a golden-haired and blue-eyed young man in shining silver armour, a rescuer as striking and unusual in his own appearance as in his original method of avian-powered water transport.

In his chronicle written about 1500, Gerd von Schuren describes the stranger as standing upright in the little craft and holding a golden sword in his right hand. A hunting-horn hung from his belt and upon his finger a ring of great value sparkled in the light. His shield was red and bore a silver heart-shaped device with eight golden sceptres and white lilies, bunched together with a jewelled golden clasp. I am not certain what the College of Heralds would have made of such an emblem, but at least we have it on good authority that the young man was none other than the knight Lohengrin, guardian of the Holy Grail. Or was he? For already the tale is becoming confused, and there seems no doubt that the tale of the swan-hauled knight was originally located upon Nijmegen; or perhaps it began in earliest medieval times without any precise location. However, by the eleventh century it was Lohengrin wooing Elsa at Nijmegen and some little while later Beatrix being courted by Helyas at Cleves, to which castle he brought his own coat of arms.

Elsa (or should it not be Beatrix?) was Duchess of Cleves, and a less operatic version of the tale presents her not as a widow but as the heiress of her father Count Dietrich of Teisterbart, a noble and worthy lord in Carolingian times. His sons had all been slain in one campaign or another and that was how it had come about that when the old count died his daughter was richly endowed with lands and property which included the city of Cleves. But it matters little which account we accept, for the point is that Beatrix was very rich and she was also very beautiful, so it was only natural that when her adored husband (or father) died, one of his vassals – the wicked, covetous, dark-haired and brown-eyed Telramund – claimed the duchy of Cleves for himself, ingeniously pointing out to Beatrix that the only way of remaining duchess would be to marry him. And being a very tough young man he openly declared that he would fight in single combat any knight who wished to take up the challenge on her behalf.

In vain did Beatrix (or was it Elsa?) appeal to those within her realm. None was courageous enough to risk being cleft to the navel by Telramund's mighty sword, and so the day came when the whole population of Cleves, some of whom had the decency at least to weep, gathered before the castle to watch her led off as an unwilling bride. Some hundreds of knights were present, but in the days of chivalry it was not considered chivalrous to rise in a mass and chop down even the most atrocious bully.

So Telramund came out, defiantly repeating his challenge three times over. Nobody stirred, except for a few women who wailed bitterly. It was then that Elsa remembered that on her rosary there hung the magic bell which could be heard to the ends of the earth when danger threatened, and she had no sooner tinkled it than the swan-drawn craft appeared. The hero landed, perhaps near the jetty of the Cleves sailing-club, and, dismissing the swan (which sailed gracefully away, towing the empty boat behind it), he took up the villain's challenge.

Fierce and long was the fight before Telramund fell, run through by Lohengrin's sword. The people cheered, the knights rattled in their armour. Here was a fine young fellow indeed, they agreed. As for Elsa, she knelt before her deliverer, but he raised her up and asked her if she would marry him. It would have been unchivalrous and against nature for her to refuse.

Soon the pair were passionately in love, and only one little cloud lay on their horizon – the fact that Elsa had to promise never to ask her deliverer who he was, whence he came, or how he had learned such an unusual method of navigation. All went well until their family of three sons reached adolescence – for even in medieval and legendary days children sooner or later began to be worried by those difficult childhood problems of the where-did-I-come-from-Mummy kind. Alas, their unfortunate mother had always to parry their inquiries, being unable to explain their father's antecedents or why it was that she herself had always to refer to him as 'You, dear', or 'Darling', or 'the Duke your father'.

Gradually the sons grew up, and all three became counts. No doubt they ruled their domains justly, but as they were unable to say who their father was gossip began to spread. Somewhat sensitive about being considered bastards – even if quite pleasant bastards – the young men demanded of their mother that she should tell them the secret. She did not do so, but in turn she asked Lohengrin whether he would not wish to explain to his sons their strange and noble origin.

Lohengrin made no reply, but after a last long kiss on the lips of his beloved Beatrix he rose from his bed, put on his armour, and leaving the Schwanenburg's portal he strode sorrowfully down to the river bank and blew on his silver horn. Fearful and silent the people watched as once again the swan came gliding round the bend, the boat trailing astern. Lohengrin (or Helyas) gave his eldest son the mighty sword which had slain Telramund. To the second he presented his shield and to the youngest his silver horn. Then he blessed them and stepped aboard. He never looked back as the swan turned and began to draw him away down the river until he had passed out of sight.

Thus Lohengrin returned to the Graalsburg, to continue his faithful watch over the Holy Grail. As for the sons, they ruled their lands in contentment, now that their illustrious parentage could be revealed, and they became the ancestors of many noble and battle-hardened knights of the Rhineland. The stately swan vanished, except from the Cleves weather-vane and the coats of arms of many a noble, until Wagner's youthful and schizophrenic patron, Ludwig II of Bavaria, tried out swan-powered navigation for himself at his castle of Neuschwanstein in Bavaria and (if I remember aright) got into trouble with his family when the water came through the ceiling of one of the better bedrooms.

Yet so great was the sorrow of the knight's true love and spouse that even now Beatrix–Elsa of Brabant haunts the rooms of the Schwanenburg, converted though they may be into the local government offices and museum. At least, that is what is said, although on our way up the winding staircase of the tower we met no white lady but a pair of English teachers who had strayed in there by a mistake.

For, on a second visit, we actually reached the city itself. It was some months later that we were returning from the Mediterranean to Holland, and having a day in hand we once again turned into the Spoy, walked up through the cows to declare ourselves to the German officer at his post, and made our way up the old river arm towards the clump of trees which marked the grave of Johanna Sebus, set on the dike. It was a morning in late September, and the reach reflected the glow of the autumn sky as though we were sailing into a Turner canvas. An aged fisherman was moving over the water in a boxy sort of boat of his own making, pulling up the lines which were attached to little pieces of floating wood. Far to the left we could hear the ceaseless throbbing of the ships approaching the Lobith customs roadstead, and every now and then a succession of hoots as a vessel signalled to a fuel boat or chandler, clearance agent or customs cutter. Their waterway was busy enough, but ours was deserted.

This time Brienen lock was open, and having paid a modest due we locked up to the higher level of the Spoy Canal which appeared beyond the gates as a straight and narrow line of water aiming directly for the city of Cleves, a mere twenty minutes distant. To our surprise an empty 600-ton barge was bearing down for the lock, and when we had turned the slight bend just before the town itself we were even more astonished to find the *Thames Commodore* entering a respectable port with warehouses and silos, and a steam crane busily chuffing away to unload one of the five large ships lined along the quays. Margarine oil by tanker seemed to be one of the commonest imports to Cleves, and a pipe-line led to a big factory which worked night and day to keep up the flow of packets to the shops of the Bundesrepublik.

Cleves was almost annihilated during the Second World War. It has been rebuilt in good market-town style, and is still crowned by the splendid mass of the Schwanenburg which towers so high above the houses and market that from its upper windows one can see far across the plain to the Rhine. And it is impossible to look down into the mellowed courtyard without thinking not just of Beatrix but of Anna, daughter of the Duke of Cleves, a young girl destined to become the victim of power politics.

King Henry of England had decided to take as his fourth wife the sixteen-year-old Christine of Denmark, a lovely girl who even at that early age was already a widow. She happened also to be a niece of the Emperor Charles V, so the marriage would have been a wise one diplomatically, at least from Henry's point of view. But the Pope, still furious over the treatment of Katherine of Aragon, neatly stopped the king's intended fourth marriage by excommunicating the bridegroom, who therefore had no choice but to turn to the protestant stable instead. Anna was eligible; she had money, and her brother-in-law was the powerful Duke of Saxony. Chancellor Cromwell made up his mind to induce Henry to marry her.

Somehow the news had gone about that Anna was not in the top class of European beauties, so King Henry commissioned Hans Holbein to go over and paint her portrait (which is now in the Louvre), and it seems probable that the artist at least did his best with a somewhat unpromising subject. Certainly the king was prepared to go forward, and he must have been relieved when a message was at last received from Calais to say that Anna and her retinue were there, awaiting better weather for the crossing. The letter was written by the Earl of Southampton, who went on to describe her excellent presence and exemplary table manners, and finished by praising her outstanding beauty which, he said, was every bit as great as it was reputed to be.

Whether Southampton was trying to court favour or was merely myopic in vision may never be known, but when Henry advanced to meet his bride upon her arrival at Greenwich he received something of a shock. Having told Cromwell what he thought about being saddled with a Flemish mare who could speak no word of either English or French, the monarch at once set about planning his freedom. It was not too difficult to assemble nineteen bishops and nearly two hundred other clergy who could be induced to sign the divorce order. As for Anna, she became the king's 'adopted sister', and lived her life under such comfortable conditions as would not directly antagonise her important protestant connections abroad.

II

St Victor of Xanten – the young Siegfried – Wesel –
Duisburg, the world's largest inland port – metallurgy and
gnomes – Kremer and the charts – the Stinnes empire – the
first Rhine lighthouse – Neander and his valley – Düsseldorf
– the Landgrave's horses – the bargemaster's adventure

EARLY in the morning the *Thames Commodore* hauled up her
anchor below Brienen lock, cut back in Lohengrin's wake,
turned the point of the confluence, crossed into Holland, and a few
minutes later was chugging past the waterfront of Lobith to dodge
between the customs cutters, chandlery ships, fuel boats and
floating butchers and bakers which twisted in and out of the
scores of Rhine ships that had dropped anchor in the customs
reach. Considering that there once were more than sixty customs
posts along the course of the Rhine one may be thankful that there
are now only three, yet one who is as ignorant of economics as
myself inevitably wonders whether there is any reason which
prevents these stations from being closed except perhaps the
difficulty of sacking the officials. Germany, France and the
Benelux are all Common Marketeers; why then was it necessary
to stop every ship on the Rhine and issue forms on which the
exasperated skippers had to enter such ridiculous items as the
number of boxes of matches on board their ships? However
speedy the clearance – and it is not always rapid, for the offices
close down at night – it seems pointless. Yet every load of gravel,
grain, cement and timber, fuel oil and bricks has to be certified,
checked, stamped and sealed. Even the *Thames Commodore* has to
declare the quantity of cocoa carried and state how many horses are
hidden in her engines, each time she passes this frontier on the
Rhine. Twelve years earlier her predecessor had even been asked
at a customs post on the Weser to declare how many undetected
stowaways there were on board.

So many ships plough the Rhine that the two neighbour

countries have at least established joint customs offices at Lobith
to clear the downcomers and at Emmerich to cope with the up-
runners. And Emmerich is a pleasant place, a town with a waterfront of cafés and skipper pubs, of chandlers and agents, average
adjusters and chart suppliers. The air resounds to hoots and toots
and the sound of heavy motors throbbing, and along the promenade
there sit or walk such very old or very young people as like to come
to Emmerich for no other reason than to watch the ships.

Throughout the centuries travellers by water have stopped at
Emmerich. It may have been to clear the customs, or to change
ships and (in the old days) tow-horses. Or just because of weather
which made further voyaging difficult or dangerous.

'I stopped at Emmerich and spent three pence on a good meal,'
wrote Albrecht Dürer, whose diary was remarkably commonplace
and domestic. 'I also drew there a goldsmith's apprentice, Peter
Federmacher from Antwerp, and did a woman's portrait. The
reason for our stopping was a great storm wind. I further spent
five pence and changed one guilder for food. I also drew the
landlord.'

There is a pleasant tale to the effect that Dürer was once up a
ladder, sketching on the wall of a church the outline of a mural
which his patron the Emperor Maximilian wished him to execute.
As he reached over to one side the ladder began to slip, and
quickly Maximilian ordered one of his attending nobles to go and
hold it fast. The courtier hesitated to undertake such a common
task, so Maximilian brushed him aside and himself stood holding
the ladder.

'Idiot!' he exclaimed. 'Can you not see that art is of much
greater worth than noble birth? You fool – I can any day raise a
hundred simple peasants to ranks of knighthood and nobility, but
where among you is there a single noble that I can make into such
an artist as this Albrecht Dürer, whom you have grudged even the
simplest service?'

If Emmerich has long been used to international travellers, it
has a special and long-standing connection with England in that
the church which stands just behind the Rhine wall is believed to
have been founded about the year 700 by Willibrord, the same

English missionary who established the great abbey of Echternach in Luxembourg. Nowadays the town is one of manufacture rather than of monks, but first and foremost it is the scene of the Rhine customs clearance. Every minute of the day another Rhine ship arrives, and with a rattle of heavy chain in the hawse-pipe an anchor goes down to grip the bed of the stream. Ships will continue to arrive throughout the night, and as none are cleared until early in the morning the dawn at Emmerich comes up over an armada which extends for a mile or more, the hundreds of thousands of tons of ships and cargo miraculously held firmly in the considerable flow of the stream.

Swinging into the harbour at the edge of the town we cleared ourselves with the smart patrol boat of the water police and then with an almost equally spotless one of the customs men before setting out across the park to acquire the fuel-receipt book which would allow us to tank duty-free throughout our voyaging in the waters of the Bundesrepublik.

As advised by the police we called at the office of a clearing agent. 'You need a *Bezugsscheinheftchen*? But certainly.' The agent turned to his cupboard and found the blue triplicate pad we needed. Then he dictated the details to his secretary. 'Ship *Thames Commodore*. Home port London. Coming from Holland. Two persons aboard. Two motors, diesel, Perkins – Pairkeens, ja?'

'Correct,' I said. 'But how. . . .' For up till then I had not so much as mentioned the ship.

The agent smiled. 'I saw you pass,' he said briefly. 'I thought you might come in.' He picked up his telescope and looked out again across the room and over the promenade where visitors were walking their dogs between the rose-beds. 'The *Wilma Two* is coming,' he said to the girl at the typewriter. 'Are the papers ready?'

We had to have our forms entered at the customs house, and there also we found that the officer had our names and ship and port typed on a form even before we entered the office. Every man in Emmerich seemed to have a telescope or binoculars within reach, and we realised that it would not be easy for any skipper to slip through the throng of ships without stopping. More than that, within minutes of a young man of Emmerich putting his arm round the waist of a girl, the news must be known from one end of the town to the other.

Somewhere upstream of Emmerich there once stood a church which served the farms far and near; but there came a time when the younger generation were sick and tired of the ways of their parents and decided to throw out the tiresome conventions of the establishment. All this long-faced piety and church-going, what was the point of it all? I suspect that if marijuana had then been known these young people would have sat on the ground smoking it, occasionally taking time off to smash up a university; but the era I am telling of was pre-college and early medieval.

The priest was naturally concerned about this new paganism spreading over the young, and eventually decided that the time had come to be outspoken. One Sunday he mounted the pulpit and delivered to his dwindled congregation a stern warning against such foolish ways. The message was aimed at the young and with-it set of whom hardly any were present, but the few who were there were stung by his words. They rushed out to summon the rest, who flocked into the church and began to barrack and jeer.

'I have warned you,' the old man shouted above the din. 'Judgement is nigh!' They were his last words, for a well aimed cobble-stone struck him on the temple and felled him. Dragged outside, he soon expired.

Not that his hearers were particularly sorry. There was now no Jeremiah to prophesy their doom, so the youngsters sent out for crates of beer and a barrel of wine and settled down to a party. The church rocked to the sounds of revelry, but if the reader expects to hear that they started to swing the bells and brought the whole structure about their heads he will be disappointed. They were too congenially occupied to consider ringing the bells at all, and they were still carousing when the thunderstorm broke overhead, a flash of lightning struck the tower, the earth opened, and the church vanished into the cleft. Over the place a deep, dark pond appeared, which has been there ever since. Some say that on Christmas Eve one may even hear the faint tolling of the church bells from deep down below its surface.

The lower German reaches of the Rhine are no different from the Dutch, and the only noticeable change at the frontier is that the tugs haul down the red flag with the white square and replace it by the German equivalent – a yellow barrel with black and white bands at either end. Scenically the landscape is as flat as before, with only once in a couple of hours some small town such as Rees perched nervously at the edge of the stream, well protected by massive bastions from the possible onslaught of the river in the early spring. More often the plain is scarred and cut away with gravel pits, and only in the distance can one see the tips of churches reaching skywards, towers such as the twins of the cathedral of Xanten away in the haze to starboard; Xanten, or Ad Sanctos as once it was, for there the great revolt of the Theban legion began, at the time of the Julian persecution. Victor – now St Victor – was the name of their officer who refused to bow down and worship the image of the Caesar, and who with his men was martyred in the amphitheatre of which the remains are still to be found. But the revolt was not quelled. Quickly the news spread, and the contingent under Thyrsus which was stationed in Trier followed the example of their fellows in Colonia Trajana (as Xanten then was called). For the Theban legion, oddly enough, was composed almost entirely of Christians, and it was on them that the fury of the Roman governors fell. For several days the blood flowed, and if the water of the Moselle is said to have been tinted scarlet for more than twenty miles by the blood of the Christian soldiers and civilians massacred at Trier, the Rhine down to Embrica (Emmerich) was no doubt only spared a similar colouration by virtue of the fact that Colonia Trajana was not situated so squarely upon the river.

St Victor was to become one of the great heroes of that age of German history where truth and legend blend. Helena, the indefatigable relic-collecting mother of Constantine the Great, attempted to recover his bones and may indeed have done so, but it seems more probable that the authentic remains (for Helena would buy anything offered to her) were those dug up in the twentieth century beneath the foundations of no less than eight successive churches built over the site.

If Victor is historical, Xanten's other and better-known hero is more a product of German romanticism. Siegmund the king and Sieglinde the queen lived at Xanten, and if they had a special appeal to us this was for the accidental reason that the old *Commodore*'s sailing dinghy was a clinker-built craft with the name *Sieglinde* carved on her transom. Through this connection with his mother we had a link of a kind with that brawny young man Siegfried, who was very modern and twentieth-century in one respect – the fact that already by the age of thirteen he was thoroughly bored by his home, fed up with his parents, and determined to have done with the establishment and to experience the world for himself instead of being told what was what. As an early adolescent he was of course more interested in adventure than anything else. Sex in the lovely and operatically massive form of Brunhilde the brunette was to make its entry later.

The strong and rebellious lad – for Siegfried was a powerful young fellow – set out upstream, wandering along the towpath toward the lands of medieval chivalry. At length he came to the Siebengebirge, the group of volcanic mountains which still lay eighteen hours away for the *Thames Commodore* as she left Xanten away on the starboard beam. Crossing the river, the boy came upon the workshop of old Mimer the armourer, to whom he bound himself as an apprentice. The newcomer proved a somewhat difficult employee, however, for he had a way of lifting his workmates high over his head and bouncing them on the ground, not from any desire to hurt them but simply to give vent to his exuberance. His violence was, one must suppose, merely the early medieval counterpart of throwing bricks at a British Consulate, but it worried Mimer greatly. The day Siegfried struck the anvil so hard that he knocked it right into the ground the armourer had had enough. He ingeniously thought up an errand which would take Siegfried through the woods where he knew one of those dreadful man-eating dragons of German romance to lurk, fire-spitting and invincible.

Of course Siegfried was not in the least perturbed when the latter-day Tyrannosaurus rushed upon him. Having slain the beast he chopped off its head and threw it in the fire. Soon a stream of melted fat flowed out, and a little bird told him that he need only smear himself with it to develop an impenetrable ecto-derm. This he did, and we all know that he was later to be undone by the lime leaf which fell upon the nape of his neck during the process and so left him locally vulnerable.

Having slain the dragon Siegfried left it dead, and with its head he went galumphing back. He quickly sought out Mimer and killed him also, and then set out on the long round of epic adventures which were to take him far away from the Rhine and the cruising grounds of this book. It was many years before he returned to Xanten, to bring joy to his parents in their old age before, as Dr Wilhelm Ruland put it, his own tale ended 'in a pitiful wail of grief'.

Three quarters of an hour upstream of Xanten's spires the *Thames Commodore* was bearing up to the point where on either side of the river an embankment stretched away across country, all that remained of the railway bridge which once had leaped the stream. On our previous voyages she had found one derelict pillar still standing in midstream and decked out in warning lights, but now not even that dumb and dismal memorial remained to mark the spot of the extraordinary adventure described with such splendid English understatement by Sir Winston Churchill in his account of how he and General Montgomery went over the Rhine in a small boat and then returned and made their way to this bridge, already dynamited, and climbed up among the twisted wreckage to watch the show. For even then the two mighty armies were shooting at each other across the Rhine, and the German shells were flinging up columns of water which crept ever closer to the observation point the two fearless men and their companions had chosen. It was not until the barrage began to fall among their cars behind the bank that they decided it was perhaps time to leave the bridge and return to headquarters, two hours' drive away.

The railway bridge had carried the line to Wesel, a town which was to be almost entirely destroyed during that modern battle for the crossing of the Rhine. But such a fate Wesel had at least expected since the time of the Romans, for Wesel on the Rhine corresponded very much to Sedan on the French Meuse, a stronghold built just at the point where the invaders would try to force a crossing. The Romans first established the place as a fort, and more than one thousand years later the Spaniards built it up as a citadel and the Prussians turned it into a regular fortress. Yet nowadays one can only discover this from reading, or from old prints, for the modern Wesel is a market town with a smattering of industry, a modest commercial harbour for coasters and Rhine-ships, and a most excellent municipal 'sport-harbour', presumably developed from gravel pits.

It was into this welcoming port that the *Thames Commodore* turned her nose on the Sunday afternoon to rest before she set out next morning for the greatest inland port in the world at Duisburg. We ourselves climbed to the look-out restaurant which the thought-ful town council had provided so that those who liked boats could sit outside in the warm evening air and look out across the rows of yachts and the dinghies sailing in the wide waters of the harbour. Beyond the further bank lay the splendid, majestic curve of the Rhine, ploughed ceaselessly by ships not only of the West but of the East also, for just above the town of Wesel the canal to Datteln led away to the links through which the barges of Poland and the German 'Democratic' Republic made their way to the Rhine on their way to the sea-ports of the Netherlands.

We slept well in Wesel's harbour, although my ears may have been alert even during sleep for the sound of a cannon. For it is told of Wesel that a young girl of the town once fell in love with a soldier of the garrison – Wesel being near the frontier and there-fore throughout history a somewhat military place. The soldier loved her too, and the young pair swore always to be true to each other, and to marry as soon as they might. Unfortunately the girl's parents had no wish to see her mixed up with a trooper who would have no permanent home and might at any moment be posted away to meet his death in some foolish battle; they would much have preferred her to have chosen a good, solid, worthy young fellow with good prospects of advancement, a craftsman apprentice perhaps, or a white-collar young man. But a soldier – certainly not. And however much their daughter might beg them in floods of tears to change their minds, they refused. The matter was closed, and they would discuss it no further.

This is rarely a good way of settling the affairs of the hearts of others, and across the ages parents have rarely realised that a *verbot* is likely to lead to tragedy. In this case the fate of the young couple was particularly drastic, for the soldier primed one of the cannon on the rampart, lit the fuse, and then held his beloved in his arms while both of them placed their heads in a final kiss, right against the muzzle of the gun. The explosion woke the garrison and also, I presume, the unbending parents; and as this unhappy incident occurred in an age when suicide was held to be a sin (as it still is, by some who have little understanding of depression and despair) the girl and her gallant lover could find no rest in their graves but would appear from time to time on the rampart and reload the gun. A tremendous report would follow – for some reason beyond my understanding the bang usually coincided with a thunderstorm – and the lovers would vanish before one had time to notice their renewed decapitation. But so far as I am aware the gun was not fired the night we lay in the harbour; or else I slept too soundly.

Upstream of Wesel and the junction with the canal which leads to the east, the open country soon begins to give way to the sprawl of Westphalian heavy industry. Passing under the soot-laden sky of Walsum it is hard to realise that this landscape now made majestically hideous by the tip heaps and smoke-stacks was once farmland where people ploughed and tilled, sowed and reaped behind the shelter of the outer dike which served to keep the Rhine at bay when the floods of early spring brought the snow-water of Switzerland and Bavaria to threaten the land. That was in the time of the Deichgrafs, men who – like the one who warned Johanna Sebus – were elected to take command of stretches of the rampart bank and see to its preservation.

One such Deichgraf was patrolling his section by boat at a time when the river had already risen beyond the top of the bank and was spilling far and wide across the fields. Deichgraf Gerd Wardmann was conscientiously inspecting the bank to detect any slips or leaks when he heard a cry for help. Looking round he saw sitting in the branches of a willow tree a tiny man whom he at once recognised as a Diekmänneken or dike-mannikin, a species of dwarf which lived in holes in the river bank. Rowing up to the tree Wardmann took the little fellow into his boat and ferried him to safety. In gratitude the mannikin promised to undertake all the repairs to Wardmann's length of the bank and in particular to watch for mole-runs and the holes of field mice, which he would stop up to prevent any possible breach – for it was usually through such holes that the water first found its way under the dike-top and quickly eroded a dangerous gap. The only condition was that the Deichgraf was not to tell anyone that the mannikin was caring for the bank and doing the official's work for him.

And so the years passed safely for the villagers of Walsum until Wardmann was an old man, when he began to feel pangs of conscience about having had his work done by another, or perhaps to wonder whether the mannikin might not be involved with the devil. At last he went to the priest and confessed what was on his mind. I do not know what the priest had to say about the matter, but the Deichgraf's indiscretion had the immediate result that mole-holes and mouse-burrows multiplied as never before, and as the mannikin no longer closed them the water streamed swiftly through the runnels and the bank became waterlogged. Even the Diekmänneken only just escaped with his life, and in his fury at Wardmann's foolishness in giving away their secret agreement he seized his staff and worked it round and round in one of the holes until he had augered an opening which the Rhine rapidly enlarged. The whole bank slipped, and the Deichgraf's own farmstead was swept away in the torrent. What became of the mannikin I could never discover. Perhaps he moved upstream to the safety of Duisburg.

At Walsum we are already within the orbit of Duisburg, the quays and unloaders of which extend for more than an hour of the journey upstream. Smoke white, grey, green or black, purple and bright orange rises so dense from the tall stacks of the foundries and furnace halls that the sun gives up the attempt to break through. The Rhine is iridescent in hues compounded of reflections and mill effluents topped with a shimmer of interference colours from the diffraction of the thin film of oil and diesel fuel heaving on the waves. I have always found Duisburg's bustling and clanging industry one of the finest sights on the Rhine, even if the air is somewhat irritant to the nasal membranes.

Duisburg was certainly a Roman foundation, and when the Merovingians later worked their way steadily up the Rhine they selected it as the place for a royal residence. From this base on the Rhine they swept across to defeat the Romans at Cambrai and so gain control of the whole land as far south as the Somme. So Duisburg was an important place, but it was left high and dry when in the thirteenth century the Rhine deserted it and decided to flow further west. Ruhrort developed at the new confluence, and when today one speaks of Duisburg one probably means Ruhrort.

Set at the junction of the Rhine, the Ruhr, and the busy Rhein–Herne Canal which leads through Essen to the Dortmund–Ems Canal and the route eastwards to Berlin and Poland, Duisburg–Ruhrort is one of the most immense waterway junctions in the world. It very nearly became an even larger one, for under Article 361 of the Treaty of Versailles the Belgians were given twenty-five years in which to decide whether or not to build a canal from Antwerp and the Meuse to the Rhine at Ruhrort. Should they do so, Germany was to construct at her own cost but to Belgian specifications that part of the link which was on German territory. In fact the Belgians never put the work in hand at all, and the shipping bound from Antwerp to the Rhine still has to make the long detour through Zeeland.

Earlier, a similar canal had been begun, but for a different reason. When in the sixteenth century the Dutch rose against their Spanish overlords and drove them out, the Spaniards found themselves in difficulties over their communications, for the rebellious Hollanders controlled the whole of Zeeland with the approaches to the Scheldt, the Meuse and the Rhine. Isabella Clara Eugenia, daughter of Philip of Spain, had been entrusted with the rule of the province of Gelderland and she decided to have an all-Spanish canal built outside the Dutch border, partly for the merchant shipping but also to form a great fortified ditch near the frontier. The Marquis Spinola was ordered to survey the route, and work on the 'Fossa Eugenia' began in 1626. Sixty feet broad, it was designed to run from Rheinberg, upstream of Wesel, to the Meuse at Venlo.

In spite of raids by Dutch commandos who destroyed the locks and shot down the navvies whenever they could, Isabella herself was able to sail along almost the whole of the waterway a mere two years later. However, the Dutch eventually succeeded in capturing both the canal termini, and the Spaniards very naturally closed the works. Part of the canal was later used for a local waterway near Venlo, and the whole line was still in sufficiently good shape in 1804 for Napoleon to inspect it and consider whether it might not be resuscitated as a shipping route safe from the interference of the abominable British. He decided on a more southerly route which would reach the Rhine at Cologne, but a few years later these works also became superfluous when he solved his problems by annexing Holland.

None has written better of Duisburg than the man who penned the leaflet put out by the city for the benefit of English-speaking visitors. 'This town has no idylls, is by no means elegant for making you a mirage of something not being there,' he points out. 'Maybe Duisburg gets publicity by facts otherwise generally being typical to prevent somebody from starting a visit there, for example: smoke and noise, cold steel, soot, fabric walls and its work. Grey everyday, complication of traffic and not understanding power, this world even gets its own dynamic vitality. Everywhere interesting, you don't need a guide.

'Duisburg is a working town, where the motors of the ships are crewing oily water of the large Lower Rhine to white spray. Blast fournaces pricked off let become night to bright red day. Herein is situated its character. Duisburg cannot cash itself, because all its chemneys are smoking.

'People is unable to mark surely, how many millionaires are living here. No one can name the number of managers, who call Duisburg their home. In every case they are numerous and herewith, not respectfully, we are at the top of money-making. The last one takes a great part of life in this town, because Duisburg has grown up out of coal, iron, steel, ship motors and the spirit of Duisburg's undertainers.'

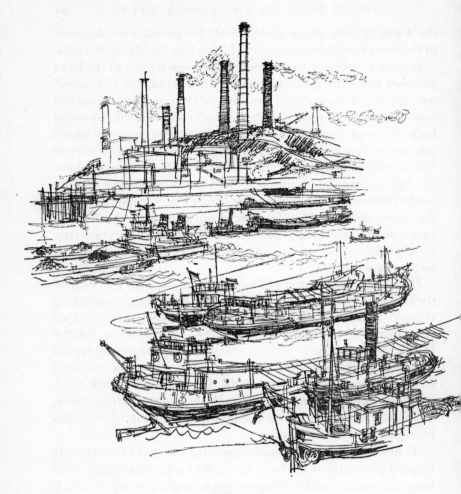

Duisburg

In fact Duisburg is the main iron and steel producer of Europe, and with its twenty miles of Rhine quays and the vast sprawl of its canal basins it is the largest inland harbour in the world. And such a port has its problems, particularly where it is spread along a river such as the Rhine, which has current enough to scour away its own bottom. Even as far downstream as Duisburg the cut-down is more than an inch and a half every year. Multiply this by a few decades, and the drop is considerable. Along the river frontage the fall in the level of the river is not so serious, for the only result is that the quaysides become rather higher, but in the huge canal basins of still water the bottom is not eroded and so the port has to be artificially deepened by dredging. Yet at Ruhrort, where most of the shipping lies, the dredgers and diggers are not necessary. Coal-mining has come to the rescue, for so much of the black wealth has been excavated under the town and port that the whole place, docks, railways, quaysides and fuel tanks, ship chandleries and sailors' pubs, sinks down into the ground at just the right speed, the subsidence almost exactly matching the drop in the Rhine bottom. Presumably the three lakes are also dropping, with their promenades, seats, rose-beds and all, together with the entire park presented to the city by Herr Krupp for the recreation of Duisburg's population. The Barbara, Bertha and Margarete lakes are named after his three daughters.

If the lower reaches of the German Rhine are untroubled by water spirits, I think this is in no way connected with the subsidence. Maybe any water-nymph daring to dive and swim in such heavily ploughed waters would run a risk of being chopped by the propellers of the ceaseless shipping, the coasters from Norway and Britain, the German and Dutch tramps, or the hugely powerful tugs which lie ready to haul the convoys of coal and oil to Switzerland. Or if once they disported themselves where now the river is flanked by the quays of Thyssen and Krupp, it may just have been that the pollution eventually became so acute that they were all killed off by phenol poisoning. Yet ashore, and particularly beneath the surface of the ground where all is comparatively peaceful, the little people are, I presume, as active as ever.

The importance of these beings to the metallurgical industry is usually overlooked, and yet in one way and another goblins good and spirits mischievous have played a vital part in developing the immense complex of industry surrounding the River Ruhr, which pours its café-au-lait-tinted stream into the Rhine at Duisburg-Ruhrort. From earliest times the miners were helped by the Kobolds, who were not by any means the demons that they are sometimes said to have been. Like the knockers in the Welsh mines they were well disposed towards the men who tunnelled into their domains, and they tried to help them. Knowing more of geology than did the humans, the Kobolds would warn of imminent roof-falls and they had sharp noses for carbon monoxide too. Provided one was nice to these little men of the mines, and occasionally shared a sandwich or a few pfennigs with them, their goodwill could be relied upon. For example, if a miner should strike upon a seam of hard rock he could call up a Kobold, who would get to work with his little pick and hack away furiously at the obstacle until he had demolished it.

Sometimes the men and the little gnomes would work together in harmony for years, but eventually the partnership was sure to be ended by some foolish young miner deciding to play a trick on his willing helper – holding back his pay, putting tacks on the floor of the mine gallery, or scattering peas to trip him up. The Kobold would not be amused. He would turn the coal to stone, the copper ore into some harder material. Then with a cry of impish laughter he would leave for ever.

Similar to the Kobolds were the Nickels – little impish fellows, who, however, had a tendency to be mischievous just for the fun of the thing. They would play tricks on the copper-miners of the Ruhr by bewitching the copper in such a way that they altered its chemical properties. Perhaps they were really trying to help, because the magical ore they produced was actually far more valuable than the copper, though the miners did not realise this. The men were angry to be deceived when their baskets of ore turned out to contain *Kupfernickel* – copper which had been wizarded by the mischievous Nickels. Nor were they any more pleased when the Kobolds revenged themselves for some real or imagined slight by kobolding the copper ore in the seam. Nowadays, many an industrial magnate in the Ruhr is thankful that these two species of sprites are touchy enough to tamper with the copper. Both of the bewitched forms – nickel and cobalt – are very well worth the mining.

Duisburg has one particular claim to fame which dates from long before its undertainers became so active, for it was thither that Gerhard Kremer fled to take advantage of the freedom of worship guaranteed in 1552 to protestants. From that year until his death Kremer lived and worked in Duisburg, in the employ of the Duke of Cleves. Primarily a geometrician, he built mathematical instruments, including globes, but his lasting fame was to be as a cartographer.

Until that time ships' captains had been dogged by the difficulty of navigating with charts on which a line of constant bearing (a rhumb-line, as sailors called it) was not straight but spiralled toward the pole – as in fact it does in nature. The problem was to make a straight course *appear* straight on the map, and by distorting the scale progressively with increasing latitude Kremer produced the system of charting which is still used today. Being so successful a map-maker he put his own name (which meant 'Merchant') into a suitably classical form as 'Mercator'.

Mercator's patron hoped to turn Duisburg into a university town. The academy was to be built up very largely around the fame of his own cartographer, and a charter was obtained from emperor and pope. Yet the worthy duke never succeeded in getting his enterprise launched. When at last it came to birth a century later the favourable opportunity had gone. Professors and students were easily tempted away to the excellent universities in the nearby Netherlands, where facilities were very much better, and after 163 years of not very distinguished academic effort the university eventually closed its doors. Duisburg's future was not to be adorned with great professorial names. Its famous men were to be more down to earth or water.

Duisburg and its neighbours have certainly produced many men of enterprise, and Mülheim – the first town up the course of the smutty River Ruhr – was the home of a bargemaster whose son, a mere deck-hand, decided in 1808 to set up on his own with a coal-lighter which he bought for 1,240 Thalers. A mere ten years later he had more than sixty colliers working the Rhine and plying between Koblenz and Rotterdam. Stinnes – for that was his name – was quick to take advantage of the invention of the steam-tug, and he ordered one to be built in Britain.

By the end of the nineteenth century Hugo Stinnes, the third-generation owner of the family business, had the largest concern in the Ruhr, with interests in coalmines and electricity and

foundries throughout Westphalia. Hotels and paper mills, newspapers and overseas shipping were added, and although the firm
was temporarily broken by the inflation of the 1920s it is still one
of the great names of the Ruhr. Up the Neckar and Main as well
as the Rhine and Moselle, the *Thames Commodore* and her predecessor had often shared locks and moorings with the ships of
the United Stinnes concern.

Of course, Duisburg's importance as a centre of shipping did
not begin with the enterprising Skipper Stinnes and his lighters.
It had always been an important river harbour, but its sudden
development began late in the seventeenth century, when the
magistrate ordered a Wesel skipper named Koch to set up a
regular weekly service between Duisburg and Nijmegen. Punctu-
ally at eight o'clock on a Thursday morning the ships left the two
towns, and as regularity was a thing as yet unknown the service
immediately attracted a busy trade. Contrary to custom the ships
sailed whether full to capacity or not, and the skippers were not
permitted to refuse any cargo that was brought in time for loading.
The Koch line soon attracted goods away from the roads, and
Duisburg began to develop as a centre for transhipment of food-
stuffs and other materials from the Netherlands. When other
regular sailings were added to carry goods and passengers direct
to Arnhem and Amsterdam this activity increased.

Envious of the success of Duisburg, Düsseldorf also began to
operate timetabled weekly runs to the Netherlands, but the
Duisburgers knew how to deal with competition. Brandenburg
and Prussia, to which Duisburg belonged, had no less than six
toll-stations on the river between Ruhrort and Lobith. At each
of these the Düsseldorf ships could be milked whilst the Duisburg
craft passed free.

We put into the tug harbour for lunch, lying among the handsome craft which were always at the ready to haul another convoy
of coal-lighters up the river. It was, I think, a fine day. At least it
was not raining, and yet it was difficult to know whether the sun
was shining or not. For miles the tall chimneys stood like a forest
of dead trees. Suddenly there would be a glow like a ball of fire, as
one of the coke-ovens was opened up in a steel works. In the

distance the wheels turning in the air marked the pit-head gear of the collieries.

Gasholders, oil tanks, a regular spider's web of high tension cables – yes, it was an ugly place, this town of half a million people. Hideous, but curiously fascinating. The long harbour basins curved away like great fingers to clutch the products of the Ruhr, and watching the traffic streaming down from the canal we could see a barge with two electric locomotives aboard, new and shining in plastic packaging as though they were for the toy railway of a giant. In fact they were bound for South America – by barge from Duisburg to Rotterdam, and then by an ocean ship across the Atlantic.

As we continued on our way upstream, whichever way we looked there were warehouses, wharves, grain silos and cranes, railway sidings, huge piles of scrap metal, and black mountain ranges of coal waiting to be shipped away. Barges lay at anchor or alongside, loading, unloading, or just waiting. There were hundreds of them, and plenty more under way in the Rhine itself too, sweeping round the bend toward the Friedrich Ebert bridge, or forging ahead in the other direction, plugging away against the stiff current. For mile upon mile the turmoil of shipping continued until at last the Rhine led out into a clearer sky and we found that the sun was shining after all. Once beyond the chemical quays of Krefeld we were out in the country again, heading up for Kaiserswerth, a neat little town perched on the port hand a few miles below Düsseldorf. This pleasant place was once reputed to have the particular property that no corpse floating down the river would ever pass it by. In this there is a curious connection with England, for it was from that primitive land that there came to the shores of the Rhine toward the end of the seventh century a monk of noble birth named Suitbert. Fleeing from the tough and unpleasant Frisians he at last reached the river, and took refuge upon an island which is now part of the dry land and constitutes the settlement of Kaiserswerth itself. One day he happened to meet Pipin the Short and his queen, who presented the island to him and requested him to set up a monastery.

Like so many of the missionaries to the Rhineland Suitbert was a practical man and he set about burning and ploughing the scrub on the land beyond the river and helping the people to improve their agriculture. He was a particular friend of the shipmen too, and he built on the upstream end of the shoal above his island a little beacon which he lit at night to guide ships and rafts into the deeper water. Probably his was the first navigation light ever installed upon the Rhine.

Suitbert also cared for the shipwrecked, of which there must have been many in those days of clumsy navigation, and whenever he saw a body floating down the river he would retrieve it for burial. Probably it was this which gave rise to the later belief that no corpse could pass Kaiserswerth without stranding. Suitbert is said also to have restored to life some 'who appeared drowned', so it is not impossible that he practised the kiss-of-life method of artificial respiration. Medieval writers stated that when at last Suitbert died the whole river was flood-lit that night by a luminous glow where it flowed around Suitbert's own island, and the very next day a new process began. The Rhine began to sweep mud and gravel into the space between the island and the right bank and soon it was firmly and permanently united with the mainland.

At Kaiserswerth the distant outline of Düsseldorf is already in sight, a sign that we shall be able to draw in for the night at one of the very best yacht harbours on all the Rhine. Modern Düsseldorf is renowned as a town of wealth and economic miracles, but once the place was no more than a village (or *dorf*) on the banks of the Düssel brook. Today that stream stinks of effluent, but once its beauty moved deeply the spirit of a young man who was something of a mystic. He lived in the seventeenth century.

Close by where the modern autobahn cuts a swathe through the woodland above cliffs which echo to the dynamiting gangs of the hungry Mannesmann works, the Düssel still cuts through a quiet gorge at the foot of limestone crags green with scrub of alder and oak, beech, and a few conifers. It was there that the restless young man would climb to look out across the land where it fell away to the Rhine a few miles distant. A storm swept in from the west just as it did the morning we headed up the stiff current above smoky

Duisburg. In the thunder and lightning, the violence of wind and rain, the grandeur of the cliff and the stillness of the forest, the young visionary saw only the might and wonder and goodness and majesty of God in his creation. I like to think that he stood there fearless and soaked to the skin as the words of his great hymn took shape in his mind. '*Lobe den Herrn* . . .' We still sing it in our churches, splendidly translated. 'Praise to the Lord, the Almighty, the king of creation.' Certainly it is known that he stood on that crag above the brook one Whitsunday, weak with tuberculosis, as another storm broke over the land which now is merely an industrial sprawl.

'That is my Father,' he cried as the thunder pealed and the rain beat upon his face. 'My Father with His fiery chariot and horses. I rejoice – for though the mountains may quake and the hills fall, His covenant is unbreakable, His mercy endures for ever!'

Three days later Joachim Neander collapsed and died. Yet he and that craggy bend in the Düssel brook had become so intimately linked that the place came to be known as Neander's valley, the Neanderthal. And there, two centuries later, a quarryman came upon some bones in a narrow cave, the first known remains of an earlier type of man, a side-branch from the sprouting shoot that was already expanding as *Homo sapiens*, our own species.

The bones were shown to the owner of the quarry, who at once informed J. C. Fuhlrott, a secondary school teacher of Elberfeld who was already known for his researches. Fuhlrott realised at once that the remains could only belong to a more ancient type of human, but when he dared to put forward this theory he was attacked from all sides. Some said the bones were those of a man distorted with rickets, others that the individual had been a malformed idiot. And, as Russians were feared and mysterious beings, it was seriously suggested that the remains were those of a cossack who had crept into the cave to hide there during the campaign of 1813–14. The scientist Virchow also set himself in vigorous opposition to Fuhlrott, but eventually finds in other caves – particularly in the south of France – confirmed the theory that the individual who had lived by the banks of the Düssel

fifty thousand years ago was indeed a more primitive type of man
than our own.

As we looked at the model of his low-browed form in the local
museum, I wondered what Joachim Neander would have thought
about the place of that simple hominid in the divine scheme which
so filled him with awe and praise. For in Neander's day nothing
was known of evolution. Darwin's *Origin* was published three
years after the bones were found, two centuries after Joachim
Neander.

Darwin was bitterly opposed by a small and vocal minority of
clerics. He still is by a few. Over the years I have discovered that
nobody ever sends me rude letters when I write about waterways
and boats, but the mere mention of affinity with the rest of the
creatures which enjoy this earth and tear each other to pieces upon
it is enough to make some people very angry. They like to feel
that God keeps a sort of toy-shop and turns out fluffy bunnies and
(at a price) humans, all ready equipped for the business of living
and working, boating and loving and dying; and if I write back to
them and say please will they tell me what they think about
mongoloids or hydrocephalics they get angrier still – though they
do not answer the question.

Neander's vision was immense and glorious. So was Darwin's,
and he liberated the human spirit and imagination for ever from
the small-minded notion of special creation. Nowadays we can
be aware of the immense span of time against which life has
developed on our own little planet (amongst many others, we
must assume) and at an ever increasing rate; onward and upward,
from nucleo-proteins in the primeval sea to single cells, then to
larger forms endowed with movement. The invention of nerve
conduction opened a whole new dimension. Bones and closed-
circuit blood-flow emancipated creatures from the water. Up to
the trees, and down again, erect on two feet and with the hands free
to work tools – and mischief, too. Mutation, selection, the weakest
to the wall under God's incredibly daring scheme. A century ago it
certainly seemed an impious idea, but now we can accept it as
just such a revelation as would have stirred Neander himself.

Neanderthal man ate, loved – or at least mated – and died. I doubt if he ever wondered about God in creation. Behind that low receding forehead, above the massive eyebrow ridges, there was nothing comparable with our own awareness. When the thunder rolled in from the Rhine our simpler cousin was perhaps just a bit frightened, but only as a dog is. He did not understand. Comprehension was beyond him. It belonged to the new species which soon was to supplant him, and hold the future precariously in its neat prehensile hands.

Down in the narrow cleft where the stinking stream still flows past the cave Neanderthal man inhabited I tried to imagine him creeping along by the water, watching for danger or prey. A man almost, but terribly limited in what he could do, and think. Was he really nothing more than an evolutionary dead-end kid, a piece of callous cosmic wastage? I thought not, for in a very real way his existence was fulfilled in our own. Without mutation and selection not one of us would be here today. The process which could produce a Shakespeare and a St Paul, an Einstein and a de Chardin, necessarily involved side-lines, culs-de-sac, Neanderthalers. They were part of the price. And that, I thought, would be a fine subject for a hymn. Had Joachim Neander lived two centuries later he might have produced it.

Many people are delighted with Düsseldorf. It is Germany's shop-window, just as it was half a century ago. The shops almost drip with affluence, the ladies of the men of industry and thrombosis drive in splendid cars, wrapped in sleek furs, and the place is quite the embodiment of what manufacture and materialism can do. Nevertheless, the rebuilt older quarter of the city has a surprisingly pleasant market-town atmosphere, and the country people range their stalls of eggs and fruit, flowers and fungi around the statue of their beloved ruler Jan Willem as though the economic miracle of the mid-twentieth century had never taken place. But best of all – at least to a boatman – is the curving waterfront with the watch-tower and crooked spire which are Düsseldorf's special mark, the river lashed by the Rhine-ships thrusting upstream where the channel runs swiftly within a few yards of the shore. Downstream of the tower a long and sinuous water-serpent guards the promenade, and beyond him are the three harbours cut away inside the dike. One contains the yachts, smart and spanking and affluent, another the small motor-boats, and the third a floating inn which is as pleasant a place as I have found along all the lower Rhine for a meal and a glass of wine on a summer's night. The upper deck is open to the stars and to the lights of the traffic soaring over the river on the new bridge further downstream. Most of the ships pull in for the night, swinging a deckhand ashore on a boom to slip a noose of hawser round a massive bollard and using the anchor to hold them off the stony shore, but some go pounding past Düsseldorf whatever the time of day or night. There is hardly a moment when the red port light of a lone up-comer or the double mast-head lamps of a tug are not visible down the long reach which stretches down toward Kaiserswerth.

Immediately above the sharp bend where the Rhine sweeps past the dock basins of Düsseldorf's inland port, the Erft Canal cuts away to starboard to the town of Neuss a short way from the Rhine. Although now a mere harbour cut, this is in fact the remains of Napoleon's 'Canal du Nord' to link the Rhine with the Meuse and Scheldt, and after it had been abandoned the course was dug out and improved by the Prussians as far as Viersen, near Mönchen-Gladbach. The enterprising Stinnes firm immediately rented the waterway from the state and used it for coal-boats, but they also had a passenger packet which ran from Neuss to Viersen.

Neuss is not the sort of place that one would visit for choice, but hidden in its past is a curious incident. In the 1470s the land was as usual the scene of a struggle for power, this time between Archbishop Ruprecht of Cologne and the people of that city. As neither side was militarily very effective each began to seek allies; the prelate found an ally in Charles the Bold of Burgundy while the city won the support of the somewhat impecunious Landgrave Heinrich III of Hessen. The Burgundian troops invested the town of Neuss and in the course of only ten months they attempted to storm its walls no less than sixty-five times, at the end of which the soldiers were becoming somewhat dispirited at their lack of success. The citizens, however, had been obliged toward the end of the siege to send the Landgrave's horses one after the other to the mincing machine to keep themselves well supplied with sausage.

The Landgrave could ill afford to see all his chargers disappear, and when the siege was over he presented a bill to the mayor and corporation of Cologne, who declined to pay. Courteously but firmly they shelved the matter, declaring it to be just one of those unfortunate things that can happen in a time of crisis. So the Hessian had to go without his compensation, but he entered the eaten horses in his accounts as a charge against Cologne – and never for a moment forgot the item. No doubt the burghers thought that they had got rid of the claim, but there they were wrong.

One day in 1480 a number of merchants from Cologne had been with their wives to the Frankfurt trade fair – for that particular institution is one of the oldest in existence – and at the end of business they merrily returned home by ship down the Rhine. They were obliged to put in at St Goar in order to pass one of the many customs posts then in existence, and they had only just stepped ashore when a band of the Landgrave's men appeared, took prisoner the entire party, men and women, children, servants and clerks, and locked them up. The men were all required to sign papers swearing under oath that they would present themselves at St Goar again on the first day of May and deliver their own persons into captivity if by that time the debt for the eaten horses had not been settled. Then they were allowed to go on their way.

After much exchange of correspondence the city had to admit that it was beaten. It was unthinkable that the merchants should go back on their word, and no doubt it was they who at length persuaded the councillors to come to terms. A sum of 7,000 guilders was agreed, and paid in four instalments.

Half a day is enough for the voyage from Düsseldorf up to Cologne, through a not very interesting countryside scarred with pylons and overhung with a light drift of smoke tinted and tanged by the strange effluvia of the stacks of such places as Leverkusen. We never attempted to stop at Leverkusen, partly because of the pharmaceutical aromas spreading down wind of the vast Bayer plants, but also on account of the strange adventure which befell a Dutch barge-master there and which, I thought, might easily be repeated.

Late one night this Dutch skipper was drinking his beer in an inn when all the other guests prepared to leave and the landlord started to bar and bolt the shutters. When the Dutchman said that he was not yet intending to return to his ship the guests all began to warn him that Leverkusen was terrorised by some strange sort of doglike monster which roamed the streets at midnight and so alarmed all good people of the locality that they locked themselves in their houses. That was why they themselves were now going home, before the dreaded hour. The Dutchman made some wry comment about the effect upon the mind of second-rate liquor. Although he was obliged to leave the inn he had no intention of returning to his ship like a chicken-hearted Leverkusener, he said. So, pulling on his nautical cap, he paid his bill and left.

He had not gone far before the monster suddenly appeared and leapt upon him. Though strong, the Dutchman was soon over-powered, but just as the creature had him upon the pavement he managed to pull one hand free, and drawing his ship's knife he plunged it with all his might between the monster's ribs.

The creature collapsed, but as the captain was struggling to his feet he heard a human voice and was amazed to discover that it came from the bleeding corpse of his strange assailant. Then there stood before him a man who said that he was a werwolf, doomed to roam the streets by night and assault people, and being a werwolf he had phenomenal strength. As the skipper seemed to doubt what he said, the man took hold of the nearest house and shook it so furiously with his hands that the tiles came rattling from the roof to fall in the street. This was more than enough for the skipper's nerves. He ran to the quay, leapt aboard his ship, cast off the hawsers and set off at full speed downstream toward Holland. He never slackened knots until he had reached the frontier at the customs roads of Lobith.

III

The tale of Reinhold – the Three Kings – Ursula and her maidens – the absent cats of Cologne – Archbishop-Electors and their victims – Bonn – birth of a nation – Bad Godesberg and the Godesburg – the inn at Plittersdorf – horsetowage on the Rhine

FROM Duisburg to Cologne, here and there some small waterside town has managed to survive among all the smell and smoke without being entirely obliterated by the overpowering collection of factories, gasholders and chemical silos, which look down upon the humbler buildings of an earlier age with undisguised contempt. Then at last the great cathedral of Cologne comes into view, vast and twin-spired, a monument to the tenacity of the builders who persevered for such ages that the crane erected to hoist stones up to the towers was four hundred years old when it was finally dismantled in 1872, more than six centuries after Gerard the master-builder began his great edifice. It is not surprising that such an enterprise should be surrounded with tales of how the job was only completed with the help of the devil, but there is also a medieval legend which connects the building with Reynaud, the dashing leader of those four sons of Aymon who, on their brave magical steed Bayard, were continually outwitting poor old Charlemagne. When Roger Ascham visited Cologne in 1550 he noted that everyone was still talking of how the hero had been slain by his fellows.

The legend to which Ascham referred told of how Charlemagne at last defeated the brothers and demanded the surrender of Bayard. The noble steed was led to the bridge in Liège and there flung into the river with a millstone round his neck, but it is pleasant to know that he shattered the weight with a single blow of his hoof and escaped from the pursuing horde to gallop for ever in the forest of the Ardennes – where his hoofs can still be heard by any boatman on the Meuse who has a reasonably sen-

sitive ear. But his gallant master had done for ever with traditional
heroics, and, turning his back upon courts and lovely ladies and
even on his own fairy godmother, he put off his knightly clothing
and wandered far away to live as a peasant.

One day Reynaud (or Reinhold) heard that a mighty cathedral
was to be erected in Cologne, and laying down his hoe he promptly
betook himself thither to offer his services. Signed on, he set to
work to lift the heavy blocks of stone from the barges and carry
them up to the site, and so conscientious a workman was he that he
would never knock off for elevenses or draw out his lunch hour
into two. He even slept rough on the site so that he might get
started each morning without delay.

The attitude of his fellow workers was no different in the middle
ages from what it would be in the twentieth century. The fact
that this outsider accomplished as much as seven men and yet
voluntarily worked overtime and even declined some of his pay
was enough to damn him in their eyes. Reynaud was a black-leg,
and that was enough. The other navvies ganged up against him,
and lying in wait for him they pelted him with blocks of stone and
crushed him to death – the first recorded victim of restrictive
practices. Then they tied his body in a sack and flung it into the
Rhine. Eventually the corpse floated, and of course a number of
duly attested wonders accompanied its discovery and bringing to
land. It was only when the people found the golden-embroidered
belt under his jerkin and read the inscription upon it that they
knew that the over-zealous labourer was none other than Reynaud
of Montauban.

Reynaud was enshrined in the cathedral, and there he remained
until the time when a crowd of pilgrims came to the city and
begged for some suitable relic to protect their own town of
Dortmund. The clergy of Cologne were not at all inclined to part
with anything, but during the discussions the shrine of St Reinhold
(as he had now become) leapt unaided into the midst of the company. When this had occurred three days running the chapter at
last took the hint, and carrying the shrine across the Rhine they
set it on a cart without horse, ox, or other motive power. So
determined were the remains of the saint to go to Dortmund that

the carriage rattled away without assistance and never halted until it reached that town. Naturally St Reinhold became Dortmund's patron saint and could be relied upon to defend it. In times of siege he would often appear in shining armour upon the walls and fight alongside the burghers.

Ecclesiastically, the vast cathedral of Cologne derived some of its medieval importance from a gift made by the Emperor Barbarossa to his chancellor in the year 1164. In order to reward him for his valiant support in the struggle against some of the cities of Italy, the emperor bequeathed to him the bones of the Three Wise Men of the East, which were placed in a reliquary and became so greatly venerated that Cologne almost outdid Compostella as a place of pilgrimage. To the non-bone-worshipper it may seem odd that the remains of the men from such varied areas of the Middle East should have been recovered more than one thousand years later, but that is to overlook the Arab genius for making a bargain. Nowadays it may be hashish and transistor radios that are peddled on the quayside to travellers willing to part with money. In earlier centuries it was bones, or wood from the cross. The Arabs knew very well what the crusading knights could be tempted to buy, and just what immense wealth many of them possessed.

Cologne has a particular connection with Britain through the eleven thousand English girls slain there by the Huns – the same whose story was enshrined in the name of the canal barge bought by R. L. Stevenson after he had made his canoe trip from the Scheldt to the Oise. *Les Onze Mille Vierges de Cologne* was destined never to roam the waterways under his command, but the girls themselves have a more lasting memorial in Cologne, where their remains used to be shown to the curious. Roger Ascham was taken by a nun to see silver figures of forty or more of the girls, many of the effigies reproducing fearful wounds. But there were also skulls and heaps of bones carefully arranged in cupboards – two cart-loads at least, he estimated. Many of the skulls were those of small children, and when Ascham asked how this could be so it was explained that not all the eleven thousand virgins of Cologne were physiologically such, but were married or pregnant before their departure from England.

It is said that the eleven thousand girls and their leader Ursula were slaughtered in the year 451. Ursula herself was Cornish and a girl of astounding beauty. Shortly before, a particularly tough English warrior had been busily sacking Brittany and was faced with the problem of repopulating the countryside, for though he had men enough in his own soldiery he needed wives for them. Knowing of Ursula's wondrous beauty he sent a deputation to her father to see what could be arranged, and an agreement was reached by which Conan himself should have Ursula, who was to be accompanied by her ten most acceptable girl-friends, each attended by one thousand maidens of lesser status for the ordinary rankers. In return, Conan would agree to be baptised.

So Ursula and her vast following of females set out, but either because of a storm or through sheer faulty navigation they made their landfall not on the Cherbourg peninsula but at the Hook of Holland. No doubt they were glad to be out of the open sea, for they carried ahead up river as far as Cologne. Hearing of this, Conan called off the deal, and the girls found themselves unprotected and unprovided for in the country of wild Germanic tribes. Ursula at once decided that they had better march to Rome to ask the Pope what they should do, and so they crossed the Alps on foot – an undertaking as remarkable as Hannibal's.

After the audience the crowd of girls set off in the direction they had come, but unfortunately their path led them through the camp of Attila at the edge of Cologne. The Huns promptly slew the ten high-class girls and the eleven thousand common ones, leaving only Ursula alive. Attila asked her to marry him, and when she declined he drew his bow and shot her dead. But, as a German book so sensibly remarks at the end of this gruesome tale, 'there may be an element of legend in the story'. In fact it seems that there may have been some such incident but it got multiplied out of proportion when the inscription *XI M. Virgines* was translated not as Eleven Martyr Maidens but as eleven thousand.

Of the Roman Colonia only traces remain, but at least the fearful modern war which destroyed so many of the treasures of the great city brought to light the magnificent mosaic floor close beside the cathedral. It was already on view when, twenty years earlier, I

had visited Cologne by train. Then the station was all but derelict,
some of the huge spans of the Hohenzollern bridge still lay tangled
in the river, and where now the city centre is a riot of bright
discharge-tube signs by night there was then a landscape of weed-
grown mounds through which rough lanes had been carved by
bulldozers. It was three years after the terrifying raids which
reduced almost all of the city except Master Gerard's cathedral to
rubble, but the smell of dead bodies beneath the scarred heaps of
rubbish still hung heavy in the air. Old men and women, very aged
and unable even then to grasp what had happened, still crouched
demented and weeping over the places where once their homes had
been. The deep-toned bell of the cathedral tolled unceasing
through an air strangely quiet from the almost total absence of
traffic as tens of thousands of pilgrims picked their way across the
landscape of debris toward the shrine of the Three Kings, for
amid the surrounding destruction Cologne's cathedral was
celebrating its seven hundredth year.

I was walking through this wilderness with a German biologist,
and every now and then he would point out some curious freak of
the disturbed ecology, a delicate shrub growing in the crook of a
ruined pillar or the invasion of a mound by such a pretty and
improbable plant as the heartsease or wild pansy. He stopped and
picked one of the wide-open blue-and-whitish blooms.

'See,' he said. 'So we should find owls, should we not?'

'Should we?'

'Yes. You remember what Darwin put forward in the *Origin of
Species*?'

I did not. I had never read the great work, though my companion's remarks as we trailed on through the sad waste-heaps of
what once had been a great city prompted me to do so as soon as I
was back in England.

Darwin traced a correlation between the abundance of a
particular species of owl and the prevalence of the heartsease, as
an example of the interdependence of species. His argument, if I
recall it correctly, ran as follows: the heartsease multiplied by
seeding, but on account of the shape of its calyx the ova could only
be pollinated by the intervention of the humble-bee. Humble-bee

nests were devoured by field-mice, and the field-mice in their turn were heavily preyed upon by the owls. More owls meant less field-mice and more humbles, and therefore better fertility among the heartsease. It was as simple as that – or would be if other factors such as cats and deep frosts were not involved.

We walked on. It seemed impossible to believe that this destruction could ever be cleared away. Twisted girders roughly cut away at the edge of the street, a single water-pipe rising solitary from the ground to a tank which balanced upon it three storeys high above the ground. The sparkle of shattered glass in crushed basements, the dust whirled up by the wind at the intersections of what once had been streets of shops. Sandstone fused and smoothed by the intense heat of the raging fire. It was as though we were walking through the relics of a vanished world.

'Do you notice anything about the fauna?' The question brought me back to the practical biological present. I thought hard.

'Yes,' I said. 'There are dogs roaming over the ruins but I haven't seen a single cat.'

'Exactly. You see, the dog will adapt. Rather than die he will eat anything – potato peels, garbage, even grass. But not so the cat. The destruction brought an end to the saucers of milk and meat, and titbits of fish. The people were starving and they could not afford to feed cats and let their own children die of hunger. Oh yes, there were rats, of course, and for a while the cats ate them. But soon they had to compete with the humans, for a fat rat made a better meal than an empty plate. And the owls came too. With rats running free over the ruins the owls forsook the country and became city birds for a while, pouncing on the rats and flying up to perch on some ruined wall to tear them apart. The rats didn't last long. They had too many predators.'

'And then?'

'When the rats were finished the days of the cats were numbered. They were too rigidly fixed in their carnivorous diet. But the dogs – they adapted, and to supplement the scraps they probably helped themselves to a starving cat whenever they found one. It is just a case of changing environment, and natural selection happening right before our eyes.'

It was a very different Cologne into which the *Thames Commodore* carried my wife and myself on this early afternoon of a warm day in July. The cathedral bell was tolling, but no longer in the desert air. The unbelievable had happened, and where once there had been only desolation there had for years already been a bustling city, a Cologne teeming with traffic and shoppers. Probably the cats had been installed again in luxury flats.

At the jetties below the cathedral the vast white passenger ships were taking aboard their complements of holiday visitors. Beyond, a cut led off to starboard into the Rheinauhafen, high over which the trams and cars soared on the slim, green and beautifully proportioned new bridge of St Severin which leaped the Rhine and harbour in one single confident bound. On the bullnose at the entrance stood St Nicholas, the patron of bargemen, reliable and undaunted. We slid out of the current and passed beneath his upraised hand to draw in at the foot of the steps.

The Rheinauhafen is a pleasant place to lie. Ships come and go, blowing off for the bridge to be swung away from over the entrance, and dockside cranes whine as they hoist the cargoes from the holds. The water-police are at home there, and so are a few poor old steamers, turned out to grass like horses in a home for old nags provided under the will of a rich animal-loving spinster. All the same, it was not without misgivings that I let the *Thames Commodore* snug into the corner, for I had heard about the affair of the local boat-owner and the archbishop.

It was Easter when Archbishop Anno invited the Bishop of Münster to stay, and at the end of the visit he told his servants to find a boat to take the bishop down the river. The servants saw a handsome barge alongside and ordered the hands to unload the cargo and make the ship ready. But the owner's son quickly called his young friends, and they set about the archiepiscopal servants and sent them packing. The servants called the police, who in turn called out the military. There would have been a bloody battle if Archbishop Anno had not called a halt by threatening with excommunication any who resorted to violence.

However, he took the opportunity to preach a public sermon on the insolence of any who refused him a boat when he wanted one.

c

It happened that the boat-owner's son was among the congregation, and he quickly collected a strong force of young men who were thoroughly sick of the ways of the establishment. They raced to the palace where the prelate was holding a banquet, and threw bricks through the windows. In their fury they brushed aside the servants and killed or trampled down any who resisted, then broke into the dining-hall and pelted the ecclesiastics with cobbles. The two bishops narrowly escaped with their lives, while the crowd set about the palace so thoroughly that several were drowned in the immense flood of wine when the great tuns in the archiepiscopal cellars were stove in.

Disguised, Anno escaped from the city under cover of darkness and raised a force from his castle of Siegburg. The city authorities were now alarmed at what might happen, and they sent an embassy which promised to pay for the damage. But Anno was not to be put off. He conducted a High Mass in St Gereon's – near where the *Thames Commodore* drew in to her berth – and demanded that the riotous young men should attend upon him, walking barefoot and in white sheets. He told them that he would announce his intentions next day.

Six hundred of the wealthiest citizens had the foresight to flee the same night, whilst Anno's men pillaged any house they chose. Those who fled escaped just in time, for after a night spent in prayer (if we may believe the record) Anno ordered the young man who had started the trouble to have his eyes dug out, and the same to be done to all the leading rioters. The remainder were merely flayed in public or driven from the city for ever.

Anno was canonized after his death. As Sabine Baring-Gould remarked, 'If these things were done in a green tree, what were done in the dry?' But perhaps I should add for the benefit of boatmen who may be worried about visiting Cologne that all this happened in 1074, since when the rights of shipowners have been regulated by international agreements, and archbishops are not necessarily archfiends.

All the same, Anno was not the only episcopal tyrant Cologne has known. Konrad von Hochstaden was another who caused havoc in the city and along the waterfront. He bombarded his own

citizens with catapults from the opposite side of the river and sent
blazing fire-ships to drift down among the merchant vessels
moored along the quays. But he also has a particular connection
with England in that he came over to London to persuade the
second son of King John to accept the crown of Holy Roman
Emperor – and also, incidentally, to contribute 12,000 marks in
silver toward the cathedral which he was just beginning to build.
'Richard of Almain', as the English were to call him from his
chosen empire of Allemagne, was duly crowned at Aachen beside
Charlemagne's tomb, but being a rather feckless individual he
could never bring himself to journey all the way to Rome to have
his coronation confirmed by the Pope, and so his appointment
lapsed. Instead of lording it over all the German nobles – a tough
assignment for any man – he lived for the most part at Berkhamsted
and passed away into comparative historical obscurity.

The Archbishop-Electors of Cologne often came into conflict
with the merchants and aldermen of the proud Hanseatic city. One
of them, Archbishop Engelbert, decided that it would not be
impossible to get rid of the person of the mayor of the city,
Bürgermeister Gryn, so two members of the chapter were detailed
to invite the mayor to dinner, and in the course of the meal their
conversation turned to the lion which had been given as a cub to
the archbishop, and which now was a handsome and fully grown
beast. The burgomaster very naturally expressed a desire to see it,
so his hosts led him down to the cage and then, after murmuring
further politenesses, suddenly opened the gate and pushed him
inside. For two days the lion had not been fed but had been sus-
tained with promises of a good juicy mayor for his next meal.

The lion opened his jaws and roared, then drew back to spring.
But Bürgermeister Gryn did not wait. Wrapping his thick robe
around his left arm he thrust it into the lion's gaping mouth, and
drawing his weapon with his sword-arm he ran the beast through
the heart.

The mayor then drew back the bolt of the door and strode out of
the cage and past the two canons without so much as bidding them
a good evening or thanking them for the dinner. Instead, he went
straight to the City Hall, gave his orders to some of the servants,

and sent them to the archiepiscopal palace. Within the hour the
two clerics were hanging from one of the cathedral gateways, to
encourage the rest to refrain from such crude trickery.

At Cologne the Rhine scenery changes. The long lines of
bankside poplars have gone, and if from time to time the banks
break out in a rash of tanker jetties and oil-flecked unloading bays
the river is mainly rural, overhung no longer by the coke-oven
tinted clouds of the reaches nearer the Ruhr. And as if to remind
the boatman that the stream has been a highway since long before
Bessemer invented his converter or Stinnes plied his coal-lighters,
here and there a pleasant little town lies sprawled along the bank,
its half-timbered inns recalling the days of the *Halfen*, the men
who rode the tow-horses as they plodded laboriously up the river.
That was before the coming of the terrible steam-engines imported
from England.

Only one year after Waterloo, a London-built steamer appeared
on the lower Rhine. She was rightly named the *Defiance*, for she
operated in spite of the hostility of traditional shipmen. Shortly
afterwards the *Caledonia* appeared, the first steamer to penetrate
the Rhine above Cologne. It is said locally that James Watt himself
was aboard, but this I have always doubted, for he would have been
in his eighties at that time. But whoever may have travelled on that
first voyage, the slim and stately ship puffed and wheezed as she
chuffed and churned the water, doggedly crawling her way up the
swiftly flowing stream toward Koblenz. Along the course the
villagers turned out in their thousands to watch her and their
cheers ran along the river banks, but the old salts shook their heads.
This mode of progress was unnatural. It was also a menace, for if
ever the day should come when a steamy monster could tow the
barges, what would become of the *Halfen* and their horses? Yes,
the steam-driven ship was something to be disapproved of and
resisted.

This curious, quiet, and for the most part unspectacular stretch
of river above Cologne is also the scene of one of those strange
voyages of an unpowered vessel which are a feature of the rivers of
a legendary Germany emerging from the dark ages. Adelheid was
the girl in this case, daughter of the tenth-century Duke Megingoz

The Oscar Huber, last of the paddle-tugs

of Berg. As a girl she was sent to the convent of St Ursula in Cologne, and she was still there when news was received that her only brother Gottfried had been killed while fighting for the Emperor Otto III in his campaign against Bohemia. Her parents decided to give their son's inheritance for a religious foundation, and so the convent of Vilich came into existence with Adelheid as the abbess. Later she removed to Cologne again, and it was there that she died in the year 1015.

Very properly, Adelheid was buried in Cologne, but each day her coffin would rise out of the ground unaided, a clear enough indication that she had no wish to remain interred in Cologne at all. So the people loaded her coffin on a barge and pushed it out into the stream. To their very understandable surprise the boat set off smartly against the current and did not slacken speed until Vilich (across the Rhine from Bonn) was on the port beam. There the bells immediately began to peal of their own accord, so the craft put in to the bank and Adelheid was unloaded by the pious villagers. In Vilich she was duly buried, and if any should complain that the tomb of St Adelheid is not to be found they will at once be assured that the wicked Napoleon made off with her remains and took them to Paris.

In fact none of the riverside towns and villages above Cologne is particularly notable until Bonn comes into view, a city which has somehow managed to sit on the very edge of the Rhine itself and yet has forgotten to equip itself with a harbour or quay of any description. Some of the government offices are raised on legs so that at least the bureaucracy can flourish unimpaired in times of exceptional flood, but that seems to be the only thought which the central government casts in the direction of the Rhine.

To most people Bonn is Beethoven, and at least there is a real charm about the modest house in which he was born. Besides, it is a pleasant change to visit a German town which has so close and personal a connection with some other great man that it is quite ready to forget that Goethe may have spent a night in the place. Queen Elizabeth I herself cannot compare with Goethe for having every lunch, dinner, bed and breakfast he ever took commemorated by a plaque or mentioned in the local guide-book.

It is impossible to draw in to the shore within several miles of Bonn, and that is a very good reason for omitting to make a detailed tour of the capital of the Bundesrepublik in the pages of this book. But as we sent our bow-wave to roll across the water and lap the sloping and inhospitable shore I could not help regretting that, although there were trip-boats in plenty, all with their separate landing stages, even to draw breath in the neighbourhood of these was *verboten*. The Beethoven house and all the other exhibits had to remain unvisited while we continued upstream. Even if I had a curious desire to see the department of zoology in the museum, that also would have to go unsatisfied.

There was a particular reason for my wishing to see this museum, which had nothing to do with my own background as a zoologist. The interest was more historical. Except in Africa, where new countries have a tendency to arise like the bubbles on the skin of a rice pudding, the birth of a new state is something of a rarity, so it was impossible for me to chug past the particularly uninteresting waterfront of Bonn itself without remembering that it was there that on 1 September 1948 the Bundesrepublik came into existence. To prevent any possible jokes the skeleton of a mammoth at the entrance to the museum was decently hidden by brown-paper and potted palms, but otherwise the stuffed or unfleshed animals and birds of the zoological department looked on, dumb and sightless, as the pale Konrad Adenauer set the great nation he loved and served so well on course again as a parliamentary democracy. Exactly ten terrible years had passed since Adolf Hitler had been in Bonn for another event of immense political importance, the meeting which Neville Chamberlain believed would surely establish 'peace in our time'.

Godesberg itself is only half an hour upstream. Beside the shore to starboard we could see the white and rather faded mass of the Hotel Dreesen, with the wash of the upstream traffic breaking on the groynes at its foot. On the left of the side which faced the river the first-floor room with the balcony was No. 118, the famous room in which the British Prime Minister stayed, waiting for the summons to cross the Rhine and attend at the Hotel Petersberg among the woods of the Seven Mountains and there meet the Führer face to face. As for the Hotel Dreesen, there is nothing very special about its appearance, and probably the room itself would be ordinary enough had it not been thus thrown into the glare of the limelight of history. As a German said to me, 'The room is often used for conferences, some of which are indeed successful.' And others only apparently so.

That great and omniscient geographer Alexander von Humboldt declared Godesberg to be the eighth wonder of the world, thereby rating it slightly lower than Hannoversch Münden on the Weser, which he reckoned to be 'among the first seven'. It is not really a very exciting place, but maybe that is because it is now chiefly a haunt of the diplomats and politicians whose presence is so necessary in the immediate vicinity of Bonn. There are forty-four diplomatic missions in Bad Godesberg, ranging from those of the greater powers and neutrals to the embassies of the banana-republics. But the place is given an air of grace by the Redoute chateau of the Elector Max Franz, youngest son of Maria Theresa, who founded the reputation of the town as a spa in the seventeenth century. Much older and in some ways more striking is the Godesburg itself, the tower of which still dominates the town from the summit of its own steep mound. Nowadays the base shelters one of the best restaurants of the mid-Rhine, and over a glass of one of the splendid wines of the Ahr valley one may sit and look out across the plain, forgetting the antlike diplomats in the town hundreds of feet below and enjoying the incomparable view up and across the invisible river to the rounded shapes of the Siebenge-birge.

It is all very peaceful, very different from the ancient times when human sacrifices were probably performed upon the sacred hill-top site of Odin's hill, or the troubled era when the Godesburg itself was erected by the Archbishop of Cologne to prevent the recurrence of raids by other worthies upon his territories. That was in 1210, and the money to build the fortress is said to have been extracted by the archbishop from a Jew who had extorted it in the form of loan interest from Christians. The burg proved useful during the ensuing centuries, sometimes as a prison for those who had fallen foul of the archiepiscopal power, sometimes as a pleasant residence for summer parties, when perhaps the jolly songs and clink of glasses would carry down through the grating to some unfortunate inmate of the dungeons who would be lucky if ever he were again to see for himself that splendid view to beyond the great river.

Then came the day when one of the Cologne archbishops deserted the establishment and went over to the protestant faith. The proud Godesburg was invested by the staunchly catholic Bavarians, who managed at last to tunnel under the walls to place charges of gunpowder. Several loud explosions shook the valley, the walls came tumbling down, and the new and catholic archbishop's Spanish mercenaries were able to slaughter every man, woman and child in the place before spreading their terror as far as Unkel, burning every house they met with and slaughtering the peasants in the fields. It was just the sort of occasion that mercenaries right up to the present day have always appreciated.

Upstream of the town and its row of villas and hotels a very picturesque half-timbered inn stands among the limes at Plittersdorf, its terrace looking over the water. This is the Schaumburger Hof, a place of some distinction in British history for it was there that Victoria sat at a stone table beneath the trees and 'exchanged her first words of love' with the handsome young Albert of Coburg-Gotha, a student at Bonn University. Later she was to ride out to the inn and renew those early memories when she visited Bonn for the unveiling of the Beethoven memorial. In those same years the inn was the fashionable venue of many a poet and writer, and the Maikäferbund (Cockchafer Club) of the poet Gottfried Kinkel regularly met there.

Kinkel was a theology lecturer at Bonn who became an assistant priest, but as he was sufficiently independent in mind to marry a catholic girl he was dismissed from all his religious posts and turned instead to the history of art. He was already thirty-three when the political unrest of 1848 broke upon the land. In the balmy security of the Schaumburger Hof Kinkel plotted with the twenty-year-old student Karl Schurz and a former army lieutenant named Annecke, and together they raised a crowd of a hundred demonstrators who crossed the Rhine to raid an arms depot and seize weapons for the militant workers in Elberfeld. The party was soon overtaken by a company of dragoons which quickly scattered them, but Kinkel escaped to take part in another rising further south. This time he was caught and sentenced to life imprisonment, and was taken off to the Prussian prison of Spandau.

His friend Schurz was also a prisoner, in Rastatt. Schurz realised that it was only a question of time before he would be brought to trial and – as a Prussian subject – executed for treason. He therefore decided that he must escape, and his batman Adam set about finding a sympathetic lieutenant who was prepared to help. Together the three men crept down a sewer and hid there,

C2

waiting for darkness so that they might climb up an air vent into a street outside the fortress. Unfortunately, heavy rain began to fall, the water in the sewer rose, and the fugitives had no option but to wade down it to its end, where they had to dive under a grating to escape into the open – only to find a short way in front of them a detachment of Prussian guards.

The three men managed to make their way back into the town unseen, and for three days and nights they hid in their wet clothes in a barn. Then the lieutenant managed to reach a workman's cottage, the owner of which provided some provisions and promised to make a rendezvous with the refugees that night. Having checked on the disposition of the guards he would lead the way to the Rhine, where he would have his boat in readiness.

Thanks to the help of this good fellow, Schurz and his companions escaped. It was only when dawn came that they discovered that they were not on the further bank of the river but merely on one of the many islands which littered its course. However, by shouting and waving they attracted the attention of some French customs men, who rowed out and took them over to safety in Alsace.

No sooner was Schurz free than he heard that his friend Professor Kinkel had been sentenced in Berlin to life-long imprisonment in the same fortress of Spandau which more recently has held the unfortunate Rudolf Hess. Hiding in the Schaumburger Hof he carefully worked out a daring rescue operation, and with a forged passport he crossed into Germany again and betook himself to the vicinity of Spandau, where he hatched a bold scheme. A pub-keeper introduced him to the prison warder, who agreed for a considerable sum to provide wax impressions of all the vital keys of the prison, and Schurz also found a sympathetic landowner who was to have his carriage ready for a breakneck dash to the frontier of Mecklenburg. The warder was to unlock Kinkel's cell himself.

Bearing his keys Schurz forced his way far into the prison as arranged, only to be met by the warder with the news that the chief officer had gone off with one of the keys by mistake, and it had proved impossible to reach Kinkel's cell.

Schurz suspected that he had been tricked, but next morning the warder brought him a cigar-box containing the bribe intact. Reassured, Schurz thrust the money back, saying he wanted the professor, not the money. And that very night Kinkel was smuggled up to the roof, eased out through the tiles and lowered sixty feet to the street on a rope, while the land-owner's carriage rumbled past to drown the noise of falling tiles and Schurz stood ready with a band of friends to overpower any curious watchman or mere passer-by who might appear at an injudicious moment.

Leaping into the carriage, Schurz and Kinkel drove toward Hamburg then doubled back by another road to reach the safety of Mecklenburg. Another friend had a carriage in readiness for a dash to Rostock, where a shipbuilder had one of his own fast sailing vessels ready to cast off. A stormy journey brought the men safely round the Skaw and across to England. Schurz then made his way to the United States, where a brilliant future in politics awaited him. It is pleasant to know that the turbulent and revolutionary democrat Kinkel was joined by his wife and children in London, where he was appointed lecturer in German literature at London University. When in 1866 a general pardon was issued he returned home to his fatherland.

If the inn beneath the limes was to become famous for poetry, plotting, and royal romance, it began its days with a very different purpose. It was built in 1755 for the towing-trade, for there was a guild of *Halfen* at Plittersdorf. In the inn the rough towage-riders would wait for the arrival of an upstream barge, playing cards and drinking enough of the home-made and fiery red wine to keep them warm when they at last set off upstream. For the job of a *Halfen* was not an easy one. Often he had to wade where the towpath was flooded or broken down, and he might be obliged to ride for hours, soaked to the skin.

The Plittersdorf inn was a relay station. Here fresh horses were brought out from the stables to replace those of the *Halfen* who had brought the ship up from Wesseling, several hours downstream. The men of the Plittersdorf guild would haul upstream to Kripp, below Remagen, and then ride back again on the horses. All along these reaches the towpath was only on the left bank, and to prevent their taking fright the horses all had a blinker over the left eye. There was one man to every harnessed team of three or four horses, and always he rode with an open knife in his hand. This was not to protect himself against rivals but so that the tow-line could be instantly severed if the ship should yaw away from the bank and start pulling the horses and *Halfen* into the river.

When the first steam-tug appeared, the drovers of Plittersdorf decided to act. The inn-keeper found his livelihood as much threatened as theirs, and he joined them in an attempt to intimidate the steam-skippers. The first ships to steam up the river past Plittersdorf were greeted with a salvo from a number of small cannon charged with nails. It was a brave attempt to keep things as they had been, but it could hardly succeed. A detachment of hussars was sent up from Bonn and quartered in the inn. The drovers were forced to behave, and as the steam-tugs multiplied so the members of the guild fell on hard times. Soon they were penniless, and they deserted the pretty inn on the bank of the Rhine to look for other work.

Elsewhere the story was the same. So enraged were the drovers and haulage men at the sight of the puffing monster cutting away their livelihood that at Neuwied and Mainz also they would fire at the steam-ships with muskets. The first tug of the Matthias Stinnes concern had to be protected with armour along its sides, and in particularly dangerous reaches it was always accompanied by a troop of cavalry riding along the towpath. Resistance to progress was hopeless. As at Plittersdorf the *Halfen* were driven into extinction.

With their departure one of the most picturesque periods of Rhine shipping came to an end, and today we can only see it preserved in such drawings as those of Wenceslaus Hollar, the private artist employed by Lord Arundel to accompany him on his leisurely journey up the Rhine on his way to Bohemia on a diplomatic mission to the Emperor Ferdinard II. This was a century before the inn at Plittersdorf was built, but the towing practice was much the same, and one of Hollar's sketches shows the diplomatic ship approaching Oberwinter, only a short way above Godesberg. Nine horses towed that English ship, and the ambassador's clerk recorded that they cast anchor for the night opposite the Drachen-fels castle. The *Thames Commodore* was pushed along by 260 horses, but she did not stop at the foot of the Drachenfels. Instead she continued a little further ahead and slid in behind the point of the Grafenwerth (Count's Island) to the pontoons of the Honnef yacht club, a society which must have the most romantic outlook of any along all the course of the Rhine. This was to be our port whilst we visited the nature reserve of the Siebengebirge or Seven Mountains, which we had just skirted on their western side.

IV

The Siebengebirge – the monk of Heisterbach – valley of nightingales – Drachenfels and its dragon – Königswinter – rafting on the Rhine – Rolandsbogen and Nonnenwerth – death of a hero – the age of Sister Gertrud

IT is said that long, long ago the Rhine flowed through at least two great lakes besides the Bodensee. One of these covered the land upstream of where the city of Bonn was later to be built, and when in early summer the Alpine snows thawed to send a flood of water down the river the lake would rise and flow over the fertile land on either side. The people who lived there were very concerned at such a state of affairs, and as the hydraulic problems involved were outside their own competence they sent an embassy to the land of the giants asking them to give an estimate for cutting a channel through the rocks at the northern end.

A bargain was made, and a gang of seven navvies from the country of the giants came to the Rhineland and dug a cleft. The water streamed through the gap – no doubt to the great embarrassment of those who lived further downstream – and a proper river-sized channel was quickly eroded. Soon the lake had gone, and only a plain remained, except that to one side of the channel the seven mounds of rocky rubble were ranged, the spoil which the seven giants had shovelled. Cartographers call these heaps the Siebengebirge or Seven Mountains. Those who live in the neighbourhood say that the hills will not necessarily be there for ever. Giants are tidy-minded folk and they are likely one day to return and clear up the debris of their digging.

The Seven Mountains are in fact thirty in number; but the name is fair enough, for from a distance only the seven highest peaks can be distinguished. The whole group is a collection of volcanic hills, some of which have yielded the stone for such distinguished buildings as Cologne Cathedral. Naturally, the quarrying was undertaken where suitable stone was close enough to the river for easy shipping, and as a result the famous Drachenfels or Dragon Cliff was so heavily preyed upon that in 1788 the one side of the castle at the top of the rock was no longer supported and crashed into the void below. The Emperor Frederick William III later stepped in and bought the top of the mountain together with what little of the castle still remained. Otherwise it would certainly not be there today to provide one of the finest outlooks in all the Rhine valley. At the back of these hills are the remains of Heisterbach abbey, where a monk is said once to have had a curious adventure. I have often wondered whether the tale might not be true, and that this good brother broke through the sound barrier of time, that elusive line which perhaps all of us will one day cross in another way.

Brother Petrus Forschegrund was reading in 2 Peter 3. '*Ein Tag vor dem Herrn ist wie tausend Jahre,*' he read. 'One day is with the Lord as a thousand years, and a thousand years as one day.' The verse puzzled Brother Petrus, and he wandered into the woods to meditate upon it, listening as he did so to the romantically stirring song of the nightingales. As dusk drew in he returned to Heisterbach and was surprised to find a porter on duty who did not know him. Led before the prior – who had also changed during his absence – Petrus gave his name. They looked him up in the register and found that it was three hundred years since he had walked out to meditate and had disappeared. Sad to relate, the discovery that the text from 2 Peter was correct was too much for the monk, and he died.

In more modern times we are beginning to realise that the railway-timetable way of measuring events in hours and minutes and centuries has only a significance within the very limited sphere of our own time-tabled affairs. Or, to put it another way, that whatever 'time' may actually be it must surely run on some kind of logarithmic scale. Viewing the immediate past we can see that an hour of events today is comparable with one hour of what happened yesterday, but nobody can seriously think that a year in the era of Neanderthal man was comparable with a year in the mid-twentieth century.

If we look at the history and pre-history of the world as revealed by geology and radio-carbon dating it is obvious that the importance, the events of each hour or day have continually increased. The world of 1970 or 1980 is as different from that of 1900 as 1900 was from the year 800, when Charlemagne was crowned at Aachen. Further back, it took hundreds of millions of years for the single-celled aquatic creatures to be replaced by even the simplest ones complex enough to live on land. And before that came the long ages of silent hit-and-miss amino-acid in the primeval soup of the sea.

Long ages? Only if looked at from our own parochial and shipboard view-point of Greenwich Mean Time. For in fact time has been accelerating. Teilhard de Chardin was well aware of this, and as a scientist he was naturally inclined to extend the curve of the graph and see where it led. Of course it did not lead to the billions of years of slow roasting or slow cooling of a decaying planet but to a time measured within only thousands of our year-units when humanity would, as it were, take off spiritually into a new level of existence, a spiritual state as much above the present one as our own civilisation is beyond the cave life of Aurignac and the herd-hunting of Solutré. Perhaps he is right.

Nowadays, I hope, we are no longer so scared by time. We accept its elusiveness, we are aware that it cannot conceivably be a straight line. And if any of us should, like that monk of Heisterbach, be tempted to meditate on the Bible as we read it I doubt if we should need to wander in the woods to convince ourselves of the truth of the text from 2 Peter.

Yet it might still come as a shock to us to realise that we ourselves have to live by the twenty-four-hour day, and if one day this year is equal to a hundred a century ago we have that much more to achieve in the same unit of local time. Once, things were run by evolution (or by God, if one prefers the term). Since *Homo sapiens* there has been a change to a partnership of ever-increasing closeness, and of ever greater urgency as the time-graph becomes more and more vertical until finally . . .

Finally, what? Perhaps the moment when, like Brother Petrus, we pass into a dimension of which we yet know only such little as the visionaries have brought back to us from their travels beyond the barrier of time – a frontier which still bounds our physical existence in a niche of evolutionary current.

But to return to the legend of the monk of Heisterbach, this pensive fellow had, it seems, spent no less than three hundred years fascinated by the song of a bird in the woods. Obviously such a thing could not be allowed to occur again, and St Bernard of Clairvaux, already known for his successful banishment of nightingales from the monastery garden of Himmerode to an island in the Moselle where the rather more kindly nuns of the convent of Stuben willingly received them, was called to rid Heisterbach's woods of the menace. He ordered the nightingales to pack up, and he banished them to the Nachtigallental or Nightingale Valley above Königswinter, to which they return happily each summer from their winter quarters.

As for the monastery, it was dissolved under the great military wave of Napoleonic materialism which rolled across western Europe at the beginning of the nineteenth century. Eventually the buildings were sold by auction, and if the choir of the church has survived that was partly because the work on the Canal du Nord, where the stone from the abbey was to be used for the lock walls, was brought to a halt just in time by the demolition of the ambitions of the great Corsican himself at the hands of the British and their allies.

The Drachenfels – Dragon Cliff – is undoubtedly one of the great sights of the Rhine, and I suspect that the quarrying which nearly demolished it went far to improving its outline by giving it an almost sheer face on the side towards the river. The view downstream from Unkel or Oberwinter toward the crag topped by a crumbled castle keep is one of breathtaking beauty, especially in the early morning when a silky shining mist of the palest blue lies over the river and the faint outline of the volcanic hills protrudes mysteriously from the sea as though they were the mountains of Tahiti. There is something age-old about the shape of these wooded hills, and their sheer insularity hints that men have lived there for a very long time indeed.

Some believe the Drachenfels to have been the scene of Siegfried's adventure, but this is doubtful. There were many dragons in

Germany during the era of such beasts, and that of the Seven Mountains met its death in a different way. The event occurred during the lifetime of Maternus, one of the three men sent by St Peter as apostles to the Rhineland and the one who died in Alsace while on his way there – an event which so distressed his colleagues that they had to return to Rome and fetch St Peter's staff with which to revive him. After this – if we quickly pass over a few centuries – Maternus reached Trier and later became the first Bishop of Cologne. But his success was confined to the left side of the Rhine, to the province of Gaul and the lands to the north. Across the river the terrible German pagans were still intransigent.

Worse still, these horrible heathens would raid across the river to take prisoners. One such capture was a girl of such rare beauty that the two toughest of the chieftains each sought to have her as his own. Horsrik was an old warrior whose club had already smashed in countless skulls, Rinbold was younger and fearless. He was also handsome, so it is already possible to guess which of the two is to win the prize. That, however, would be to miss out the bit about the dragon, for when the two warriors raised their weapons to have at each other the venerable priest of Odin stepped forward and held the men apart. It was foolish to lose one or possibly both of the leaders for the sake of an argument about a Christian beauty, he said. She would be sacrificed at sunrise next morning to the insatiable dragon who lived in a hole on the cliff and terrorized the area. This decision was greeted with applause, though Dr Ruland when he set down the story added for the sake of his readers that 'Rinbold, the proud young chieftain, looked sorrowfully at her angel-like face.'

So, next morning, the girl was garlanded and garnished in a way likely to appeal to the monster's appetite and then tied to the tree to which the dragon fodder was customarily attached. The people retired to a safe distance, and then as the first rays of sunlight came over the forest to light the maiden's golden hair the scaly beast emerged with bloodshot eyes and flaming breath, and licked its steaming lips at the sight of such a dish. Just as it raised itself upon its tail to strike, the girl pulled out her golden crucifix and held it aloft, an act which had such a dramatic effect upon the dragon that he reared, pitched over backwards, and was precipitated into the Rhine far below. As the cords loosed themselves from her body two strong arms seized her – but only gently, for Rinbold was at heart a good man, as befits such a tale. He and the old high priest were the first two to be converted. They were quickly joined by thousands more. Even Dr Ruland does not tell us what became of Horsrik, but being rather a horrible old man I expect he remained perverse and obdurate until the end of his days.

At the foot of the Drachenfels lies Königswinter, where the massive car ferries swing across the river from Mehlem and the hotels which look out across the promenade are still as busy and almost as self-consciously distinguished as they were in the days of the Grand Tour. It is a popular place with Rhine and Ruhr families as well as with foreigners, and no doubt this is partly because of its position and also because it has some excellent wine-inns. Indeed, there is nothing wintry about Königswinter. The second half of the name comes from *vinitorium*, and on the volcanic slopes behind the town the German kings had some of their far-flung vineyard terraces. The volcanic soil produces a very drinkable red wine, even if its name of Dragon's Blood is a little too popular for my taste. As Königswinterer Mönchspfad or something equally medieval and evocative it would perhaps appeal to me more. Yet a boatman who does not like wine, however excellent, can easily lose himself in contemplation of the fine model of a medieval Rhine ship hidden away in the back room of the Jesuiter Hof, one of the pretty and jumbled inns which has served visitors since the seventeenth century.

The easy, sensible and mundane method of scaling the Drachenfels is of course by the rack-and-pinion railway, the oldest in Germany. But Königswinter still has its carriages – or more properly carts – and once when I happened to spend a land-bound night of early spring at that riverside town it occurred to me that the sensible thing would be to go up the Drachenfels early enough to hear the dawn chorus of woodland birds, and to make the ascent by cart. It was then that I discovered the curious system of calculation on which the carters worked.

It was not altogether easy to find a man prepared to turn out at half past six, but when one of the drivers was told that the client was English that in itself was enough to explain any such eccentricity as wanting to go for a drive before breakfast, and he agreed to take me. The fare, he explained, would be twenty-eight marks if I was alone, but only twenty-five for two people.

'You mean twenty-five each, of course?'

'*Aber nein*! Twenty-five altogether.' If there were three of us it would only be twenty-three for the carriage, he added.

I thought of the horse plodding up one thousand feet of mountain with a cart-load of English. Surely the creature had to work harder, consume more oats for every extra passenger. I told the carter I did not quite understand the system of calculation and asked him to repeat the charges, which he did.

'And how much for four people?' I asked.

'For four it would be only twenty marks – five marks each.'

It seemed that the horse was even prepared to take five passengers as well as the driver, but at this point an innate consideration for the brute creation stopped my pressing further. I easily found two people who were willing to be my guests, and when a third was dubious about getting up early I pointed out to him that by lying in bed he would not only be missing a pleasant outing but actually costing me three good solid gold-lined German marks. A generous man, he at once agreed to sacrifice an hour and a half of sleep and accompany me, and early next morning I set off with my three guests.

I had expected the drive to be pleasant, but I had not imagined just how idyllic that slow ascent would be as we wound along the lanes between the orchards of pear and apple blossom with the dew sparkling in the forerunner light of an early dawn. The cart had rubber tyres so that the only sound was that of the clip-clop of our horse and a creaking of the shafts. A good strong aroma of horse drifted back to us, supplemented by a tang of stale wine from the coachman.

The dawn chorus, if there was one, was already over, but a green woodpecker flashed over the meadows and laughed in the clear light. From down on the river the bell of the ferry rang faintly, and somewhere in the hills a church tolled for early service. When we entered the tall woods of beech there was silence except for the squeaks of tits almost at the upper limit of audible frequency. It was a ride intoxicating in its loveliness, in the sheer improbability that such crystal sharpness of the air could exist uncleft by the jet fighters of the Americans – who, fortunately, were still in bed – and that here and now in the twentieth century one could crawl slowly up a long woodland path, horse-drawn and without even the sound or smell of one of Carl Benz's horseless carriages or their sleek descendants.

And how splendid is that view over the Rhine in the early light, the river still lying in the shadow of the bulk of the hills themselves. Below, a Dutch ship and a Belgian, each throwing its symmetrical wedge of ripples across the rough grey surface of the river. To the right Godesberg and the world of sleeping diplomats, in the background the strange volcanic hills piercing the rolling land of the Eifel. Left, the view extends over the comma shape of the Nonnenwerth, and in the distance the light gleams upon the harbour of Oberwinter with its riot of pink cherry blossom as a smudge of colour visible through the binoculars. Then the river runs straight, the swift reach leading up to Unkel and disappearing round a sharp bend hidden in mist and mystery. Years ago, I thought, one might have been lucky enough to see a raft emerge from the dimness toward Remagen and Sinzig on its way down river. Rafting on the Rhine was now at an end, but I remembered as a boy seeing a sizeable float running through the gorge, and as late as 1960 we had met two or three rafts one sixth of a mile in length when the *Commodore* had taken us up the River Main. Even those were humble compared with the rafts of earlier days.

Modern traffic on the Rhine is enormously impressive, and it is an unforgettable experience to stand by the ruins of the Drachen-burg and see a giant tug thrusting up to Switzerland at the head of a tow-train which extends through Godesberg and beyond. Yet if anything could possibly be more awe-inspiring it would be the timber raft of a century or two ago, an assemblage of logs vast almost beyond belief. Smaller rafts were floated down from the Black Forest and the woodlands of the Taunus and Odenwald, and at certain villages below Koblenz these were combined into one huge consignment which would be sent on its way to Rotterdam,

serving as a passenger and cargo carrier at the same time. Sketches
of such rafts have survived, and also a few descriptions such as
that of a journeyman apprentice who noted the details in his diary
written in the early nineteenth century.

It was so extraordinary a sight that he would never have believed
it if another had told him of it, he wrote. There were five hundred
oarsmen aboard the raft, half of them in front and half at the rear,
whose business it was to steer the raft in the fairway. There were
no oars along the sides; but in the centre of the raft, which
measured 1,700 feet in length and 250 in breadth, there stood a
tower-like structure six to eight storeys in height, on the top of
which sat a man with a flag. The understeersmen watched the
signals of the overseer, and gave their orders to the rowers
accordingly so that the raft was always kept in the channel. On
approaching a town the band would strike up, and hundreds of
men and women streamed to the shore to wave with their hats and
kerchiefs. He discovered that the raft would draw in at Irlich,
downstream of Neuwied, to take in a further float which was 120
feet long and 40 broad, and next afternoon he went with a crowd
of people to see it. The raft had already come to a halt and he noted
the immense pieces of bank which had been torn out by the
anchors flung ashore to bring such heavy floats to a stop.

For one kreutzer the public might view the raft, and along with
hundreds of others the apprentice went aboard. Thirty wooden
houses were ranged along the raft in the manner of a narrow street,
and through the windows one could see fine ladies and gentlemen
sitting at their ease. Some of the hutments were offices, but those
which contained the bedrooms had curtains. The army of labourers
who performed the rowing were housed in simple and low huts
without any windows at all.

Naturally, provisions had to be available for the people making
the journey either as crew or passengers, and several hundred
barrels of beer and wine were lashed in rows. In a canvassed stall
there was a herd of oxen. The band was gathered at the foot of the
steersman's tower and as he went aboard it began to play – music
being handed out to those near enough to join in the singing. He
sang heartily with the rest.

'It was just like being in a village at fairtime,' he wrote in his diary. 'One could step up to a gaming table and throw dice, or buy whatever one wished at the stalls. The range was burning brightly at the back of a large restaurant, where many people were already sitting at the tables. I joined them, and ordered a Mannheimer beer.'

Another account written about the same time tells how the duty paid out by the captain of such a raft at the seventeen frontier toll-posts between Andernach and Dordrecht amounted to 35,000 guilders. Naturally, such a colossus of the river could not easily be brought up sharply, and it was essential to have a clear run. On the day before the departure a warning craft was sent down the river to prepare the keepers of the bridges of boats, the millers with their water-mills anchored in the stream, and the fishing craft and other vessels that the raft was coming. Then, when all was ready for the departure, the seventy-year-old skipper 'whose very appearance inspired awe' inspected the sweeps and the men and held a formal muster of the whole company, addressing them on the importance of good behaviour. Finally he climbed into his tower or pulpit, took off his cap, and ordered the entire complement to pray.

Every man bared his head and prayed to God for a safe journey. Then the anchors on land and in the water were raised or let go, and to the shouts of the understeersmen the floating island got under way. At Cologne the mid-Rhine steersman handed over the raft to a Dutch pilot who took command until the voyage reached its end at Dordrecht. There the crew were discharged and the men had of course to find their own way back. The raft was put up to auction as a single lot and would realise five or six hundred thousand marks.

Today the rafts have vanished. They would be too dangerous to manoeuvre among the throng of merchant vessels. But the view of the river from such a ruined nest of robber barons as the Drachenburg is as splendid as ever, so alluring indeed that it is difficult to tear oneself away from the terrace rail. At length I set out with my three willing ballasters to return to Königswinter on foot, and dropping through the dark woods below the castle we crossed a gentle meadow of hairbells and knapweed, scabious and buttercups, and plunged into a deserted little valley cut deep in the beechwoods, the hidden cleft of the Nachtigallental to which St Bernard had banished the warblers he considered so improper and erotic.

On this morning they were not there. It was too early in the year for their Rhineland philanderings and they were still dallying in southern lands before returning again to their own vale to nest and to sing in all the exuberance of impending summer as their forefathers had done ever since Brother Petrus fell down dead in the doorway of Heisterbach, slain by the realisation that time might not be just what it seemed.

The trouble with the romantic Rhine is just that. It *is* romantic – so much so that it manages to crowd into the relatively short stretch of its middle reaches as much legend and history, chivalry and dastardy, true love and bastardy, noble devotion and blind hatred as the rest of Europe put together. Sweeping down upon the current, any steersman who is not completely insensitive to the past has to divide his attention between rocks, the signals of upcoming ships, and the tales of the heroes and heroines, villains and haughty adventuresses who inhabited – and perhaps still haunt – the ruined towers and keeps on either hand. And these castles come so thick and fast that he has scarcely identified one crag-bound watch-tower or keep before the next is already on the beam.

Fortunately the *Thames Commodore* is now heading upstream, and the stiffness of the Rhine current will itself hold her back sufficiently to allow her crew to see those sights which have inspired poets and artists across the centuries. Besides, we are still short of the gorge itself where the castles begin to form an almost continuous line of battlements and strongpoints, so we can settle comfortably on deck with the Drachenfels to port, the sun ahead, and note on the summit of the wooded hill on the starboard bow a single solitary arch of crumbled stone through which we can glimpse the brilliance of the sky behind it.

This arch is the Rolandsbogen (Roland's Arch), and the slight bend of the river above which it stands is the setting for one of the greatest and saddest tales of the era of medieval chivalry, a story sung by minstrels in the great halls of many a castle, a tale which varied much with the years and the particular troubadours who sang it, but which was probably one of the most favoured themes of all. For the Song of Roland was perhaps even better known than the great epic of The Four Sons of Aymon. Certainly the ballad was sung on the invasion beach when the Normans landed in England and it fell to the minstrel Taillefer to bolster their morale by striking up the tale of Roland the mighty, the fearless and chivalrous, the knight who with his handful of companions stationed himself in the Pyrenean pass to hold at bay the hordes of Islam while Charlemagne's army, badly mauled in the battle, withdrew to the safety of the Frankish lands. One by one the men were slain, then Roland himself, and only with his dying breath did he blow one single blast upon the great horn Oliphant. Yet it was a blast so penetrating that Charlemagne heard it across France. It caused him to stop, rally his men, and march all the way back again to slash and rip and slaughter those pagan hordes who had slain his twelve noblest and most chivalrous knights.

However, in the Rhineland the version sung by minstrels to the tough knights in their craggy nests was different. Roland blew his horn, yes; but so great was his natural strength, so powerful his blood, that although he had been left by the Moors for dead in the gorge of Roncevalles he regained consciousness, bound his own wounds, and set out in great pain to limp and struggle homeward, bound for the Drachenfels and the castle in which lived the lovely Hildegund to whom he had sworn eternal devotion. The journey took him some years, as well it might, but at last he came to Königswinter and dragged himself up the long path which led to the Drachenburg.

Yet all this effort was in vain. As Hildegund's own ageing father explained to the travel-worn and emaciated knight, her lover had long since been reported as slain and the girl in her sorrow had vowed that she could never look upon another man but would enter a convent. She had got her to a nunnery, right there in the Rhine, on the Nonnenwerth (Nuns' Island). See, down there in the trees, where the river curves round the foot of the hill and splits into three separate channels – that is where she is to live her days, in sadness perhaps, but in devotion and charity and prayer.

The news is of course terrible to Roland, a blow so fearful indeed that from the sheer shock the wounds caused by the Moorish swords and lances in the pass of Roncevalles re-open and his blood flows out. He is carried into the Drachenburg, and though weak from the haemorrhage he eventually recovers enough to make his way down to the river and have himself ferried across. He orders a small and simple castle dwelling to be built, and built quickly, right on that shoulder of bluff where he might look down upon the grounds of the convent in the stream. There is to be a bay window where he can sit, weak from his wounds and wanderings, his only wish to watch for the form of the fair Hildegund as she passes every day from the refectory to the chapel.

A more ordinary mortal might devise some means to rescue Hildegund from the convent and whisk her away to Rome to seek release from her vow. But not Roland. He is the flower of chivalry, of acceptance of fate. He will never love another, but nor will he break into the new life of his love. For the rest of his days he will live only for those brief recurring moments when the veiled figures cross the courtyard in the spring sunshine, in the falling leaves of autumn or in the powdery snow of a crisp winter's day when the Rhine itself is near to freezing.

And so the years go by. Roland's bodily wounds will never heal. Nor will the wound to his noble heart. It is as though his own life is dripping away as he strains to catch the singing of the choir borne up to him on the breeze. One of the voices is Hildegund's and now and again he thinks he can distinguish it. And of course Hildegund has long since heard of the knight who has built the tower in order to be near her. Little by little the unbounded spiritual joy which was to attend her in the nunnery ebbs away. One day, heartbroken, she dies. Her companions bury her in the convent.

Roland hears the bell tolling for a funeral. He knows whose it is, for as the sisters file across the court there is only one missing, his Hildegund. He sits there at the window, motionless as the chanting wells up from among the trees. The nuns file back to their cells. Roland sits there still, his head rested on his hands. It is dark when his one servant comes into the room to summon him to his evening meal.

But the knight does not answer. The servant steps forward and touches him on the shoulder, only to find that he does not look up. The only thing for which Roland has desperately clung to life itself has gone, and his great and broken heart has simply stopped. There at the bay window overlooking the Nonnenwerth he has quietly died, to be with Hildegund eternally as he had vowed.

The arch is easily visible from the river and it is sad to know that, quite apart from the fact that the noble knight was himself a legendary and almost Homeric character, the castle ruin at Rolandseck really has nothing to do with Roland, the hero of Roncevalles, for it was not built until three centuries after that famous battle. But it may well be that another knight named Roland loved a girl who had retired to the Nonnenwerth at the foot of the crag. The castle itself eventually decayed, and in 1839 even the famous arch was destroyed in a violent storm. However, the poet Freiligrath happened to notice its absence when he was travelling by post-chaise down the valley, and he wrote such vigorous verses of appeal in a Cologne newspaper that money to rebuild the arch poured in and the Rolandsbogen was soon restored to the condition in which it stands today.

As for the Nonnenwerth, that fair island has a particular connection with England as the place at which Edward III stayed on his return down the Rhine from a meeting with Louis the Bavarian. There the monarch held his court in the river, and in his honour a singing contest was organised, but who the Mastersinger on that occasion was and what his prize song may have been I have never discovered.

Centuries later the French, burning with iconoclastic zeal, dissolved the convent. After a score or more years as a beer-hall and place of assignation it became a convent school. All this while an aged nun had tolled the bell morning and evening, and under the new order one of the sister-teachers asked the wrinkled woman how old she was. But poor old Sister Gertrud did not know. She could only say that she had come there as a child, long, long ago. The years had slipped away just like the waves of the Rhine. She had counted neither the one nor the other. To her, time did not matter.

In the Seven Hills

Out of curiosity the novices persuaded the abbess to hunt through the records of admission, and so it was discovered that Gertrud was well over one hundred years old. When the young nuns told her this and congratulated her, instead of being pleased she was dismayed. A century was too long for any reasonable woman to live. Early next morning she tolled the bell for the last time. She was found dead, her hands still clutching the bell-rope.

Later the romantic isle was to have musical connections of a curious kind, for when Franz Liszt discovered it he was so delighted with the wooded Nonnenwerth that he thought of building there a summer residence for his mistress and the children she had borne him. The girl was the Countess of Agoult, a notable Parisian beauty who fell violently in love with Liszt, leaving home and husband and children to accompany her lover through Europe. She gave birth to two daughters, of whom the younger – Cosima – was eventually to marry Richard Wagner. Yet if Liszt found the Nonnenwerth just such a place as caused the music to flow from his muse, he eventually abandoned his idea of taking over the island. The cost of coping with continual erosion by the Rhine was too great for him.

V

Yacht clubs of the Rhine – Bohnenfeld shoal and Unkel reef – the ferryman of Erpel – Remagen and Apollinaris – the wayward girl from the castle – from Linz to Andernach – defence by bees – the value of a Neuwied wife – Deutsches Eck and Ehrenbreitstein

JUST upstream of the Nonnenwerth the harbour of Oberwinter lies to starboard, a port of refuge where scores of Rhine-ships can put in to flee from the ice-floes driving down the river in a sharp winter. It is a noisy place, because the main road runs along one edge of it and the trailer lorries bump and clatter all night long on their way to the cities of the Ruhr; and it is also one of those harbours where the bank is so carefully protected with shoals of rock that one can only hope to draw in against a work-boat or the jetty of a yacht club.

German yacht clubs are for the most part very hospitable, offering their facilities most willingly to the rare bird from abroad. But one can have adventures there just the same, as the *Thames Commodore* and her elder sister were both to discover. It was an April day when we drew in at one of these friendly places aboard the *Commodore*, and the janitor was busily painting the railings. The local yachtsmen were summer boaters only and they had not yet begun to be active, so apart from one or two members sitting in the clubhouse none were about. The only ship as yet in commission was ours.

We went out for the evening and it was not very late when we returned. The jetty gate was locked and there was no answer when we rang the bell. I noticed however that there was a light in our own boat, and it was not difficult to guess why. Unwilling to be locked out for the night I climbed round the barbed wire, loosed a small day-boat, and used it to ferry Miriam the few yards from the rocky shore to the nearest pontoon. Then I returned the launch to its mooring and together we marched along the planking toward the *Commodore*.

The janitor was certainly startled, but he did not come ashore. In fact he was unable to climb the companionway but was half standing, half leaning on the bulkhead, one hand holding a whisky bottle three parts empty. It had been full and sealed only three hours earlier, and so had the wine bottle which I saw on the saloon floor together with a rum and another whisky, both of which had been broached by ourselves but were now dry. I marvelled at the man's capacity.

Rising with difficulty the guardian of the yacht club addressed us in what would, in Anglo-Saxon, have been four-letter words but because of the complexities of the German language ran to about two dozen letters apiece. No simple *Himmeldonnerwetternocheinmal* either, but good solid lower-deck stuff, sounding like Wagner after a night out. In this curious lingo he set about us for daring to disturb him.

He made a sort of lunge at me with the bottle, and when I side-stepped he went full length on the floor. Not wanting to have him encumbering the bilge all night we shoved him up the companion way and tipped him over the edge. The man fell like a sack of rotten apples and rolled on to the next pontoon.

'If he falls in, I can tell you someone who's not going to help him out,' said Miriam. As he scrambled up, cursing, she pointed down the line of pontoons toward the clubhouse and addressed him with one word only – '*Heraus!*'

German is a good language in which to shout and order people about. The man gaped, and began to shamble away. I wanted to follow him to the end of the line, but Miriam restrained me. A ducking would not hurt him, she said. It seemed doubtful if he could become more sodden than he was already.

The sequel to this was that I wrote a letter to the club, thanking them for their facilities but mentioning finding their man aboard and too drunk to get off the ship unaided. In reply I had a note which said that for a long time past the club yachts had been drunk dry, but in spite of suspicions the guilt had never actually been pinned on the waterman. However, he had now been sacked, and everyone was glad. In fact I myself was not altogether happy about it, for however foolish it may be to abuse a position of trust there are many – of whom the club janitor was one – who are so hooked on addiction of one kind or another that merely to sack them solves nothing.

Then there was the occasion when we left the *Thames Commodore* out of the high season at another Rhine yacht club. In fact we were so outside the normal yachting period that for the last few weeks she lay alone, without even a gang-plank connecting the clubhouse and jetty to *terra firma*. She was absolutely safe from outside interference.

That same thought occurred to two men who must, I think, have been fugitives escaped from a jail. Whether they swam over or used a dinghy and set it adrift I do not know, but they lived aboard for perhaps two weeks – to judge by the chipped whiskers in my electric razor and the count of empty soup packets, beer cans, tins of meat, baked beans, coffee and sardines and vegetables. They did not trouble even to help themselves to the radio or my camera and binoculars – or indeed to anything which might have been identified had they later been caught. And one of them at least must have been a very accomplished house-breaker, for their entry was so well executed that we never discovered how they found their way into the ship at all. The men were reasonably tidy but not the best of cooks, for sometimes they had let the curry or stew burn on the bottom of the pans. However, they could easily have cleaned out very much more than the food cupboards, so we bore them little ill will. Certainly they deserved to get away after showing such ingenuity in the choice of a hiding-place.

At a third club an elderly naval man came and took our lines, then superintended our mooring with a very experienced eye. Approving of the way I had set our ropes he introduced himself as the retired captain of one of the famous German warships of the Second World War. We chatted of the Rhine, and boats, and wine, then as I was preparing to climb aboard again he said casually, 'Do not be worried if in the night you see a searchlight.'

I assured him we would not be in the least alarmed.

'Good. You see I have installed one. It comes on automatically and sweeps the harbour. We lost a dinghy. Thieves. Yes, two young men – you know the way it is. The boat was on a trailer and they towed her away in the night. But they are now behind the bars. Ha! That is good. Yes, one year behind bars. Very good!'

'Very,' I said.

'But it will never happen again,' the captain said. 'Not now that I have fixed up the searchlight. It's a powerful one, a naval searchlight. It comes on, sweeps the moorings and banks, and that's that.' He was about to turn away when he added as a sort of afterthought, 'And by the way, do not be alarmed if you hear shooting in the night.'

'Of course not.' I tried to sound as though the firing of revolvers was my usual lullaby. 'I wouldn't give it a thought,' I said.

'Excellent! There is no need to be worried, you see. It is just that if I wake up and hear a sound on the bank I call "*Wer ist da?*" And if there's no answer I fire, twice. That should keep them off, you know. Either that or. . . . Well, only two weeks ago I heard a sound and I shouted a challenge. No answer, so I fired. Yes, twice. And got one with each bullet. Ha! That was good, wasn't it?'

'Yes.' I wondered if he had killed them.

'In the leg,' he added. 'And they couldn't get away, so they are behind the bars too – Ha! After a term in hospital, of course.'

'Of course.'

'They won't try it again.'

'I shouldn't think they would,' I agreed.

'Though others might, of course. That's why I have my revolver at the ready. So, if you hear shots do not give it a thought.'

I promised. And when after dark we came back on board we did so in our bare feet, our ears straining to catch the challenge which would precede the shots. But the officer slept soundly, and next morning as we chugged away up the Rhine I pondered what would happen to a yachtsman in Britain who blazed away with a gun and winged a brace of petty thieves. There was not much doubt who would be the one to end up behind the bars, ha! Nor could I help wondering what the annual bag might be of deaf individuals, or of young couples strolling under the trees too lost in each other's love to notice the tone of earnest triggering intent in the sudden hail from down among the boats.

Oberwinter is not a notable place, but like Königswinter it holds

D

a medieval vineyard tucked away in its name. Outside the harbour
the Rhine runs almost straight between Honnef and Unkel, and in
this reach there is a shoal only visible at very low water, a bank
which goes by the curious name of the Bohnenfeld (or Bean Field).
The villagers in Oberwinter will assure one that the old maidens
and bachelors and childless couples come there and are harnessed
to a heavy iron harrow which they must drag up and down to
cultivate the field. Why? That remained a mystery, but doubtless
it was intended to make them fruitful.

A little further ahead and immediately before the sharp bend to
port round the pretty town of Unkel there used to be a rock known
as the Unkelstein. Sadly, the needs of navigation caused it to be
blasted away, though even now there is a very swift passage and to
starboard the water swirls and breaks over the inshore end of the
rocky bar. Of course the Unkelstein accounted for many a stout
ship in its day, and the passage by Unkel could sometimes be one
of those for which a skipper brought out his holy candles and lit
them, but more picturesque was the custom of leaping from the
bow onto the rock with a bottle of wine in one hand and a glass in
the other, and drinking the healths of the remainder of the crew
and passengers with sufficient dispatch to be able to leap back
aboard before the stern had passed. In those days the ships would
of course be travelling more slowly, but they were also considerably
shorter than the 300-foot craft of today.

The bend above Unkel is dramatic. The cliff rises almost
vertical on the starboard hand, and above where the busy roadway
is built up on stilts over the edge of the river a shrine is carved in
the rock, no doubt to assist the devotions of captains fearful of
being washed against the deadly Unkelstein. Then comes Erpel to
port and ahead on the starboard side the town of Remagen, which
tries very hard to convince one that it is something of a resort.

Erpel has of course long been a ferry point, and it is one of
several in Germany where the ferryman was once wakened in the
night by a tapping at his door. Thinking perhaps that the doctor
needed to be taken over the river for some emergency he rose and
dressed, but outside he could find nobody. He was just about to
shut the door with an oath about these damned teenagers being up

to their tricks, when he heard someone calling from the direction of his boat down at the shore, a thin voice which requested him to push out and haul over – for the craft was a chain ferry and not a rowing-boat.

He did as he was asked, and although he could see no customers on either bank he began to pull on the chain in long, hard heaves. The boat seemed heavy, and after a while he took off his muffler and cap to pull the harder. It was only when he arrived at the other shore that he realised that his craft was filled with hundreds upon hundreds of the little people who, for some reason, had decided to emigrate from the right bank to the left. As each of them left the boat a silver coin tinkled into his cap until the good ferryman had a pile of good solid money. And – which is an interesting side-light on the habits of the little people – they had all paid in coins minted by the Electorate of Cologne.

Across the river from Erpel is Remagen, one of the few Rhine villages to have its name indelibly printed in modern history. The remains of the pillars of the railway bridge across the Rhine (there are no road bridges between Koblenz and Bonn) still stand battered and forlorn in the stream, and I hope they will always do so, for it was by that bridge that the Americans crossed the river and sealed the fate of the Nazis. The lieutenant who should have blown the bridge but failed to do so was escorted to Berlin, it is said, and there a psychopath Führer, screaming with rage, personally tore the insignia off his uniform. Of course the bridge was later destroyed, but by then the damage was done. The Rhine had been crossed – the last great barrier before Berlin.

A short way beyond Remagen the delicate gothic Apollinaris church stands by itself on the starboard hand, resting confidently upon the rocky cliff. In fact it is a nineteenth-century building which replaces an older one erected at this unlikely spot at the particular behest of one of those self-willed and waterborne deceased saints which are a feature of German rivers.

Apollinaris himself is said to have been an actual disciple of St Peter. His remains were acquired by the same Archbishop of Cologne who brought home the bones of the Three Kings, and as the combined cargo of relics travelled down the Rhine from

Switzerland so the bells in the riverside town swung into action of their own accord, all the way from Strasbourg to Cologne. This was enough to make the townspeople run to the bank and fling themselves upon their knees until the barge had passed out of sight.

So the triumphal voyage proceeded to the continual accompaniment of bells of church and chapel, abbey and cloister, until the craft was approaching Remagen, where it ran aground. At first this seemed to be due to bad steering, but a more mysterious reason was soon revealed. Apollinaris wanted to go no further. All efforts to float the vessel off the shoal were in vain until the bones of the saint had been off-loaded and carried ashore to a chapel which happened to be dedicated to St Martin but was of course transferred to the protection of Apollinaris himself a short time after.

If the name of this saint suggests mineral water, it is for the very good reason that when the famous spring in the Ahr valley was discovered in 1852 it was naturally named after the hill where the saint had been buried. Soon Bad Neuenahr was attracting royalty, and as in the course of time other hot springs were opened up through boring, the place became one of the leading establishments in a country where even nowadays the business of drinking salty waters is taken extremely seriously. And of course Goethe – an almost compulsive cure-taker who made frequent visits to springs – set his seal of approval on them and so ensured the future of such places at Neuenahr. Stomach, pulse, small intestine, liver and gall-bladder, kidneys and heart and ureter – there is not much of the body which a real cure-believer cannot have improved by a visit to Bad Neuenahr. But, as the town's PRO so wisely insists, it is not necessary to become ill to visit the place. One may even enjoy Neuenahr when healthy.

The Chapel of St Martin which gave way to that of Apollinaris is connected with an unusual tale of a haunting. Somewhere above the town there lived a noble knight who, like so many others, went off to the Thirty Years War and was slain, probably by the Swedes. His widow was inconsolable, and she sent her young daughter every day to the Martinskapelle to pray for her dead father. The girl was not very attracted by this doleful and devout occupation, and as she reached her teens she developed a tendency to go on past the chapel and have a good time in Remagen, returning late at night with every appearance of having spent the day in tearful piety. One day when she was enjoying herself with the boys a violent thunderstorm came over the valley. No doubt the mother was relieved to think of her dearest daughter safe inside the chapel, but I doubt if the girl thought of her mother at all. There is nothing like a thunderstorm for making one want to be held in strong and masculine arms.

In fact the lightning struck the castle, which collapsed in ruins. The water streaming down the hillside from the cloudburst swept away the debris and stones and timber, furniture, and the corpses of cattle and servants. When the storm had at last abated the gay girl decided to go home, and she made her way toward the castle ready primed with the usual tale of sorrowful hours spent before the altar. But the place had vanished. Hurrying to and fro with her lantern she could find no trace of it. She called her mother, but there was no answer. All night she sought in vain. And still does so, if we can believe what is said locally.

Another thunderstorm on the Rhine left a more solid memory. Among the bargemen of Remagen was a certain Captain Jonas Jülich, who was voyaging heavy laden when the storm broke and the wind drove down the reach to raise sharp waves which began to swamp his craft. Instead of lighting a candle (which would no doubt have been blown out) he prayed earnestly, adding that he would give peas and bacon and bread to the poor of Remagen if he survived to do so. His ship made home in the port of Remagen, and the skipper was as good as his word. He founded a dole of pea soup and bacon to be dished out to the poor of the town every St Agnes day.

Further up the Rhine at Bacharach there is – as we shall later see – just such a tale about a Jew as might have been invented by Julius Streicher, the professional anti-Semitic inciter of the terrible 1930s. (I used at one time to take his paper *Der Stürmer* out of sheer curiosity, but years later I burned them all from a feeling of respect toward my own friends in Germany.) It is pleasant – and in Europe decidedly rare – to find a story which is favourable to a Jew, but this is one of the exceptions. Once again, the time is the Thirty Years War. The Swedes have visited Remagen and set the town in flames when suddenly a small boat is seen coming down the river. It is rowed swiftly toward the bank and the boatman drops his oars and jumps ashore. He runs to the town gateway and quickly cuts three strange signs in it, then jumps aboard and goes on his way downstream. None know who he is, though all can see that he is a Jew. But when the flames reach the point where the man cut his mysterious marks they halt. No more houses are consumed, and the fire dies out. The unknown Jew has saved the town.

To starboard Remagen, then next on the port hand lies Linz, a pretty little town of the kind the Germans call *weinfroh*, or wine-happy. It is a pleasant place (though without a harbour) to visit in September when the vintners are holding their festival and the wine booths are set up all round the market-place. The mayor makes a brief speech, the band plays, the fireworks race aloft in the evening sky and the town is, in a word, *weinfroh*. And very good the wines are, for here again the rock is volcanic, and there is just a slight tang of Vesuvius or perhaps of hell in the local vintage.

However, the volcanic fault has produced another useful substance, for just above the town the cliffs are of basalt and the scars on the hillside show where the hexagon columns have been hewn and blasted away to provide the neatly fitting blocks which form the surface of river and canal banks, harbour walls, docks and locksides throughout the low countries. Only recently has concrete come to take the place of basalt, but it is not necessarily as satisfactory. If a concrete wall should break or subside, to restore it is no easy matter, whereas the hexagons of basalt are as easily rearranged as a child's set of building blocks.

With the stately cliffs rising higher, the two Brohls next face each other across the stream, Rheinbrohl to port and just plain Brohl to starboard. Brohl itself is a loading point for stone and it has a very respectable harbour, but otherwise it is a dull village cut in half by the roar of the main line expresses. Rheinbrohl is probably no more picturesque, but at least it has a claim to fame through the extraordinary incident which occurred in that apparently quiet little place toward the end of the nineteenth century.

A child aged two had died, and when the villagers were gathered at the grave the mayor of Rheinbrohl gave orders that the bell was to be tolled. The priest and his parochial council immediately refused, because it was the business of the incumbent and not of the mayor to decide when the church bell should be rung. The mayor promptly turned to the representative of the county council, who ordered a troop of soldiers to be brought to Rheinbrohl to enforce the will of the burgomaster. The priest had the church bolted and barred, but eventually a special train arrived at the station, bringing a whole company of soldiers and a picket of police. This force set about the church door with axes and crowbars until they had battered their way inside; they then seized the ropes and tolled every bell in the tower for a whole hour without interruption. Naturally this was not the end of the affair, for the parties carried on a lengthy dispute before the courts until the battle was finally decided in favour of the priest and his parishioners.

High on a rocky bluff to port the ruins of Hammerstein next stand out against the sky, a castle which is said to have been built originally by Charles Martel. However that may be, an eleventh-century lord of Hammerstein married his cousin Irmingard. The emperor and the pope both declared such a marriage to be invalid, and Otto of Hammerstein was obliged to give an undertaking both to the emperor and also to the Archbishop of Mainz to put away his wife. This he promised to do, but instead he made a raid upon the archbishop, who had to flee for his life. The emperor was thoroughly roused by such impertinence, and laying siege to Hammerstein he starved the castle into submission. Irmingard and her devoted husband were stripped of their possessions and turned out of house and home.

Two years passed before Otto appeared before the synod at Mainz and promised to put Irmingard away and behave himself. The bishop ordered that the lady should undertake a penance and retire to a nunnery, but he had not reckoned with the woman's spirit. She refused to have anything to do with a convent, and setting to work upon Pope Benedict VIII she used her charm to persuade him that the most reasonable thing to do was to let her live with her Otto. So successful was she that the pope came over to her view of things and actually sacked the Archbishop of Mainz, sending Irmingard triumphantly home in the company of a guard to protect her from any attack by the prelate.

As we thrust upstream beneath the vast cliff of Hammerstein, with its vineyards clutching the rocks in defiance of Newton's laws, I wondered as I had often done before at the perseverance of the German vinedresser, who seems ever prepared to scale several hundred feet of almost vertical rock to tend the vines on a pocket-handkerchief of terrace from which the yield, even in a good year, cannot be very great. The same surprise was felt by Baring-Gould when he travelled up the Rhine.

'When we consider the labour undertaken in cultivating the vines one is disposed to ask what the British working man would say, were he transported hither and offered a job at vine culture. He would decline the task, thrust his hands into his pockets, light his pipe, and wait for town or district council to find him an easy job at good pay, with the confidence that therewith it bought his vote.' And that was written more than sixty years before the *Thames Commodore* carried us up the river below the same terraces toward the cluster of chimneys and silos a mile or two ahead which told us that we were nearing Andernach, where a splendid medieval crane still stands on the bank of the Rhine as though waiting for the *Halfen* to haul a barge to beneath its jib. Probably Goethe slept at Andernach – he certainly visited it – and maybe he visited the Jew's bath also. Whether or not Andernach still has this curious feature we could not tell as we chugged past the waterfront, but here as also at Speyer this amenity had long survived from the middle ages when it was in regular use. It consisted of a shaft or well with a spiral staircase leading down into the natural ground water, and as the level changed with that of the river the Jews reckoned it to be 'flowing' within the meaning of the Law, which ordained that women were to bathe in running water at the end of menstruation.

Andernach once had a narrow escape. The men of Linz, always

their enemies and rivals, decided to attack the Andernachers while
they were still sleeping, and after a night march up the river they
came in sight of the town just as the first streaks of light were
paling the sky. At that early hour the bakers would be at their
ovens and the delivery boys already on their bread-rounds, but as
all these proceedings took place behind the stout town wall the
Linzers were not likely to be detected as they crept silently up
from the river bank.

However, two baker lads had already finished their deliveries,
and had climbed to the top of the gateway tower to watch the dawn
rise beyond the hills of the Westerwald. They at once noticed the
moving shapes down below, and hastening to the storm-bell they
tolled it to rouse the townspeople.

The Linzers had the choice of retreating or of trying to rush the
town before the Andernachers had pulled on their trousers and
snatched up their arms. They took the latter course, and charged
up to the foot of the walls. But Andernach like many other places
was a town whose citizens kept their skeps on the walls, and the
two lads now raced along the parapet tipping them off. Infuriated
bees have often proved more effective than artillery, and soon the
brave Linzers were fleeing in disorder, their arms flailing round
their heads as they raced to plunge their swollen faces in the river.
The Andernachers stood on the walls and laughed, but afterwards
they commemorated the event by carving statues of the boys on the
town gateway.

However, the faces were probably put there for a special reason.
It was the custom of guilds of tradesmen to put distinguishing
marks in their towns, in order to have some way of checking the
statements of wandering apprentices. If a young man alleged that
he had been indentured to a master craftsman in Andernach, then
his prospective employer would ask him what was carved on the
gateway. Sometimes the signs were much less obvious and were
only communicated to the apprentice when he had served his term,
and the fact that he knew them then served as a passport within the
craft throughout the country.

Less pleasant than the story of the baker boys is the recollection
that once, when Andernach was undergoing one of the sieges that

were such a feature of life in a Rhineland town, the mercenaries who were waiting encamped outside the walls managed to seize one of the nuns, although it was common practice to regard them as outside the whole business of war. They stripped her, painted her over with honey, and rolled her in feathers before leading her on horseback through the camp to show what a comical bird they had managed to trap. However, their commander was far from pleased. Such goings-on were not to be tolerated. Burning, sacking, pillaging and raping was fair enough, but to honey-and-feather a nun was going too far. He had the guilty men dropped in a cauldron of boiling water and then proceeded with the greatest complacency to burn down the town and himself destroy the church and convent.

From Andernach the Rhine is for a short while a river of the plain, wandering casually from side to side and letting the hills retreat to a distance. We drew in against a fuelling boat at Neuwied, a dull industrial town; even its history is not inspiring, except for perhaps one item connected with a diplomatic mission.

Neuwied was once a petty (and short-lived) princedom on its own, and as its rulers proclaimed freedom of religion it was a haven for every conceivable oddity of denomination from Anabaptists to Shakers. Once when the princedom was involved in litigation the chancellor was sent off to Vienna to present the case for Neuwied. After a very lengthy hearing the dignitary returned and handed in his expense account, which included the sum of 2,000 florins for 'loss of conjugal rights'. The prince questioned this item as being surely rather excessive, but the chancellor ingeniously explained that it would upset his dear wife if the figure were any lower. And so the bill was paid – by the citizens, as was usual.

At Neuwied, the junction of the Rhine and Moselle is little more than an hour's chugging distant. There can be no doubt that the confluence which gave its name to Koblenz (= confluentes) is one of the most splendid anywhere, and it is best seen from the frowning height of the ramparts of Ehrenbreitstein on the right bank of the Rhine.

Ehrenbreitstein must have been a formidable defence for the

crossing of the Rhine, and when the French attacked Koblenz in 1688 the fort on the opposite side of the river kept the enemy at least partly at bay. Yet little by little it came to be noticed that some of the shells fired from the Ehrenbreitstein cannon were not exploding, and when to this was added the discovery that the French seemed to be extremely well-informed about the fortifications and the strength of the garrison it occurred to the commanding officer that the master gunner was playing a double game. Accordingly, just as he was about to fire toward the enemy he was seized and the shell extracted from the gun. Sure enough, it contained a detailed plan of a sortie which was planned for the coming night.

The gunner was quickly court-martialled, sentenced, and decapitated. A plaster cast was taken of his head to swell the collection of intriguing objects in the museum of the Electoral Palace, but the head itself was put into a mortar. A note written by the garrison commander was placed inside the mouth, then a soldier touched off the fuse and sent the unusual missile flying into the French camp.

The note was short and formal: 'With the compliments of His Excellency the Elector, to the Marshal Boufflers.'

The fortress perched above the river is one of those immense bastions which proved too costly to dismantle entirely, too solid to crumble, too militarily utilitarian to convert into a pleasure park, and so has become an odd and rather desolate mixture of government stores, ice-cream counters, palm court, and for all I know a prison also, but its depressing atmosphere is altogether redeemed by the view from the edge of its walls. To the right the Rhine sweeps away round the long bend by Vallendar, past which the tow-trains creep on their slow way upstream. To the left the Rhine disappears into the cleft which leads to the castled gorge, and straight across the broad stream Koblenz lies in the angle which ends in the acute point of Deutsches Eck. The extreme tip of the promontory is formed of a gigantic granite whatnot, a sort of two-tiered wedding cake of masonry the size of which is only appreciated when one realises that those ants crawling over the steps are parties of holiday visitors. More than thirty feet in height are the

Ehrenbreitstein and Deutches Eck

great pillars hewn from Black Forest rock, the shafts which surround a massive raised plinth upon which stands, martial and splendid, nothing at all. Before the Second World War the Kaiser Wilhelm was in position, mounted on horseback and with flowing cloak, accompanied by a winged genius. Up to the roof of the emperor's helmet the whole affair was almost 130 feet high, so even without the mighty statue itself the memorial is impressive enough.

'*Nimmer wird das Reich zerstöret, wenn ihr einig seid und treu!*' So runs the inscription of Max von Schenkendorf: Never again will the empire be destroyed if you remain united and true. This is a modest enough sentiment to have survived from the days of the Kaisers, and it has not been removed. As for the Eck, there are three opinions – that the Kaiser should be resurrected, that the rest of the structure should be taken down, or that things are best left as they are. I incline to this last, for the base gives a sort of finish to an otherwise flat promontory. Besides, I like to have people reminded that even the greatest and most pompous of military men can quite easily be disposed of.

At the foot of the Ehrenbreitstein fort is the 'old' electoral palace which the archbishops of Trier used before the last of them built, just too late, the new one across the river in Koblenz. The last but two of the Cologne electors – for the French Revolution was to sweep them away – lived in the usual high style and had a jester, dwarf, beautiful Italian sopranos and every possible delight, and when on a journey in 1761 he came up the valley he was very naturally entertained for the night at Ehrenbreitstein by his counterpart of Trier. It seems he was not well and ate little of the sumptuous banquet put before him, but when the band struck up he began to shuffle in the rhythm of a minuet. A noble lady kindly invited him to dance, and soon he recovered his spirits. Round and round the dance-floor he twirled with one lady after another until he was in a state of collapse. The electoral leech bled him, but to no avail. The dancing – and perhaps a whole life of self-indulgence – had been too much for him, and next day he died.

Koblenz belongs more to the Moselle than to the Rhine, and as the *Thames Commodore* had already visited it several times when preparing her memoirs for *Small Boat on the Moselle* she this time steamed straight past, heading up beneath the bridges toward the opening of the Rhine gorge. In twenty minutes the bright ochre battlements of Castle Stolzenfels were in view, but she was not yet to pass beneath them. Only a quarter of a mile before the castle she blew three loud and long blasts followed by two short and sharp to warn any ship coming out of the River Lahn to keep out of her way. Past the church of St John she entered slacker water, then eased off to draw in to the piles below Niederlahnstein lock, her first since Willemstad in far-off Zeeland.

VI

Oberlahnstein – Burg Lahneck – last of the Templars – the knight and the fisherman – Lahn navigation – the death-bird's wail – knockers of the quarries – Ahl and Nievern – the waters of the Ems – preparations for a voyage – bathing discouraged

THE Lahn is so inviting a river that the *Thames Commodore* has always been surprised to find that it has not become one of the favourite haunts of inland boats like herself. Reasonably safe, free of two thousand tonners racing for the next cargo in Rotterdam, it is a right little tight little stream flowing past one village after another until it finally does a double twist to the last lock at Niederlahnstein and opens up to the junction with its mighty relative the Rhine. Yet it rarely sees a foreign cruiser, and only the more enterprising and less flashy German craft deign to notice its existence at all.

Even the mouth of the Lahn is intriguing. Close on the point to port stands the ancient church of St John – but of where? Presumably of Niederlahnstein which is the nearest settlement, but I suspect that it once belonged to an abbey perched on the Rhine bank and long since vanished. Ahead the square keep of Lahneck stands a little bit tired, half asleep after its centuries of guarding the entrance to the valley, and perhaps a little horrified at the bright yellow renovations of Stolzenfels across the Rhine. The main course of the Lahn curves a little to the left along the pretty and rather tumbledown waterfront of Niederlahnstein and to starboard the cranes in Oberlahnstein's harbour are busily loading cargoes from the small Lahnships into their greater cousins of the Rhine trade. Beyond them a tower or two and some fragments of medieval town wall remind the boatman that Oberlahnstein was once a proud town and not just the rather scattered and nondescript place of small factories which it has now become.

In fact Oberlahnstein has the unusual distinction of being the place at which an emperor of the Holy Roman Empire was actually relieved of his office. The man was Wenceslas of Bohemia, an individual who paid little attention to the responsibilities of his office. That was the reason why the four electors of the Rhineland met together in June 1400 and sent him a stern letter to the effect that he was to come to Oberlahnstein on a certain day in August and tell them what he proposed to do to stop the rot which was spreading in both church and state, or else.

Wenceslas did not even reply. He preferred to remain in Prague where things were easy enough. He had no intention of visiting Oberlahnstein to explain his conduct. However, on the appointed day the four electors were there right enough, together with a great assembly of lords and knights and representatives from cities throughout the empire, and as the emperor evidently did not consider them worthy of his attention Archbishop Johann of Mainz stepped out in front of the people and read a remarkable proclamation.

'For many weighty reasons, and because of his insupportable failure, we hereby remove and depose Herr Wenceslas from the Roman Empire, declaring him useless, idle, and thoroughly inept as head of the Roman Empire, and we release all lords, nobles, knights and gentry, cities, countries and peoples subject to the Roman Empire from all fealty due to Wenceslas in the name of the Roman Empire, and from all and every such oath, and we further instruct them in their oath to the empire, never more to obey Wenceslas nor to render him any service such as would be due to a Roman emperor, but rather to reserve such obedience and service for him who, by the will of God, shall be elected as emperor. The foregoing verdict and sentence is read and delivered by us, Johann, Archbishop of Mainz, upon a throne constituted as a throne of justice.'

Cheers rose above the town, and no doubt the good wine flowed in many a tavern as the four electors returned into Oberlahnstein's castle and completed the formalities for the installation of Ruprecht of the Palatinate, who was duly elected on the following day, across the Rhine at Rhens.

Goethe was enough of an inland waterways man to take an

occasional trip by water, and it was as he rowed with his friends
down this last reach of the Lahn and looked up at the mighty
towering keep of Burg Lahneck that he began to form the lines
which I presume are diligently taught to every schoolboy and
schoolgirl of both the Lahnsteins.

> *Hoch auf dem alten Turme steht*
> *Des Helden edler Geist.*
> *Der, wie das Schiff vorübergeht,*
> *Es wohl zu fahren heisst:*
> *'Sieh, diese Sehne war so stark,*
> *Dies Herz so fest und wild,*
> *Die Knochen voll von Rittermark,*
> *Der Becher angefüllt . . .*
> *Mein halbes Leben stürmt ich fort,*
> *Verdehnt die Hälft in Ruh,*
> *Und Du, Du Menschenschifflein dort,*
> *Fahr immer, immer zu.'*

> *High on the ancient bastion stands*
> *The hero's noble shade,*
> *And bids the shipman sailing by*
> *A safe untroubled voyage.*
> *'See, once these sinews too were strong,*
> *This heart so sure and bold,*
> *Sturdy the marrow in my bones,*
> *The Rhenish in my glass . . .*
> *Through half my life I fought and thrust,*
> *To spend the rest in peace,*
> *And you, you little human barque,*
> *Sail ever, ever on.'*

Probably the tendon so strong, the heart so firm and wild, the
bones full of knightly marrow – to say nothing of the beaker filled
to the brim – belonged to the last of the Templars of the Rhineland,
whose tale is woven into the fabric of Lahneck. For however
peaceful the keep may look as it stands high in the night sky above
the lock, bathed in the glow of summer floodlighting, it has

certainly had its great moments, and none more dramatic than that which is said to have occurred in the year 1315. The Knights Templars had begun as a noble and chivalrous institution, but as time went on and there was little scope for their original purposes they became corrupt, a sort of semi-brigand society of toughs. That was why, in 1313, Pope Clement V excommunicated the Templars one and all, and Philip the Fair expelled them from France. Outlawed, these fierce and tried men of undoubted bravery had either to give up their order or to find some place where they could maintain themselves by force of arms against the rest of the world. Thus it was that twelve of these knights forced an entry into Lahneck castle and appropriated it for their own fortress.

Lahneck belonged to the archbishops of Mainz, who had built it to protect their territories from marauders, so the pope immediately sent an order to the archbishop instructing him to have the Templars ejected. An archiepiscopal army was sent to surround the castle in force and demand their surrender. The knights, however, did not trust the offer that they might keep their lives and liberty if they laid down their arms. They knew the pope too well. Defiantly they withstood the onslaught of their enemies and killed many of them. Again the archbishop demanded surrender, with the promise of a pardon, and again the knights refused. Pardon belonged only to God, they said, and God would be able to know well enough who it was who needed to be forgiven. As for trusting the men of the Roman Church, unfortunately this was something which they were unable to do. The twelve men must certainly have by now known that death faced them whichever way they turned, and they had resolved to sell their lives as dearly as they might.

So, at dead of night, the troops of Mainz were made ready for a final assault. But the scaling ladders had not yet been thrown up when the massive gate swung open, the drawbridge fell, and the twelve knights in armour poured out of Lahneck, slashing and thrusting as they came.

How many of their enemies they cut down in this last desperate sally is not known, but at last eleven of the twelve were among the heap of dead at Lahneck's gate. Only one remained, an old man in shining armour.

At this moment a messenger from the archbishop broke through to the front, calling that the fighting was to stop. The emperor himself had guaranteed freedom to the Templars, he proclaimed.

The old man stood still for a moment. Then, leaping over the prostrate bodies of his companions he cut and thrust his way through the men at arms to where the commander of the besieging army stood. Grappling with him, he dragged him to the edge of Lahneck's cliff, and flung himself and his enemy, locked together, over the precipice.

Another tragic but very different tale of Lahneck's keep comes from more recent times, when the castle was no more than a ruin and had not been restored to its present state complete with residence, inn, and summer open-air theatre. It was in 1852 that a girl who was visiting the Rhineland as a tourist ventured up the path to castle Lahneck and pushed open the door of the tower. Who this young lady was I do not know, though I have an indistinct recollection of having read that she was English. But however that may be, this unfortunate girl moved blindly forward to a fate as improbable as that which overtook the maidenly heroine of any medieval Rhineland keep.

The castle of Lahneck was not often visited, and the girl found the steps covered with the debris dropped by jackdaws, but she made her way step by step up the spiral until at last she came to the wooden stairs which led to the top, and climbing up to the sunshine she no doubt enjoyed the splendour of the view along the valley of the little river, and across the roofs of Oberlahnstein to where Stolzenfels stood proudly looking down upon the Rhine. But when she came to descend, she found that the stairs had gone. Her climbing them had put the final strain upon the rotten woodwork, and whether or not she had heard the structure collapse behind her there was certainly no longer any exit from the tower.

Of course, such a discovery would be a shock for anyone, but no doubt the girl reassured herself that help would come. She had but to call and wave, and the alarm would be raised. Yet if she did so, none saw her and she spent the night upon the roof. Early next morning she took her scarf and waved it, calling with all the voice she could muster toward the Lahn, where a boat was moving down the river. The skipper heard her call, and he answered, waving his hat to her. Yes, a lovely, clear morning was it not? A fine day for an early climb to the top of the castle keep. He waved cheerily – and passed on.

Later that day the girl saw schoolchildren playing a game down below. She called and waved to them also. People often wave to children. I have often done so myself from the deck of the *Thames Commodore*. They wave back, then return to their play. And that is exactly what they did on this occasion when the poor girl was calling and gesticulating for help. How many others saw her I do not know, but it occurred to none that she was in danger or despair. At last, weakened by hunger and terror and the exposure of the cold nights on the top of Lahneck's keep, she died there.

From Lahneck's terrace where once the last of the Templars grappled with the last of his enemies the view of the confluence of the rivers is a fine one indeed. And a little to the right a Lahnship or perhaps the *Thames Commodore* is slowly being raised by the water flowing into the lock, beyond which a not very beautiful dye-works occupies the site of an old watermill, the Weissmühle. Millers have a way of being the fathers of beautiful daughters, and the miller who ran the Weissmühle in the 1450s was no exception. Wondrous fair was his Elisabeth, the loveliest maiden in all the country round about. Many a young man had tried to win her affection; but no, Elisabeth was not interested. Secretly she was deeply in love with the choice of her own, a mere fisherman from the Lahn. She cared nothing for competitors.

At least, that was how matters stood when one day a remarkably smooth and handsome young knight appeared at Lahneck. In fact he was the son of that noble house, who had spent his youth in the service of the bishop of Mainz, and now emerging fully fledged from the archiepiscopal court he was just ready to fall head over heels in love with the miller's daughter. This he did, and he haunted the vicinity of the mill whenever he could, to catch a glimpse of her, and to lure her into his arms.

Now it is one thing to be loved by a Lahn fisherman, and quite another to have the heir of Lahneck as boy friend, so it is hardly surprising that Elisabeth found it easy enough to respond to the thrill of laying her head on a metal breastplate in preference to the homely and perhaps somewhat smelly jacket of her first true love. All the same, she did not tell the young fisherman of her new romance but met him every evening as before and lay beside him in the soft grass of the river bank, beneath the willows.

One evening, however, the fisherman waited in vain. Elisabeth did not come. Worried that something might have happened to her, or perhaps stung by the first prickings of a well justified suspicion, he made his way to the mill and peeped in at the window. What he saw there one can guess, for at once he went down to the river bank and sat there as though dazed.

He had been there some time before he heard steps, and maybe a slight clanking sound. The young knight of Lahneck saw the fisherman on the bank and commanded to be rowed back down the river toward the foot of the castle hill. Without a word, the story says – though it is difficult to see how anyone can tell – the young man pushed out his punt and conveyed his rival down-stream.

But he did not stop at Lahneck. He let the boat be swept on, out past the Lahnsteins and into the turbulent Rhine. Perhaps he did not even need to rock the boat to ensure that it was swiftly overset in midstream. Both men were drowned, as probably the broken-hearted young fisherman had intended.

As for Elisabeth, she waited in vain next day for the arrival of her romantic lover. When she heard that the fisherman had disappeared, and the boat also, she must have guessed what had happened. She flung herself into the mill race, and that was the end of her. The affair was also the end of the Lahneck line, for the gay knight had been the only son, and with his death the family became extinct.

The fisherman in this pleasant tale must, I think, have been an Oberlahnsteiner if he found himself on that side of the river, for the fishery in the Lahn was very strictly regulated. All fish caught in certain areas of water had first to be offered to the customs clerk and the castle cellarer at fixed prices – four heller per pound for pike, ten heller for perch, and so forth. Salmon and lamprey

had to be given to the lord in the castle, free of charge, so if he had
not been so impetuous the young man might even have disposed of
his rival by judiciously poisoning one. Fishermen of Niederlahnstein were not permitted to set their gear on the Oberlahnstein
side of the stream, but when the river was frozen and the fish were
stuck fast in the ice these fishermen were allowed to hew them out
with axes on both sides of the river, provided that a quarter of
what was chopped out on the Oberlahnstein side was given to the
customs clerk, whose position was well provided with such useful
perquisites.

The Lahn was always a somewhat capricious river, and it
naturally paid the riparian lords to try to improve the navigation
so that more ships would use the river and thus be subject to tolls.
The dukes of Nassau carried out some works in the sixteenth
century, and the archbishopric of Cologne also endeavoured to
make the river more amenable, so that transport between Cologne
and the archiepiscopal domains in the Limburg area would be
improved. Weirs were installed to increase the depth of water,
and these were provided with flashes like those at the mills on the
Thames. Boards could be pulled out to leave a gap through which
a downgoing barge would be swept by the current, and an upcoming ship could with some difficulty be hauled by a winch.
Dikes were also installed to divert the dangerous masses of ice
which occasionally came down the river and threatened to destroy
the houses in Niederlahnstein and elsewhere.

In 1808 the Lahn was made thoroughly navigable as far as
Limburg, and two years later to Weilburg. Then in the 1840s the
banks were corrected and supplied with groynes where necessary,
and a few years later the flashes were replaced with somewhat
primitive locks, one of which still existed below Nievern when the
Commodore passed up the river in 1961, the others having already
been replaced downstream of Limburg by their more modern
electrically operated successors.

Nowadays, the passenger shipping at Lahnstein is confined to
trip boats which run up to Bad Ems, and the daily vessels of the
Köln–Düsseldorfer line which call at their jetty on the Rhine
bank. There may also be a few small Dutch holiday-ships lying

for an evening along the waterfront of the Lahn. But in the nine-teenth century there was a very considerable traffic, particularly when the railway from Lahnstein to Bad Ems was opened. Upper-class visitors went in their thousands to take the waters, and often they made the journey to Oberlahnstein by ship. There were daily steamer services to Mannheim and to Cologne and Rotter-dam, and strangely enough there was a direct sailing by paddle-wheeler every Saturday for London, a service which lasted almost until the end of the nineteenth century.

The Nassau State railway which opened the mineral springs of Bad Ems to the outside world was a very considerable achieve-ment of engineering, and the directors had the wisdom to com-mission a notable German poet, Wolfgang Müller von Königs-winter, to prepare suitable poetry for its opening. He began with a paean of praise in honour of the new railway bridge over the Rhine at Koblenz, and then the company took their seats and the special train set out on its inaugural journey to Nassau, returning as far as the bank of the Rhine, where three great decorated ships lay ready with tables set for a banquet. And so the Nassau railway brought its puffing locomotives to the winding valley. In and out of the rocky spurs they burrowed their way, hooting for each tunnel and crossing.

'The death-bird is calling,' the bargemen used to say, nodding their heads. They could see only too clearly the menace of this brash new competitor oozing steam from its joints, and some of the clay pipes they smoked in the Lahn inns were soon stamped with an inscription which expressed the matter very differently but concisely.

Der Teufel hat den Dampf erdacht
Den Fuhrmann um sein Brot gebracht.

The Devil's brain invented steam,
And robbed the carrier of his bread.

And these forebodings were right. The locomotive's wailing whistle heralded the transfer of cargoes to the newer form of transport. The towpath fell into disuse, the horses were sold, the drovers forced to seek work in the new industries which sprang up beside the track. It was regrettable, but inevitable.

But the *Thames Commodore* could hold her own against the locomotives of the Bundesbahn, which still smoked and shrieked as they wound up the valley. For she was not in a hurry. She liked to linger, and look, and savour such sights as the row of houses on the port or Niederlahnstein side below the lock, simple dwellings which once had been those of fishermen and shippers, and which stood back discreetly from the towpath, faded and peaceful. In front of them sat the old gaffers of Niederlahnstein, elderly sailormen and river-pilots, even perhaps one or two professional fishers of time past. And just to complete the beauty of this riverside scene a group of pinkish half-timbered buildings with neatly cut slate roofs stood higher than the rest, consciously more important and better class than the neighbours. A rounded tower with a pentagon top seemed to step forward as though determined to see who was daring to come up the river, and it was not difficult to guess that this had once been the tollhouse where dues were levied. The rest of the complex was now one of the many 'old original Wirtshaus an der Lahn of the famous song' inns to be found along the river from Lahnstein as far upstream as Marburg. Naturally, Goethe ate his lunch at the Niederlahnstein hostelry, and nearly two centuries later the *Thames Commodore*'s crew ate their evening meal at the same inn – and a very good meal it was too, though I doubt if their visit will ever be commemorated by a plaque as Goethe's was. Goethe is plaque-worthy, the *Thames Commodore* is not, and I doubt if she has it in her to feel jealous about the matter.

It is, or at least used to be, a curious fact that the River Lahn could actually speak. 'I want a man! I want a man!' These are not the impassioned words of a girl left over in the discotheque, but the cry of the Lahn herself. (She is *die* Lahn, in contrast to the manly and masculine *der* Rhein.)

'I want a man! I want a man!' And even the fish are frightened, so much so that they flee in shoals straight into the nets of the fishermen who take advantage of their terror.

I am indebted for this information to J. W. Wolf, who received it from Professor Weigand of Giessen on the Lahn rather more than a century ago. And I can well believe it. Most rivers like drowning people, and there is no reason why the Lahn should be an exception. Indeed, some still assert that when somebody is to drown in the Lahn, the river calls. The millers and washerwomen who are down close to the water hear the cry distinctly. Usually the call is heard between eleven and twelve o'clock in the morning, which is also the hour at which the water-sprites dance upon the surface. First, the Lahn begins to rush and surge, then come the waves, and from the middle of the turbulence a loud cry is heard.

'The time has come, the hour is at hand! It only needs the man!'

Then the millers and the washerwomen and others who hear it nod to each other and shudder. The Lahn has called, and someone will soon be drowned – for so it has often happened.

Above Niederlahnstein the course plunges into a narrow and twisting valley, the hillsides falling steep and densely wooded to the stream and leaving barely room for the road or the railway, except where the stream has cut across and left a patch of flat gravelly plain large enough to support a hamlet with a scatter of fruit orchards. Here and there the hillsides are scored with gashes, for they have long been worked for ore and one may still see the heaps and screes of slaty spoil from the diggings. The mines were long believed to be inhabited by the sort of knockers without which no mine would be complete. Sometimes a metallic knocking noise would be heard, which each man was sure he had not himself made with his pick, and such was the effect of the echoes in the galleries that the miners thought it wise to propitiate the mysterious Hanselmännchen, who might otherwise do them harm. If there were some who doubted the existence of these goblins they were quickly silenced by the testimony of those who had fortified themselves with a bottle of schnapps before passing the workings at night and had actually seen the little fellows running about, swinging their miners' lamps as they went.

The goblins were kept in good humour with a daily dish of soup or stew and an annual change of clothes. The jacket was always a red one of the size for a boy of about six years old, and it was the duty of the miner's wife either to make it or to acquire one when she went out shopping. This system worked very well. The goblins never got in the way, and just occasionally they felled such a mass of rock as the miners themselves could not have hewn in weeks.

Three centuries ago some enterprising entrepreneurs from Belgium erected a foundry at Ahl to smelt the ore quarried in the cliffs of the Lahn. The ingots were carried away by barge, and all seemed prosperous enough until a dispute broke out between the elector archbishops of Mainz and of Trier as to whose responsibility it was to see to the maintenance of the river. Some barges carrying marble altar-tops down from Diez had come to grief on the bend near Ahl, and the responsibility for this disaster was disputed – and maybe the lack of altar slabs regretted. For a time neither side would allow the other to sanction navigation, and by the time the great men had been brought to forget their pride and permitted the shipping to use the river again, the foundry was almost bankrupt and its owners were not prepared to risk carrying on the business any longer in an area of such clerical rivalries.

Ahl's lock is the second on the way upstream, and I have always thought it the prettiest of them all. Its narrow cut is edged with a long camp-site which is a great favourite with Dutch families, and children splash and swim in the shallows. The meadow on the point between the cut and the river is bright with the flowers of summer, and the heavy scent of meadowsweet drifts across the river. Roses climb in a pinkish riot over the lock-house fence, and whether on purpose or by chance the river authority has painted all the lock gear in just the right red and dark green to make the mechanism seem a natural part of the scene. Beyond the lock comes a long and narrow cutting, purple with scabious and loose-strife to port, pale bluish to starboard where the Wandering Willie cascades down the face of the retaining wall. There are blackberries too, only accessible from the deck of a boat. It is altogether a very pleasant place in which to spend half an hour in the late summer, picking the fruit and waiting for the light at the blind corner to change from red to green.

On this lower part of the river the locks are only a mile or so apart, and from Ahl it is no great steam to Nievern with its wire-works close by the stream. One day a tailor from Nassau was walking along the towpath by Nievern when he happened to see a

light in a cave in the cliff, and thinking it must come from a pub
he went inside for a drink. He soon found that the place was not an
inn, but the dwelling of a curious being, half snake or eel and half
maiden, a sort of freshwater mermaid of the Lahn. In fact she was
a bewitched princess, and she was wearing a very fine crown of
gold.

The princess gave the tailor a present of jewels and gold, and
set before him a bottle of very much finer wine than he would have
found in any inn. In return she only asked for three kisses to
liberate her. He gave her two good embraces, but I think she must
have flicked her scaly tail in excitement, for he took fright and
withheld the third. What happened then is hard to say. The
princess vanished with a terrible wail and when next morning the
tailor recovered consciousness he found himself among the rocks,
his clothes torn and his face scratched as though a female had
clawed him in earnest.

Where the cut leads out into the river once more, there stands
forlorn and forgotten among the rotting branches and the jungle
of undergrowth a sad stone figure, looking out along the top of the
weir as though wondering who has been washed over the top.
From his mitre and the crucifix held in one hand he is easily
identified as St John Nepomuk, patron of those who fall into mill-
races, and often found in just such a strange position. He is a
pleasant baroque figure, the Nepomuk of Nievern, and I have
always feared for his safety. His position makes him inaccessible
to hooligans but he is dangerously placed to withstand floods and
waterborne tree-trunks, yet he is there still – a little mossy perhaps,
and frost-flaked and eroded, but conscientiously guarding the line
of the spill-over as any good Nepomuk should.

A short pound, another lock, a long and narrow cut with low
bridges, and suddenly the boatman emerges into the most stately
reach of all the river where it runs between lawns and walks and
formal flowerbeds into the very centre of the ochre elegance of Bad
Ems, with all the fun of hypochondria and hot springs. And the
springs certainly are hot, the water gushing out at temperatures of
up to 51 degrees centigrade, leaping high into the air and sending a
continual drift of steam to float away between the buildings.

Dr Döring, a resident physician who once was asked by an English visitor of the nineteenth century what the benefits of Ems water might be, gave a long list of diseases benefited by the cure. First came pulmonary complaints 'having their origin in other parts of the body', then loss of voice, hoarseness, inflammation of the mucous membranes, pituitary phthisis, gout, rheumatism and 'repelled cutaneous complaints'. Also on the list were 'debility of the chest, tubercles of the lungs, catarrhs, spitting of blood, scrophula, nervous disorders, congestion of the liver and abdominal organs, chronic eruptions of the skin, urinary ailments and female complaints'. Indeed, as Jerome K. Jerome would certainly have noted, housemaid's knee was almost the only complaint not on the list.

I am not sure that so much steam issuing from the hot spring in the middle of the town may not have some strange and insidious effect upon the Emsians, congesting their sinuses and driving the blood to the heads. Bad Ems is the only town in Germany which I have found it difficult to pass through without being involved in the sort of misunderstandings and exchange of comments, freely and frankly expressed, which in earlier centuries would have caused the British Foreign Minister to send a stern note to the Prussians or Hessians, or Nassau-men, or whoever was in command of the place.

Ems must of course be sad about the margraves and burgraves and landgraves and mere archdukes becoming so rare. Worse still, those that remain do not patronise Ems. Gone are the days when the Kaiser sent for the French Ambassador and told him to eff off and look to his guns because as soon as he (the Kaiser) had finished his prescribed course of baths there was going to a Franco-Prussian war, *mein Gott* there was, and may the best man win so long as it is the Prussians, *Gott mit uns*! Gone also are the carriages of the Tsar of all the Russias and the Queen of Greece – whose lady-in-waiting had a bust so comely that the English traveller Mr Quin nearly walked into the river when he had no more than a distant view of it. Instead there are the dough-faced men and women sent there by the *Krankenkasse*, a sort of National Assistance Board for cranks I suppose it must be, which pays for

them to come to Ems and be cured of a malady described as
Managerkrankheit. This must, I think, be a tendency to manage
people, the sort of congenital bossitude which I have sometimes
noticed in West Indian bus conductresses and school prefects.
The quickest cure for manager-crankiness is to push the patient
in the river, but at Bad Ems they do not do this. Instead the cases
are dear-deared and poor-thinged and take-life-gentlied and made
to listen to the orchestra (for a fee) between walks in the gardens
(pay at the gate) and a turn in the bath water (please sign the
attendance sheet. Your bill will be sent on. *Dankeschön*).

The curious thing is that those who are so selflessly devoted to
the noble vocation of de-managerising other people should not
necessarily be immune to crankiness themselves. Maybe the
disease is contagious, or perhaps the sickness is a psychosomatic
one. Whatever the reason, I know no place in the whole Bundesrepublik where the officials are so bossy as at Bad Ems.

Our first experience was aboard the old *Commodore*. It was her
first day's run of a new year, because we had left her through the
winter hanging on her own hook in the anchorage of Niederwalluf
above the Rhine gorge. The first day aboard a sailing boat is
occupied in shaking the mice out of the canvas, after which the
ship is ready to put to sea and sink because nobody has remembered
to turn off the cock through which the lavatory empties, and which
is always placed by shipwrights on the side to which the ship
heels over so that the vessel will rapidly scuttle herself if attacked
by pirates. But the *Commodore* was not a sailing boat, and the
process of getting her under way for the first time in the year was
an annual event which demanded rather more intelligence, a
spare pair of trousers, and a magnet with which to recover any
pieces of ferrous metal negligently dropped into the bilge.

I would not like to say that it was either difficult or unnecessarily
time consuming, but while the mate was putting hot-water bottles
in the bunks, going into the city like Cotta and his men in their
intervals between fighting the Belgians to buy bread, or stocking
up with packet soups and frankfurters and sauerkraut, the captain
and chief engineer had some small jobs to attend to. First he
would refill the water system which had been carefully drained to

avoid any damage by frost, and then he would empty it again because the pipe which ran above the top of his own bunk had split just out of malice and had to be removed and replaced as soon as he had hung all the bedding out to dry.

It is an odd thing about plumbing, but you can never take out a pipe until you have removed the ones on either side of it, and exactly the same law of nature applies to each of these in turn. Eventually you find yourself back at the cylinder, where the last joint is painted in so tightly you cannot free it without a risk of smashing a hole in the side of the boat below the waterline. A shipbuilder once told me it had something to do with the unions. Plumbers, he said, were so happy when plumbing, so gay and satisfied and warm-hearted when engaged in screwing up joints with Stilson wrenches, that the baser nature of their leaden souls moved them to wish, somewhat selfishly I think, to keep all the fun for themselves. This they did by having only one of those long-threaded pipe-ends with a nut thing on it, and putting it right next to the stove and if possible behind it.

So the captain and the chief engineer would next have to find the hacksaw and attack the pipe vertically, lying with heads in a drawer while they did so. And there again we can note a further odd thing about plumbing, for it is a fact that an iron water-pipe will cut a hacksaw blade much more quickly than a hacksaw blade will cut an iron pipe. But as this book is not meant to be a fitter's manual for waterworks apprentices I should perhaps conclude the remarks about the early springtime tendencies of a convection hot water system by saying that an even more inexplicable fact is that a boat-owner who starts boat-owning with a complicated system of metal piping will suddenly discover after a few seasons that there are no iron pipes left to remove. By some strange transmutation they have all been converted into lengths of rubber garden hose.

With the water system fixed, there was little else to do. It was merely a matter of filling the engine with oil, dismantling the ignition, feeling in the oily bilge for the spanner dropped in the course of this process – a non-ferrous spanner which was determined to resist all the advances of a magnet on a string and could

only be retrieved in a do-it-yourself way – trying to get the gener-
ator to work, clearing the winter's growth of algae and two dead
fish from the cooling system and a live but undersized eel from
the in-flow pump of the lavatory bowl, unsticking the non-return
valve which had taken upon itself to be a *non-aller* as well as a
non-retour, sweeping the soot from the chimney, disentangling
the willow branches and a drowned cat from the rudder brackets,
and trying to coax the airlock out of the radiator in the forward
cabin. *Quo facto* it only remained to shovel the coal from the hold,
lift up the floor traps and bale out the odd corners with a tin,
dismantle the river water-pump, fit new washers to the plungers of
the primus stoves, grease the four staufers on the water-pumps of
the paraffin engine, find out why the fuel would not flow to the
motor at all, clean the dynamo brushes, retrieve them from the
bilge and clean them again, oil the joints in the steering system,
fill the worm-gear with worms and generally prepare to give the
signal for departure. Friends or members of the family would look
on and make encouraging sounds, but as none of them could easily
distinguish between a screw-driver and a hammer I preferred to go
about these little tasks myself, humming German folk-tunes to
show how thoroughly I was enjoying it all.

There is nothing like a little ship's husbandry for loosening up
locked vertebrae and making the limbs supple. And yet such work
leaves its marks upon one, marks which often prove to be remarkably indelible. Nothing will remove them but a good hot
bath. The *Thames Commodore* has two showers but her elder sister
had nothing better than a small galley sink in which it would not
have been easy to bath a dormouse. However, as we sped down the
gorge of the Rhine lashed by a strong April wind and occasional
strikes of hail I chortled at the thought that when we reached
Niederlahnstein we only had to turn right and run up four or five
locks to reach Bad Ems, a place where I forget exactly how many
thousand gallons of piping hot water straight from the boilers of
hell itself pour unaided into the Kurverwaltung's bath-system
every day. It is usually very difficult to get a bath at all in Germany
because, like the Indians, the natives think it insanitary to sit in
water which has lapped the promontories of their own torsos and

would rather die a stoic death from a chill contracted in a cold shower than risk the mortal danger of zizzing in a steaming bath-tub; but I was sure Bad Ems would be different. Cranks went there by the thousand, fully paid up by their own municipal crank-cases, just to bath and bath and bath until they had lost all desire to manage anything or anybody. The Romans used the waters at Bath in the same way, long ago. They invited obstinate English chiefs who tended to be bossy and softened them up in the swim-ming-bath with beautiful maidens thrown in, often at the deep end. Yes, at Bad Ems, I said to myself, I would have a *Bad*, a real fifty pfennigs' worth of scrub. Or, if necessary, a whole D-mark of tosh all to myself.

With the *Commodore* berthed at the top of the town I jumped ashore and walked back into the centre. Across the lattice bridge the magnificent buildings of the bath-administration stood well kept and expensive-looking. I boldly climbed the marble steps and crossed the carpeted hall to the counter. Two very superior young ladies were counting money, like wicked avaricious princes-ses in some German folk-tale who were doomed to count until they wore their fingers to the bone.

'Excuse me . . .' I began. Neither of them took any notice. I raised my hand and brought it smartly down upon the ping-bell knob.

The head girl looked at me, started violently, but recovered enough to ask me my business.

'I want a bath,' I said.

'A bath!' The girls exchanged glances. The one who seemed to act as spokesfrau for the Bad Ems waterworks looked me up and down rather severely. She seemed uncertain whether I was dirty, or perhaps an important visitor from one of the new African banana-republics. Whichever was the true cause of my black skin I could see that she did not feel comfortable so long as I was there. Besides, the plain demand for a bath suggested I was deranged, and possibly dangerous. She glanced anxiously at her companion, then bravely faced me.

'Have you a ticket?'

'A ticket? No. I want a bath,' I said.

'You must apply to the office by the bridge. That is where the tickets are issued.'

I wondered if I ought to bow myself out in reverse, as people did to archdukes and German emperors, but fearing to fall down the steps I turned and hurried out into the street to find the ticket office. There I was confronted by an acidulated man who perhaps had been steamed too much in tending the geyser, I thought. For a while he paid no attention, as though hoping I would go away.

'A ticket for a bath, please,' I said suddenly and very loud.

The fellow peered at me over his glasses in genuine astonishment. 'A bath?' He sounded incredulous. 'Did you say . . . a bath?'

'Yes. In a hotel, anywhere, I don't mind.'

'May I see your doctor's certificate.'

'I am not ill. I just want a bath,' I explained.

'Nobody may have a bath without a doctor's certificate. Even then it would only be a very short immersion. Two minutes on the first day, a little longer on the second or third perhaps, provided the doctor prescribes it. More would be very dangerous.'

I could see that the idea of just having a bath to get reasonably clean was something foreign to the Emsian mind; but I did not at once give up. I assured him that I well understood the dangers of having a bath. Like sheltering under a tree in a thunderstorm, ascending Vesuvius during an eruption or attempting to photograph a clutch of newly hatched cygnets, it was an undertaking upon which one embarked only at one's own sole risk and peril. Nevertheless, I felt brave enough to try. See, I had even brought my own soap and towel with me so that the Emsian Kurverwaltung should not be put to unreasonable trouble.

'Soap?'

'Yes. It is very useful in the bath,' I said. And I added that in my own country people often used soap in the bath. What was more, the hotels actually dished it out free. He would be able to check that for himself if ever he came to England.

Suddenly his expression changed to one of real apprehension. It was the word 'England' which had given him the clue. The English – off their rockers as usual. That was it. Mad dogs and Englishmen.

E

'This is not England,' he said in a soothing tone. He came round from behind the counter. 'We have to close the office now,' he added. 'Enjoy yourself in Bad Ems.'

He eased me out into the street, darted back into his office and turned the key in the lock.

I walked back to the *Commodore*, where the mate drew off a bucket or two of hot water and scrubbed me down on the draining-board in the galley.

Up the Lahn

VII

Hazards of Bad Ems – a sex-linked spring – voyage of the Ursula – Dausenau – the Wirtshaus an der Lahn – Nassau, cradle of dynasties – the Stein donkey – trouble with anglers – Frau Marioth's fortune – Heinrich of Langenau – a journey through time

BAD Ems, *du wunderschöne Stadt!* How sad it is that the Admiralty Pilot Books do not penetrate far enough into the mysterious lands flanking the Rhine to provide you with one of their lordships' brilliant literary descriptions. It would probably run something like this:

Bad Ems is a town situated on both banks of the River Lahn. The population in 1893 was 4,201. The language spoken is German. The government of the town is stable and based upon a system of land-rats with universal suffrage for both sexes. There is a post office which is connected to the public telephone and telegraph system. Provisions and small quantities of coal may be had. Baths may be taken if prior notice is given to the authorities and a certificate of ill-health is produced.

There is a railway station at which trains frequently stop, and which is connected to the Federal Railway (die Bundesbahn). A second railway, die Malbergbahn, ascends the Malberg hill on the left bank, power being provided by a tank of water underneath the carriage. Small quantities of beer and sausage are obtainable at the station on the summit. Caution: do not lean out (*nicht hinauslehnen*).

Conspicuous objects are: on the *right* bank das Kurhaus at the end of die tulip-beds; at 1100 hrs local time (1000 GMT), an orchestra plays on the balcony. On the *left* bank, der Wasserturm, bearing the arms of the dukes of Nassau. The river is spanned by a pedestrian bridge known as die Fussgängerbrücke, and ½ cable further upstream by a second bridge, eine zweite Brücke, for road traffic.

Caution: near the left bank, and 1½ cables upstream of the decapitation cable for canoeists placed across the weir stream, a permanent waterspout is situated in the river. Experienced mariners approach it cautiously from windward and throw ballast upon the shoreward side of the float until the jet is tilted to play on the promenade.

Anchorage: Opposite das Kurhaus in midstream. Below Fussgängerbrücke on the *left* bank is a new quay (in 1965) provided with bollards. Vessels should on no account attempt to approach the quay, as the local authority (die krassen Idioten) has filled the river with rocks to protect the foundations.

Four years had passed between the *Commodore*'s trip up the Lahn and the day when her successor came chugging up the Kurhaus reach. This time I was not worried about the bath facilities, for the start of a new season's voyage aboard the *Thames Commodore* was a relatively simple and cleanly affair. The captain and mate would spend a few evening hours chatting to the dockers who came to watch them stow the stores aboard ship in the Regent's Dock, then the captain would press the starters, check the gauges, and away. There was no chance to get really dirty, and even if we had approached the Lahn in a rather oily condition the shower-baths aboard would soon have made us respectable.

Steering up past the familiar lawns I wondered what changes might have come over the town, and we had not run far up the reach before we came upon the first of them. Down near the blue onion domes of the Russian Orthodox Church the management of the spa had introduced a sort of miniature floating island from the centre of which a fountain shot a single fire-hose jet high in the air. The purpose was, I suppose, to discourage water-borne visitors even more, for the direction of the prevailing wind had been carefully noted and the waterspout anchored in such a position that the whole output would fall squarely across the navigation channel. But intrepid mariners such as ourselves were not deterred. We found the water-jet exhilarating. It gave a sort of Conradish feel to the journey up the reach, and added a do-and-dare-or-be-sunk atmosphere to the attempt.

Bad Ems

With the palm court orchestra on the port beam I told the *Thames Commodore* that a brand new quay awaited her. I had seen a newspaper photograph of it only a week before, the picture showing the immaculate new quayside, bollards and all. The Minister for Culture, or Wharves, or Inward Affairs or something had opened it and made a speech about what a great day it was for Bad Ems to have such a nice new facility. It had never occurred to me that in order to prevent the new quay from sustaining any possible damage from anything so unreasonable as a boat the city fathers would have protected their wharf by pouring truckloads of rocks into the water alongside it until there was not enough depth to give a safe approach for a minnow.

We anchored in mid-river, lowered the dinghy and I rowed near enough to the shore to be able to jump. Once again I presented myself in the plushy hall of the *Kurverwaltung*. I was so neat and tidy that the girls (they were new ones) stopped calculating the profits and beamed.

'Can I help you, Sir?'

'Yes, 'I said. 'My compliments to the burgomaster, and tell him that if he is responsible for the new quay he is a thundering ass

117

and should be taken to the bridge and dropped in his own bloom-ing river,' I said.

The girls were evidently worried.

'The burgomaster?'

'Yes, and all the burgraves, echevins, town-rats, building-rats, secret-rats and anyone else responsible,' I said. (A secret-rat or *Geheimrat* was still almost as much of a holiness in Germany as when I had stayed in the house of one thirty years earlier.)

'The quay is not our responsibility,' said one of the girls des-perately. 'It belongs to the water-rat.'

'Rubbish,' I said. 'No water-rat would be such a geblasted idiot as to foul his own wharf. Besides, I read the newspaper about the opening.'

As the girls could not produce the burgomaster I was referred again to the man in the bath-ticket office. He, it seemed, dealt with all matters connected with strangers and people of possibly menacing demeanour. On account of my cleanliness he did not recognise me as the lunatic who had called upon him some years earlier, but he identified me well enough as the man who, only a few minutes earlier, had been seen not only to drop anchor in the sacred river but actually to have rowed to the shore and landed upon the holy steps of Bad Ems. Before I had even opened my mouth he began to set about me.

'You are from the ship,' he squeaked, peering over his glasses. 'What do you mean by anchoring in the river, in front of the Kurhaus? You must stop at the quayside."

'Of course you're making a joke,' I said.

'A joke! Why do you think the town of Bad Ems has spent all that money on a new quayside if boats do not use it, eh?'

Which was as good a nonsense question as ever remained unanswered.

Bad Ems is in fact so buoyed up by its own springs that it does not worry about visitors who may be more interested in the river water than in the hot gushers. One of the springs at least has a reputation which is both curious and ancient, and if we can believe the story – which is perhaps asking rather much when it concerns a tale told by Bad Emsers – the first notable visitor to take the waters was Agrippina, the wife of the Emperor Germanicus. From earliest times one particular spring at Ems was reputed to have the property of determining the sex of future children, in that pregnant women bathing in the Bubenquelle (Boys' Spring) would eventually produce a boy. Its working upon Agrippina was disastrous, for she shortly afterwards gave birth to the boy who afterwards became the notorious Caligula, probably the most revolting creature ever to have been born in the Lahn valley. Yet this spring certainly achieved a great reputation for male progeny. If a boy was born, then it was the water which had done it; but if the child was a girl, then of course the woman must have made her visit too late. No doubt this would account for the case of the English lady who, the Emsers assert, already had eleven daughters when she came to Bad Ems, bathed in the Bubenquelle, and promptly had a twelfth. Many people still believe in the special property of this gusher, whatever the rest of the world may prefer to think about sex being determined by the XX or XY mechanism of chromosome assortment. And even though I used to be a geneticist I would not wish for one moment to interfere with such a charming belief.

Bad Ems is perhaps more famous among historians for its telegram than for being responsible for the birth of Caligula. It was in July 1870 that the Kaiser was taking the waters when he was visited by the French Ambassador Benedetti, who had been sent to Ems by Napoleon III with instructions to request the Kaiser not to permit Prince Leopold of Hohenzollern-Sigmaringen to put himself forward as candidate for the throne of Spain. Not surprisingly the mission failed. One day the men met on the promenade beside the river and Benedetti raised the matter again. But the Kaiser had 'nothing more to say'. The exchange was short and perhaps not very diplomatic. The famous telegram drafted by Bismarck swept along the wires from the local post office, heading for Berlin. The Franco–Prussian war was launched, Strasbourg was bombarded, Alsace and Lorraine attached to Germany for nearly fifty years. On the promenade a discreet stone recalls this event so typical of Franco–German relations of a past age, but nobody is particularly proud of the recollection.

Yet it was not only the royalty and diplomats who frequented fashionable Ems. Along the Lahnside walks Weber spun his melodies, and in the ugly Schloss Balmoral which we had passed to starboard above the waterspout Richard Wagner once sat at his desk, poring over the orchestration of *Parsifal*. At Bad Ems Offenbach began his composition of *La Belle Hélène*. Jenny Lind sang there, a rival to the indigenous nightingales of the Malberg copses. Liszt gave concerts in the same stately Kursaal on the port hand from which the strains of Smetana's *Vltava* floated across the water to where the *Thames Commodore* lay. And these recollections combine with the very genuine elegance of the range of spa buildings on the right bank of the river to give it a very definite allure.

So in spite of its shortcomings as an inland port, after these first two visits I liked Bad Ems sufficiently to go there again. The next occasion was somewhat unexpected, for I had just walked along the Moselle heights from France to the Rhine in seven and a half days instead of the eight I had estimated when booking my return flight. Cutting across the neck of forest between Alken on the Moselle and Boppard on the Rhine I was overtaken by gusty rain, and as I reached the outskirts of Boppard and looked across to where the passengers in the chair-lift were being slowly lowered across the tree-tops in the downpour I was glad I was not one of them. I was at least somewhat sheltered by trees until I reached the town, and quickly I was at the promenade. There lay the BP tank-ship on which we had pulled in to fuel the *Thames Commodore* only a year before, and beyond it the giant Dutch passenger-ships hung at their jetties. Further up I came to another stage, that of the *Ursula*. In five minutes she was leaving for a voyage to Bad Ems on the Lahn. There were many worse ways of spending a wet afternoon than by turning it into a busman's holiday, so I bought a ticket and hurried down the gang-plank.

I wished the skipper a good day, and he looked at me strangely.

'Haven't I seen you before, somewhere? It was on a yacht, surely. On the Lahn,' he added.

This I thought a remarkable feat of memory. I recalled now that on an August day in the previous year we had indeed come

down the Lahn and had shared the Bad Ems lock with the *Ursula*.
It had needed considerable juggling with the lines, as the lock was
only six inches longer than our combined lengths, but I would
never have recognised the skipper of that vessel if he had come
tramping along with a rucksack. Nor even aboard a ship. But his
recognition – due, if I remember rightly, to my face having been
implanted in his memory because of its barely suppressed fury
when the *Ursula* bumped the *Thames Commodore* on the buttocks
– was enough to have me invited into the wheelhouse. And that is
the best place to be on any vessel. Thus it came about that I have
been through the Lahn locks to Limburg eight times, but the
first four to Bad Ems ten times over. And to negotiate the Lahn
aboard the *Ursula* was certainly an interesting experience.

The *Ursula* was built for the Bad Ems run. With 200 horsepower to stem and overcome the Rhine she had a fair turn of
speed, and to make the greatest possible use of the Lahn locks she
was built five and a quarter metres in beam. This allowed her nine
inches on either side in the larger locks, and almost two inches in
those such as Ahl, and in the stop-lock gate openings at Nievern
and Bad Ems. Negotiating these was a matter of cannon off the
cushion, the cushion being made of stone. But the greater problem
was with the headroom.

On entering the Lahn the second-in-command, Peter, had
promptly undone the wingbolts and flattened out the front and
back and sides of the wheelhouse so that he and the skipper were
left standing up in the rain, clad in plastic macintoshes and with a
tarpaulin flung over the most vulnerable bits of wheelhouse.
Even then the rain driving into the wiper on the prostrated wind-
screen caused a short-circuit, and a steamy sizzling until Peter
disconnected the wires. Down below, the passengers were having
lunch, but I stayed up to see how we would fare at the bridges, for
the *Ursula* had considerably more freeboard than the *Thames
Commodore*.

Above Bad Ems lock the three of us crouched on the floor, and
remarking that the river was a few inches above normal the skipper sighted carefully over the spokes of his wheel. He seemed satisfied, and allowing the ship to glide with its own momentum he

E2

slid her neatly under the first bridge over the cut. The wheel cleared the lower girders by about six inches. I was glad it was raining, as otherwise some stupid passenger on the upper deck who was not watching would probably have been cleanly decapitated.

'That was a near thing,' I said.

'The next bridge is lower,' said the skipper. He took the binoculars and counted the courses of stone visible, then gave an order to the mate.

Peter brought up the tools, and just before we reached the bridge the wheel was removed. A diminutive one was put in its place, projecting no higher than the flattened-out superstructure.

'O.K.,' said the skipper. He sent Peter to the hatch to prevent any incautious passenger coming out at an inopportune moment. Then we threw ourselves flat on the floor, for this bridge was so low that we could not see over the superstructure without scalping ourselves. The Lahn did not often rise, but after heavy rain it could come up enough to give the *Ursula* trouble. Only the week before, the skipper had squeezed into Bad Ems with a bare inch to spare, and during the two-hour halt the river had risen enough to prevent the *Ursula*'s return. The weir being a fixed one he had persuaded the lock-keeper to open all his paddles at both ends and cause a fall of water in the cut, and though the draw-off had only lowered the level a couple of inches, that had been enough to free the ship for her return to the Rhine. This time we had an inch and a half to spare.

'And that's plenty,' said the skipper. 'An inch is as good as three feet, surely.'

If Bad Ems is sophisticated and medicated, Dausenau a mere half-hour upstream is as natural and rural a place as one could find. It lies right down by the river bank and here and there the arches at the top of its medieval walls still survive along the towpath, incorporated into the walls of the houses. At the very entrance to the town – or, more accurately, just outside its gate – a thousand-year-old oak still casts its shade over the seats where the old men sit of an evening, no longer to judge their fellows but to discuss the harvest, taste their wine, and maybe wonder why the

Dausenau

younger generation is so restless and drives so fast and furious through the village street.

Though only two of its original seven towers are now standing, Dausenau still has the aspect of a tiny fortified town huddled between the hills and the river bank. In fact one of these towers is hardly standing, and its lean is such that some years ago twenty feet had to be removed from the top to prevent it crashing upon some unsuspecting motorist driving up the valley. That it was not taken down entirely was perhaps because it is said to have been the prison in which Charlemagne locked up his disobedient daughter, who had an unfortunate habit of falling in love with his secretary Eginhard.

Just inside the village, and right against the difficult landing

where the *Thames Commodore* lay with an anchor to hold her off
the stones, there is another of the 'only, old and original Wirtshaus-
an-der-Lahn' inns, and a very pretty one too. Looking out over
the remains of the town wall against the towpath it cannot have
changed much since the days when thirty tow-horses were stabled
there. Even now its low-ceilinged, smoke-stained rooms have
names which reflect how the shipmasters would sit round their
table in the best parlour, the *Halfen* or drovers in another, and
that lowest species of humanity the *Treidlern* or tow-men in a third.
For bank-haulage by men was the rule until horses supplanted
them for the few years before the Nassau railway robbed them and
their drovers of the chance of a night's rest at the inn by the river.
Somehow, Goethe failed to stop there, but Blücher spent the
night in this friendly hostelry before leading his men across the
Rhine in pursuit of a Napoleon retreating in disorder from Moscow.

> *Es steht ein Wirtshaus an der Lahn,*
> *Da halten all' die Fuhrleut' an;*
> *Frau Wirtin schenkt vom besten*
> *Echt Ullrichsteiner Fruchtbranntwein;*
> *Und setzt ihn vor den Gästen.*
>
> *There is an inn along the Lahn*
> *At which the drovers all pull in.*
> *The hostess' speciality,*
> *Real Ullrichsteiner brandy-wine,*
> *She sets before her welcome guests.*

The song was written by a Marburg student, and at Dausenau
they are quite certain that theirs was the inn which he visited and
immortalized in one of the best known of German songs. But the
Fuhrleute or drovers are gone, and whether or not the landlady
still serves real genuine Ullrichsteiner Fruchtbranntwein we were
unable to discover, for when we spent the night below its windows
the inn was closed for its weekly *Ruhetag* or day of rest. Yet somehow I am not so sure that this drink was ever obtainable. I have a
suspicion that it may only have made its way into the song on
account of its impeccable poetic metre.

Nowadays life at Dausenau must be quiet enough, and not particularly dangerous. Yet it has been calculated that up to the year 1660, when at last Nassau was administered by an official who thought witchcraft to be nonsense, nearly three quarters of the population of the neighbourhood died as a result of plague, witch-burnings and the ravages of marauding armies in the Thirty Years and earlier wars.

Another lock and already there comes into view the conical hill to starboard with a square ruined keep peeping from the beech-woods which clothe the slopes to the summit, all that remains of the residence of a line from which England, Germany and the Netherlands have drawn their monarchs, and Luxembourg her line of Archdukes. To please the Dutch a huge orange flag floats over the humble wreckage of Nassau. Curiously enough, the castle of Orange-Nassau was brought to ruin by no human foe, but merely by wind and storm, frost and snow, the splits wrought by the roots of trees, the attacks of juvenile hooligans, and the depredations of those in need of building materials.

The keep is said to have been built by a hunting knight who pursued a noble stag up to the top of the hill, slaughtered it, and then happened to notice that the view was a particularly pleasant one, just the outlook he would like to have for his residence when he married one of the seven beautiful maidens in Castle Arnstein, further upstream. In fact the castle was placed there in early medieval times to protect a road which was already in existence in the pre-Roman era, and its position was such that even in the stormy middle ages it could not easily be assaulted – partly because it had advance posts on the neighbouring hillsides. One of these, on a spur running down toward the river, was guarded by a family named Stein which was to give rise to the Freiherr von und zu Stein, one of Germany's wisest and most competent statesmen. A memorial to him was placed on the modest ruins of the family fort, and by some curious chance it was struck and totally demolished during the Second World War when such an unlikely place as Nassau with its surrounding woodlands was subjected to a violent bombardment – perhaps through a chance of mistaken identity. But in 1953 a new monument was put up, a ring of columns with Stein himself standing in the centre and looking out above the trees and across the railway bridge to watch the signals on the mast at Nassau lock as the green discs are changed from horizontal to vertical as a sign to the *Thames Commodore* that she may enter. President Heuss himself dedicated this pleasantly light and airy memorial, and this alone can be taken as a sure sign that Stein must have been a right-minded man as well as a famous one.

I doubt if any of the *Thames Commodore*'s crew could have made much of a showing in answering an examination question upon the life and work of the Freiherr von und zu Stein. I myself had never even heard of him. But he was an observant statesman who looked at the world around him, diagnosed its obvious faults and fearlessly set about putting them right. He noted, for example, that peasants were late with their crops because they had to work a specified number of days for their landlords. Villagers might not even move house and home without permission of the gentry, nor might they marry unless the landlord gave his permission. These and other absurdly feudal laws which had still survived into the nineteenth century so incensed him that he drove to the Royal Palace and told the Prussian King Frederick William III that the house must be put in order. The king did not receive the idea well, so Stein at once handed in his resignation as minister and retired to his mansion in the village of Nassau to draw up a work in which he set out the reforms he was convinced were necessary.

However, in 1807 Napoleon was spreading his grasp over Prussia, and if the condition of the peasants had previously been shocking their lot was now far worse. Liberty, equality and fraternity might be fair enough in France but they were certainly not for export. So, in the hour of crisis, the king appealed to Stein, who returned to Berlin to take charge. He immediately overthrew all the feudal restrictions, freed the peasantry, and gave considerable rights of self-government to the towns.

Inevitably, these liberalising actions were deeply resented by the royalty and aristocracy, but none feared Stein's influence more than Napoleon, who drove him to flee for his life. Yet after the retreat from Moscow the Freiherr returned once more and set to work to forge a single unified nation out of the jigsaw puzzle of minor dukedoms which at that time still made up the map of Germany.

Stein's family mansion still stands in the village, one of the few buildings to survive the devastating air raid. There one may note that, although the family arms are sedate enough and consist of a red rose on a golden ground, the crest is a donkey with its tongue out. This improbable device is said to have originated in the days of the Emperor Barbarossa whom the then Lord of Stein accompanied on his desperate ventures into Italy. As his horse was shot beneath him, Stein could only transport himself home upon a donkey which he managed either to buy or perhaps to steal. The poor beast nobly plodded over the Alpine passes and down half the length of the Rhine valley to bear him home to Nassau. By then its tongue was permanently hanging out from thirst and exhaustion, but its good-natured master gave it a pension of free grazing for life, without any further work, and honoured it by adopting its portrait as the family crest.

Nassau has special attractions for the boatman. It is almost the only place on the whole river where there is deep water to the bank so that one can actually moor without risk of being pounded heavily on the rocks by the wash of passing barges. It has always been one of the *Thames Commodore*'s pick-up points for her friends, because the trains of what used to be the Nassau State Railway run into a little station within easy suitcase-carrying distance. Then there is the fact that one has a garden without the labour of keeping it, a pretty little parklet of rose-beds right beside the mooring, and even more important is that the garden is well supplied with litter baskets. I have always been disinclined to throw refuse in the river, even on streams like the Rhine where it is the general habit among shipmasters to throw all their rubbish overboard and let it silt up the approaches to Rotterdam. Somehow one accumulates an astonishing amount of rubbish in a short time - especially if one has visitors who think their life is deprived if they cannot buy English daily newspapers.

And then there is the view. The splendid medieval bridge of ten arches was partly carried away by a great flood at the time of the

Thirty Years War, and later entirely demolished by Brandenburg troops who blew it up as they fled headlong from the villainous French who, like the villainous Swedes, were always inclined to spread death and destruction wherever they might. But it has been replaced by a handsome and rather old-worldish suspension bridge, the towers of which frame the outlook down the reach beside the steep slope of the castle hill to where the morning mist hangs as a white layer of fleecy cloud halfway up the hillside beyond the lock, a slope which used to produce wines of great excellence. There are few better places than Nassau in which to let the dawn chorus of the woodland urge one to be up and about, to see the beauty of the early light flooding the valley, and to fill all the litter baskets before the attendant comes round to empty them.

It is no long run from Nassau through the meadows to Hollerich lock with its tall spruce on the one side and a stately silver birch on the other. It is a friendly and remote place without so much as a road, and the lockside tap has some of the best drinking-water for many miles, particularly if one is inclined to pots of tea. We would always tank at Hollerich while rising or falling in the deep pen, and as we did so the lock-keeper's son would pore over the box of stamps we always carried aboard for just such occasions. There is not a lock-keeper in the world who cannot muster a collector among his friends or family or godchildren, and some of the *Thames Commodore*'s occasional crew save all the more interesting ones from the mail at home to help make her passage through locks in such remote places an event never forgotten.

Hollerich's gates open out to one of the Lahn's most splendid sweeps, but the great bow of meadow where the river curves round toward the foot of the spur of Arnstein monastery is a favourite one for campers, and among campers a certain proportion are sure to be anglers. Not all anglers are alert – indeed, it seems an occupation which both demands and induces a certain lethargy of the mind – and so I never approach a riverside camping site without blowing sufficient blasts on the hooter to awaken the dead, the fox from his lair in the morning, and – I hope – such anglers as have cast their lines across the channel before dropping off to sleep. On this particular occasion it was breakfast time for such shore-dwellers, and when we came round the corner most of the families were sitting in their portable palaces, taking the first meal of the day.

When I saw the pair of thin gossamer traces which extended right across the shipping channel to the further shore, it was too late. Twenty-nine tons deadweight of *Thames Commodore* took them neatly on her stem and drew out the reeled nylon with a splendid rattle of the ratchets. But what made the run-down even more impressive was that the two angling members of this particular family from Gelsenkirchen were of the kind that likes fishes to announce their presence by ringing a little bell hung on the rod, and the violence of the jangling of both bells at once must have made them think they had both simultaneously hooked such a fish as would break all records for the Lahn. They came tumbling out of the tent, mugs in hand, and raced to grab the rods before the gear disappeared into the river. In this they succeeded, but they lost a great length of line and only narrowly escaped being pulled into the water.

There followed, of course, considerable abuse, swelled by the female members of the family. But it is foolish to yell at a ship, particularly when the captain has a loud-hailer and can out-shout one by several hundred yards and quite a few decibels, too. I could see that the men's tempers were a little frayed – partly because their fellow campers found the incident so hilarious – yet I hardly expected them to take the trouble to get out their Mercedes and roar up the valley to yell threats at us from the bank at the next lock upstream. Empty threats, too, for the navigation authority is not very sympathetic to fishermen who do anything quite so silly as to lay a line right across the river.

The tents spread along the shore of the Lahn stretch round a quarter circle of meadow in which the castle of Langenau stands, skirted on its farther side by the Gel brook. It is a homely looking place in which a pleasant half-timbered manor is built against the ruin of an earlier one, which in turn seems to lean for support against a medieval keep. It has anything but a military appearance, and so far as I know it was never a nest of noble vultures as were so many of the castles on the Rhine. Even its position is unwarlike

The Lahn above Hollerich Lock

and trusting, for instead of being perched on a formidable crag it sleeps quietly among the cuckoo-pint and water-marigolds, breathing threatenings and slaughter to none. And appropriately enough, the only tales I have discovered about the place are peaceable ones.

Langenau formerly belonged to a family named Marioth, and in the seventeenth century one of the ladies of the manor was particularly known for her kindly nature. So perhaps it is not so very surprising that one night when her husband was away on business she was awoken by a light, and sitting up in bed she beheld a little dwarf-woman standing on the mat beside the bedstead and holding a lantern. Frau Marioth was not in the least alarmed at such a sight for she knew the Lahn valley to shelter a fair population of such little people. She asked the tiny woman what she wanted, and a piping little voice explained that the chief lady of the little people was about to give birth, and down in the ground they just did not happen to have a midwife.

The good Frau Marioth quickly dressed herself, and led by the dwarf woman she crept through a number of low passages in the rocky hillside until at last she was brought into a magnificent boudoir in which the mother-to-be was awaiting her. All went well, the child was born, and as a reward the noble lady of the little people presented her visitor from the outside world with a magnificent ring. Frau Marioth was to take it, she said, and on the following Eve of St John (midsummer, that is) she was to wear it on her finger and walk to the Silberberg at Weinähr, a mile or two from Langenau. She was to climb the path up the hill until she came upon a raven and a pair of hawks fighting over the remains of a dead pigeon. She should make a careful note of the exact spot, for there her reward lay buried; and provided her family never parted with the ring their fortune would never run out.

Back home, Frau Marioth awaited the return of her husband, to whom she related the whole story. He was not very inclined to believe that his wife had had anything more than a dream, but there was no escaping the fact that somehow she had come into possession of a very curious and obviously valuable ring. So, when midsummer's eve came round he was ready to accompany her, even if somewhat grudgingly. When, however, they came upon the specified birds scrapping over a dead wood-pigeon he carefully marked the spot, and on the following morning he took his men up from Langenau to excavate. Almost immediately they struck a vein of silver ore which proved so rich that the Marioths quickly became extremely wealthy.

Eventually Frau Marioth and her husband died. They left three children, who decided to share the property by taking the ring to a jeweller in Koblenz who was to divide it carefully into three equal and narrower rings. This he did – but the vein of ore yielded no more silver. The younger generation dug hole upon hole on the side of the Silberberg, but not another ounce did they find, and when one of their descendants tried once more to mine the silver he lost 300,000 Thalers in the operation.

Then again there is the tale of how, once upon a time, long, long ago – and I hope the reader is sitting comfortably in the bilge as we turn the long bend to port past the bright blue and orange tents of the families from Holland and the Ruhr – once upon a certain time another fair mistress of Langenau was walking along that very same bank where the imprudent anglers were cooking their breakfasts and disregarded our warning hoots. She held her small son by the hand until they came to a place where he could play in the grass, and there she sat down. As the day was pleasantly warm she dozed off. She did not sleep for long, but the moment she awoke she realised with terror that her child had vanished. Scrambling to her feet she searched the meadow, the river bank. Not a sign of the child was to be seen. The mother ran to the castle and at once a search party was sent out. All day and throughout the night the men combed the woodland, and at dawn the fishermen dragged the river. But never a trace of little Heinrich was found. He had simply vanished.

In the course of time the sorrow of his disappearance faded, and as the years flowed by like the River Lahn he was forgotten. Eventually his parents died also. It was seventy years after the event that a knocking on the gate of Langenau castle one evening caused the porter to open. Before him stood a small boy who told him some hare-brained tale of how he had been playing at the water's edge when a hand (that of the Lahngeist, I presume) rose from the water, clutched his arm and pulled him in. A kind beautiful lady had taken him into a hall where he had played with a host of boys and girls until at the end of the afternoon he had said he must be going home. And here he was – though he did not recognise any of the servants as those he had left only a few hours before.

The young Lord of Langenau was summoned, together with his

bride – for he was only recently married. He looked the child up and down, shrugged and said he had never seen him in his life. Yet his wife recognised a family likeness in the features, a fact which aroused her suspicions in what happened to be an entirely wrong direction. But while she was speculating on possible previous amorous adventures of her husband the chaplain remembered that sometime, somewhere, he had read something in the family archives. Hurrying to the library he began to blatter through the papers until he found what he was seeking. Yes, there it was, written in the hand of two or three generations earlier.

'My son Heinrich was lost. The silver cross on his rosary bears the date 1506.'

The chaplain raced back to the group which still surrounded the stranger boy. The rosary? Yes. The lad felt inside his shirt and drew it out. The silver cross, with the date 1506 – yes, it was there right enough, but were we not now already in the 1580s?

'It is he! Heinrich!' The lord of the manor steps forward, hesitant.

The company do not know what to do, to say. Here is the lost child, seventy years old but still a small boy in appearance, in speech and in fact.

'Heinrich, dear. Come in. . .' The young mistress of Langenau takes him by the hand and leads him into the court he knows so well. And yet as she does so the transformation begins. Within only a few moments he runs through seventy years of physiology and ends up in the realms of gerontology. He is a lad, a young man, middle-aged, elderly, then an old and rheumaticky fellow all in succession, growing and wilting like a plant seen in a speeded-up film of its development. At the door into the great hall he is already decrepit, and there on the threshold he collapses, his frail body no longer able to support him in his old age. Heinrich of Langenau dies, in the home where he was born.

Somewhere there must be a moral in this tale. Maybe it is concerned with the Lahngeist and its curious ongoings, but personally I prefer to find in it a reminder that time – as the monk of Heisterbach also discovered – is relative, that the railway time-table of school-leaving at fifteen or eighteen and retirement at sixty-five is an invention of man rather than a facet of real truth. And perhaps it also holds a hint that we are much closer to another time scale than any of us would care to admit, except in those dreams when perhaps we experience a new dimension as vividly as did Heinrich of Langenau when the Lahngeist stretched her arm above the waves and drew him down into a new level of being.

The Lahn near Obernhof

VIII

*The founding of Arnstein – the Cramberg loop – the devil
of the Gabelstein – attack on the* Thames Commodore *– an
Oxford lawn – Balduinstein – Diez and Oranienstein –
Limburg's mooncalf – figures on the bridge – the truth about
Waterloo – fate of the Nepomuk*

SPLENDID in its colourwash of white and ochre the great
romanesque abbey church of Arnstein stands upon its hill,
looking out over the reach which curves down past Langenau. It
stands upon the site of a strong castle, but in 1109 that stronghold
was inherited by a boy of such gentle disposition that when he
grew up he decided to disown the warlike deeds and habits of his
friends and neighbours and convert the place into a monastery.
Perhaps he was swayed to this resolve by the fact that his own
marriage with a noble Bavarian girl named Guda was childless.
There was no line running ahead to eternity. And so it came about
that Ludwig and his good wife Guda presented themselves one

day before the abbot Gottfried and – as a monk of the time recorded – 'stripped off all the old clothes of damnation' and donned the white of the religious order.

Ludwig of Arnstein and his knights then at once set about the reconstruction, breaking down the fortifications to form a place on which to set the institution, and adapting the remaining buildings into a monastery. For Guda they built a cell on the side of the hill, wherein 'she chastised her body night and day according to the commandment of God in the holy gospel'. Certainly it was a very odd version of the gospel to which Guda or the monkish archivist had access, for whatever the odds in the apostolic arguments about justification by faith or by works there was never any suggestion that righteousness lay in a sort of holy masochism. Poor, fair, loving Guda, she did not long survive in her loneliness of self-mortification, but Ludwig continued his humble life as a monk for forty-seven years from the foundation of his monastery. Only after his death did he come again into a brief moment of pomp, when his bier was carried into the choir by four powerful counts, Nassau and Isenburg, Diez and Katzenelnbogen.

Inevitably in the course of a turbulent European history Arnstein was sacked. At last it was secularised by Napoleon's iconoclasts, and shortly afterwards it was put up for sale as building materials. Luckily Waterloo had by then come and gone, so the church was retained for the local people and has survived until today as one of the treasures of the gentle Lahn valley. Finally, after the First World War, Ludwig's monastery was again raised to something of its original status, and the Arnstein Fathers are still there. But I am sure that these men, who spend their time in prayer and intercession, would not sentence their loved ones to die from loneliness in a cold cell of stone.

Arnstein is accessible from Obernhof, a gay little place of neat-cut slate roofs which is rather more self-conscious than Dausenau but quite as much of a problem for the boatman who wants to come to land. I had been through the place several times before I decided that I really must visit Arnstein (which proved something of a disappointment) and would disembark at Obernhof if I had to anchor in mid-river. Besides, Obernhof was the only wine village on all the length of the Lahn, so it merited a reasonable amount of effort. And here, as at Dausenau and Nassau and other places in quite other lands, something that the Nassau lock-keeper had said to me seven years earlier proved a sound piece of advice.

'Never,' he had said, 'never draw in where there is new stone-work on the shore or the landing-stages. It may look neat and smart, but why is the new stone there? Because the old has collapsed, and is lying there in the river, ready for a boat to run on it.'

I learned another truth on that same first voyage up the Lahn. It was April, and the river stood about two feet or more above its normal level, giving the *Commodore* a strong current to contend with – though seven years later her sister found the stream four feet above the standard, and that in June. So fast was the flow that below Nassau her young sister found the stream swifter than that in the whole of the Rhine gorge except at the Bingen rapids. On that first occasion there had been heavy April rain, but the lock-keeper at Scheidt looked across the river to where the wooded slopes were showing just the faintest tinge of bright green.

'The buds are breaking,' he said. 'The river will drop half a metre overnight.'

This remark puzzled me, so I asked him to explain.

'It is simple,' he said with all the assurance of a countryman. 'When the buds break and the leaves expand, the trees draw more water from the soil than at any other time, see? So, as it seeps down the hillsides the water is taken up instead of running into the brooks and down to the Lahn. You'll see.'

And see we did. Next day the woods were clothed in their Easter bonnets of brilliant green, and the level at Kalkofen (the lock above Obernhof) which is daily announced over the radio had fallen by more than half a metre.

Upstream of Kalkofen, a place which consists only of the solitary lockhouse where the Gelsenkirchen anglers came to curse and swear and let off steam, the deserted keep of the Laurenburg stands frowning upon the top of its shaly ridge. Lowering, one might even say – for that is what its name appears to mean, and there is to be no story of a fair lady named Laura who was defenestrated, deceived or despairing. In fact the Laurenburg was the original ancestral home of the family which later gave rise to the Nassau lines, and seems to have been abandoned long ago, perhaps because of its sheer inacessibility. But with Laurenburg on the port beam, or perhaps over the port yardarm, we are approaching a stretch of river where for miles on end there is no railway, no road, nothing but the deserted towpath and the song of birds in the dense woodland.

This is because the Lahn turns so complete a loop that after several kilometres it is back to within less than half a mile of its original course. This section of the river also has a considerable gradient, and, as there is a difference of more than twenty feet in the level of the river where it returns upon itself, it occurred to the ingenious engineers of the River Main Hydro-Electric Company that it would be worth while poaching into the Lahn and drilling a tunnel through the neck of land to put a generating station at the outlet. In 1930 they did so, and where the Lahnships laden with marble chips and the *Thames Commodore* on her voyage of discovery have to make a four-mile circuit and pass through two locks, the water heading for the turbines takes a swift short cut far beneath the fields which surround the village of Cramberg and emerges with a rush and roar into the river again at the foot of the sheer cliff of the Gabelstein, which rears up more than three hundred feet from the water.

This splendid crag is inaccessible to mere humans except on its top, and so it is a natural reserve in which nest kite and kestrel, and even the peregrine falcon which is something of a rarity in this part of Europe. Foxes have their earths in the narrow gulleys protected by scrub and scree, but more unexpected is the marten, which has plenty to prey upon in the security of the cliff. Curiously, the enterprise of the electrical engineers with their generating station brought a new factor into the ecology, for the bright lights in the windows of the turbine-house at the foot of the cliff attracted insects by the million. Word was quickly passed round among the various tribes of bats, and many of them decided to move in and to set up home in the disused slate workings nearby, within easy reach of an evening meal.

One of the dukes of Schaumburg was once riding home late at
night when he missed his path and came in the darkness to the
very edge of the Gabelstein, where his horse prudently dug in its
feet and refused to advance any further. After trying in vain to
urge his steed forward the rider discovered why the creature was
so reluctant, and backing carefully away from the cliff edge he
turned and found the path which led to his castle of Schaumburg.
In gratitude he gave the horse a pension (perhaps he had heard of
the Stein donkey) and released him from all duties, and at the same
time he had a horse-shoe struck in the rock to mark the place of his
lucky deliverance.

The Gabelstein with its rocky reefs on a sharp bend of the river
was always something of a terror to ships, particularly in the days
of bank-haulage. Iron ore and wood, lime and coal, glass and wool,
oil and wine, grain and salt and mineral waters were among the
cargoes which the Lahn barges carried on the river from the time
early in the seventeenth century when an enlightened Count of
Diez dredged out and improved the course all the way to the
Rhine, to make it navigable for larger craft than before. Yet the
shipmasters had many difficulties to contend with, for the river
was then without locks and ran swiftly between shoals and rocks,
and the swirling water could easily throw a heavy bank-hauled
ship against the rocky shore. Where a passage was particularly
dangerous rings and tackle were attached to the rocks, or a windlass
might be used to help haul a vessel up a swift reach. But there was
also the unfortunate circumstance that the Lahn had a devil of its
own, quite distinct from the spirit which would cry out that it
wanted a man. This devil inhabited the Gabelstein, which was a
good place for doing a bit of wrecking, just for fun or out of
devilment.

Once when a small barge was returning upstream from Oberlahnstein, the shipmaster was anxious to make Balduinstein for the
weekend, and seeing a thunderstorm coming up the valley behind
he decided to join the two hauling-men on the towpath and leave
the tiller to his daughter. The men hauled together as strongly as
they could, but the lightning drew nearer and nearer, the flashes
flickering behind the line of the forest on the hilltops. Soon they

were approaching the sharp bend at the foot of the Gabelstein, and the captain called across to his daughter to steer well over to the port side to prevent the barge from being washed into the dreaded cliff where the devil had his home.

Marie leaned with all her might upon the tiller, yet it seemed as though some inexorable force were drawing the boat across the stream, ever closer to the foot of the cliff where the devil of the Lahn had his lair. The men hauled at the line, but their combined strength could not hold her off. Suddenly a scream rent the air.

'Let go, and save yourself, father! The devil is taking me!'

A blinding flash of lightning followed, and part of the crag of the Gabelstein crashed down upon the barge, burying ship and girl at the bottom of the Lahn. And since that time, they say, the Lahn devil has never been seen or heard again. But there they are wrong. He was certainly in residence one June afternoon when the *Thames Commodore* came chugging up the reach below, without a care in the world.

I had been up the Lahn often enough to know that the bend by the Gabelstein was probably the most dangerous corner on the river, which turned through half a circle before leading up to the lock of Scheidt. The sharpest part of the bend was immediately opposite the crag, where the stream was also narrower, and the corner was tight enough to be blind. The situation was complicated by the fact that the water on the curve was comparatively shallow, for it was too far above Kalkofen lock to show any damming effect. Finally, the engineers of the Main Hydro-Electrics had placed the outlet of their power-station in what had always seemed to me an idiotic position, the entire output of water from the turbines being discharged at right angles to the stream at almost the narrowest point, and on the blindest part of the bend.

Knowing all this, it was my habit to regard the Gabelstein as one of those places, like the Binger Loch and the Unkel corner on the Rhine, and the whole of the unregulated section of the Rhone, where the captain would himself take the wheel. This was not because I mistrusted the ability of whoever else might have been steering, but for the simple reason that if any unpleasant incident should occur it would be embarrassing for any friend who happened to be at the wheel, for however impeccable his navigation he would never be able to convince himself that he was not at fault. So, about one minute short of the Gabelstein I took over. No doubt the Lahnteufel up in his lair chuckled. He had prepared things better than I could guess.

The Gabelstein bend is, of course, a place where a red-rimmed board on the bank bears a black spot on a white ground. This does not mean 'accident black spot', but merely 'one blast, please'. The *Thames Commodore* obediently blew off a piercing note which echoed up the valley, bouncing off the rocks. No answer. The passage was evidently clear. She stemmed the outflow of the power-house and began to turn the tightest part of the bend.

At that moment there came into view a Lahnship heavily laden with marble slabs. She was on the wrong side of the stream, careering down without giving a hoot, a toot, or a thought for anything unless perhaps the good wine which I suspect the skipper had taken for his lunch.

The *Thames Commodore* gave a single toot to indicate that she was taking her proper course on the starboard hand. No answer. Instead the barge seemed determined to aim straight for her. Fifty yards at the most separated us now. We signalled again. No reply. The blue flag which should have been flown to request a starboard-to-starboard encounter remained at the bottom of the staff, the flasher light for the same intention gave not a single wink. We edged over to within a few feet of the Gabelstein and turned the bow in sharply because of the turbine run-off, which was now close upon us.

I saw a sort of oafish realisation dawn upon the thick face of the man at the wheel. He began to spin it, but too late. He merely brought the stern over to reduce our passage still more. As he swept past us the gap between his quarter and the rock face was probably not more than a yard wider than our beam. With a spurt the *Thames Commodore* shot through it, then went hard astern to avoid impaling the power-station on her broad nose. All might have been well, had not the wash of the barge thrown up her stern which came down with a tremendous thump upon something very hard indeed.

I noted that one engine had stopped, so as soon as I had her clear of the run-off and into calmer water I ran her bow against the clay bank below Scheidt lock and jumped over the stern to investigate. Feeling the propeller I could count all three blades, but they did not seem to be facing in the right direction. The shaft turned freely through three quarters of a circle, and then stopped. I could feel with my fingers that one of the blades was then against the bottom of the ship. This would be a matter for a slip, I could see.

The next thing was to look carefully in all the bilge compartments inside the ship and see whether there was any trickle of water. There was not, and so it was clear that only the screw had struck the rocks. To some extent this was a relief, but to be half way up a river like the Lahn at the beginning of a summer's voyage with only one screw and the Rhine gorge still to be negotiated was not altogether encouraging. I was just pondering the situation when another barge, the *Lahnstein*, came out of the lock.

The *Lahnstein* was an old friend. She was a privateer, and I had often chatted with her pleasant captain at lock-sides. She came stolidly down the reach and began to draw off the water and pull our stern out across her path. Unaware that we could not use the starboard engine to take our rump out of his path the captain was extremely surprised – as he told me a few days later, when we were talking about the incident – to find the corner of his wheelhouse holing our dinghy and tearing it off the falls.

Two incidents in ten minutes was, I thought, enough. We would take the ship to the nearest slip and see what was to be done. The lock-keeper at Scheidt rang up the water authority at Diez, two hours up the river, and the water-rat in residence said he would be delighted to lift the stern with a crane and do whatever might be necessary. Late that afternoon a sling was put round the *Thames Commodore*'s buttocks in the diminutive harbour of Diez, and the crane began to creak and groan. It had a maximum capacity of five tons, and although his fellow workmen assured the crane driver that this was only some sort of official fiction he was not inclined to risk lifting too far. I was relieved that he proved so obstinate, as otherwise the probability was that we should end up with the authority's tower-crane on our deck and a nasty hole in the wharf where its roots had been. All the same, the crane managed to lift the stern far enough for us to see that the propeller shaft was about as straight as the neck of a swan.

So the *Thames Commodore* backed out cautiously, aided by a push or two to help her through the entrance. By the time the locks closed for the night she was far down the river at Nassau. An early start in the morning mist, and soon she was running through a Bad Ems which was still asleep, silver grey in the dead light. At half past nine she was swinging round to the foot of the slipway where the Lahn flowed into the Rhine, and while the shipwrights renewed her shaft – which proved to be bent through fifty degrees – and re-shaped her propeller I set about rebuilding the stern of the dinghy. Two days later she was steaming up the Lahn again to round the bend of the Gabelstein easily enough and slip into the open lock-pen of Scheidt.

There is something curiously English about the lock of Scheidt. After a while one realises that it is just the fact that between the house and the river there is a broad slope of well-cut, smooth, spotless grass. Such a sight is so rare on the continent that I asked the pleasant country fellow who kept the lock how he came to have such a fine spread of lawn.

'Because as a young man I was a prisoner of the English,' he said. 'Our camp was at Oxford, and I worked as groundsman to one of the colleges. Cut and roll, cut and roll, and after a century or two you have a fine lawn, they used to say. But it doesn't take that long. As soon as I came home I sowed the grass and began. Cut and roll, cut and roll, and it's no more than twenty years I've done it, and look! People always ask me how it's done, and I tell them. The director of one of the big Schlossparks in Bavaria was here the other day, and he asked me too. Ah, I said, he'd better go to Oxford and see for himself, then go back and tell his gardeners to get on with it.'

He then went on to say that he had only one regret. He would have liked nothing better than to stay in Oxford for the rest of his life. If he hadn't had a wife and baby he would never have come back to Germany. Yet he was content enough. There were not many places in the world as quiet and peaceful as the lock-house of Scheidt. Better there, by far, than in the rat-racing world of the Ruhr.

Softly the Lahn meanders deep in its cleft round the plateau of Cramberg. Before Scheidt one is heading south-west, at Geilnau north-east, and before Cramberg lock south-east. It is a long reach of herons and kites and occasionally a buzzard, and the only settlement is the straggling hamlet of Geilnau which flanks the river to port, its little strips of orchard running down to the water from behind the houses. Geilnau is not much of a place, though a few campers find it a handy spot to pitch a permanent summer tent. However, it used to have a flourishing trade in selling mineral water from its own particular spring until the Thirty Years War brought the villainous Swedes to the valley and the inhabitants quickly filled up the well with refuse. This was sensible enough, for invaders always preferred to set up a base camp wherever there was a curative spring, the water of which was beneficial to their sick and wounded. The Geilnauers were prepared to forgo the source of their wealth if they could thus be free of the Swedes, and so their village was saved from devastation.

Through Cramberg lock the river curves into the village of Balduinstein, which owes its origin to a quarrel between Arch-bishop Balduin and the occupier of the Schaumburg on the hill above it. Balduin, that aggressive Archbishop-Elector of Trier of whom it was said that he would rather set about people with his sword than bless them with his cross, was always ready to extend his own territories by a system of armed trespass, and with a view to wearing down the Schaumburg he built the strong-point down by the river. Around it a settlement sprang up which nowadays is peaceful enough and forms one of the most charming little resorts in all the valley.

Balduin's stolid tower is now a ruin, but not so the Schaumburg, which was reconstructed in the last century 'in the English style', or at least as a German architect's idea of the extraordinary palaces in which the eccentric English lived. It has a tall iron mast with an outlook platform like a giant crow's nest on the top, and our climb through the flowery meadows was well rewarded by the astonishing view over the domains of the Waldecks which is to be had from the top of the pole. And it is only from such an aerial view-point that one realises the truth about the Lahn or the Rhine, the Moselle and the Neckar. To a boatman each of these rivers may seem a stream edged by tall hills, but a wider view shows an upland extending to the horizon with narrow and curling clefts cut down into its mass by the continual erosion of these streams.

There are no longer any ferries on the Lahn, and however much they may flourish on rivers such as the Main and the Moselle where the aspect of the slopes often determine that the villagers will live on the side of the stream removed from their fields or vine-yards, the uncultivated Lahn valley can make do with a relatively small number of bridges instead. The last of the ferrymen worked the river at Balduinstein, and when he was put out of business by the new bridge of concrete somebody had the pleasant idea of putting his statue at one end of the parapet.

> *Der letzte Fährmann auf der Lahn*
> *Den letzten Groschen heut bekam.*
> *Von nun an schliesst die alte Lücke*
> *In Balduinstein die neue Brücke.*

> *The last surviving ferryman*
> *Received today his final pay.*
> *From now the new-built bridge will span*
> *The crossing, here in Balduinstein.*

Past Balduinstein the hills gradually recede – or, more correctly, the upland plateau slopes down, and softens. The gradient of the river itself slackens, the cliffs become lower. A mile or two more, and Fachingen lies to starboard, all but its bottling plant being hidden from the river. Fachingen water is well known among those who like to drink minerals, and its production still runs to I know not how many thousands or millions of bottles annually. Much of the solution of sodium carbonate was formerly carried away by barge, but this trade has now left the river and taken to the road and rail instead. Curiously enough, the discovery of the

F

wonderful properties of the water is said to have been made by a
bargee, who in about the year 1740 drank it, perhaps mistaking it
for a glass of wine. He was swiftly cured of some serious ailment
and the wonder was sufficient to cause a Diez surgeon to look into
the matter and analyse the water from the spring. Within a few
years Fachingen was being bottled to the tune of half a million
flagons a year.

After Fachingen the marble quarries begin. The industry goes
back to the beginning of the nineteenth century, when a 'work-
house' was erected at Diez in which state prisoners spent their
days in sawing blocks of marble. Many castles and palaces in the
Rhineland were supplied with marble, and the particular rose-
red stone of the locality eventually came to be seen in cathedrals
and railway stations as far away as the United States. Thin slabs
for cladding and more massive ones for tombstones are still
sawn from Lahn marble – though by machinery instead of
convict labour – but the heyday of the industry is past and most
quarries furnish either road stone or limestone for industrial use.
Yet even this is enough to keep a considerable fleet of Lahnships
running all the year round.

Diez itself is one of the great sights of the river, a cluster of
ancient half-timbered houses clustered round the base of a sugar-
loaf of porphyry, the top of which is occupied from side to side
by an astonishing grey stone castle with a purple roof of slate and
so many turrets and spikes that it looks like a set for a film of
legends collected by the Grimms. Below it the river is crossed by
a bridge which has no doubt been blown up on many occasions,
but somehow the toll-house has always managed to survive by
clinging desperately to one of the buttresses in mid-stream.

The castle of Diez now contains a youth hostel. Before that it
was certainly a prison, and it is long since the counts of Diez
occupied it. Once they were a powerful line, accompanying the
emperor of the day on crusades and other forays, for which they
were duly rewarded. In the late fourteenth century the last of the
counts died without a male heir, and his daughter married into
the Nassau line, from which was to spring William the Silent, who
inherited property at Orange, far away in the Rhine valley, as well

Diez on the Lahn

as lands in the Netherlands. If William the Silent freed the Nether-landers of the Spanish tyranny his brother at Diez was the first in Germany to abolish serfdom in his lands. But what made this brother a man for whom the *Thames Commodore* had a special regard was the fact that he brought over a Dutch waterways engineer to reconstruct the Lahn and make it navigable for barges, and it was under his enlightened rule that the towpath was built. What with that and his introducing the Reformation into his lands along the Lahn he was obviously a man apart.

Through Diez lock a magnificent baroque palace appears to starboard – or very nearly does so, because only the back of the building and a charming little waterside gazebo can be seen, oddly mixed up with army vehicles and all the debris which usually attends the presence of soldiery. For this splendid place is now the headquarters of the 5th Panzer Division, who panzer about in the grounds like children in a play area. But the elegant building formerly belonged to the Nassau-Diez family, and an earlier building on the same site was the convent of Dirstein. This particular institution was one that drew its girls from

aristocratic families, and because so many of the novices were
related to the nobles in the area they were allowed passes into the
outside world to an extent that was probably unusual. The young
knights of Diez and Nassau and other seats were not at all averse
to the decorous visits which the young ladies from Dirstein were
permitted to make.

There happened to be in the convent a nun named Jutta, who
was in fact the Countess of Diez, and being a high-spirited woman
she decided just before Lent that it would be a pleasant idea to
help her particular friend Clementia to go to the Shrovetide
Carnival in Limburg, of which they had heard so much from the
relatives they visited outside. Undoubtedly such an escapade
would have been against the rules but perhaps she bribed the
portress. However that may be, Clementia slipped out of the convent and into the Diez family carriage which Jutta's brother had
brought there in readiness. By the time they reached Limburg,
Clementia was made up as a most ravishing mermaid.

Now, girls in convents are not necessarily more immune than
others to feelings of romance, and amid all the fun of the fair the
mermaid Clementia succeeded in falling head over tail in love
with a neighbouring young gallant, Gerlach of Limburg. Back in
the convent she could not sleep for thinking of him, and whenever
she was allowed out to the Diezers or the Limburgers sure enough
her adoring Gerlach was there. One day he persuaded her to elope.

Clementia may or may not have been torn in her emotions, but
returning to the convent she stole into the chapel and hung upon
the statue of the virgin the veil which she had taken upon her
admission. Then she slipped out through the gate again and accompanied her lover for a time of decidedly human enjoyment.

And yet as the days of blissful adventure passed, Clementia
began to feel disappointed and to regret her rash action. She
slipped away from her lover (who by this time may also have been
having second thoughts, for he made no effort to pursue her) and
after some little while she stood forlorn and weary before the door
of the convent she had left. Her mind made up, she knocked at the
wicket gate and the portress opened to her.

It was then that the errant girl had a surprise. The woman who opened the door to admit her was not the familiar gate-keeper but none other than the Virgin Mary. Naturally the prodigal girl dropped to her knees, but the Virgin told her to stand up.

'You have sinned much,' she said. 'But because you have loved so greatly, it will all be forgiven to you. While you were away I took your place and did your work. Nobody knows that you have been absent. So off you go, take up your service where you left off, and sin no more!'

By now the *Thames Commodore* is chugging between the fields of grain and bearing up for Limburg. Below the weir the navigation channel skirts an ayot, the Pestinsel or Plague Island, upon which there once lived a poor Franciscan who had selflessly tended the lepers until he too contracted the disease and was banished like them to the middle of the river. Yet even in that exile which was to last until he died, the brother sang songs to cheer his fellow men, the people of Limburg, that by so doing he could forget his own suffering. 'And whatever he sang, so the people and the guildsmen sang it also, and pipers and other musicians took up his melodies and words,' relates the Chronicle of Limburg. These were the Middle Ages, stark and cruel and pitiless, and yet there is something beautiful in the melancholy of the tale. Even now as one stands upon Limburg's ancient bridge and looks out over the silvery line of the weir where the ducks dabble in the weed, it is not so difficult to imagine the townspeople standing on the towpath below the glorious cathedral on the rock, calling to the monk to strike up again, and joining in the verses of those songs which have vanished in the mists of a turbulent history which preserved not a single note from those far-off days.

In the year of our Lord one thousand two hundred and forty-eight, according to the same chronicler, Limburg was besieged by no less than eighteen redoubtable lords who assembled their combined forces around the town and every day for four and a half years continued without ceasing to attack it upon every side. Many a brave man was drowned in the Lahn, the writer added. However, in the fifth year the people of Limburg were beginning to run out of food, and had no more than twenty gallons of corn left in the stores. The end, it seemed, had come.

Yet the town council was not to be discouraged. Having slaughtered what was presumably the last donkey and skinned it, they
stuffed the skin with the grain, sewed it up and setting it on the arm
of the catapult they hurled it out over the walls into the enemy
lines.

The besiegers were puzzled as to what this unexpected visitor
might portend, and the only conclusion their commanders could
make was that the town was so well stocked that corn could
be flung away. That being so, to besiege Limburg any longer
was fruitless, and the order to strike camp and depart was
given.

This tale suggests a certain simplicity among the commanders, if
only because similar stories abound in Germany and France of
pigs and calves stuffed with corn – though usually only in their
stomachs, which was more realistic. Invariably the final bushel of
grain seems to have been used in this way, and always with success.
It is never recorded that any besieging general took the incident
as a sign that the city was in fact out of food; but then, military
men were probably no brighter then than they are now.

Of course, credibility could stretch far in the Middle Ages, far
enough in fact for sixteenth-century Limburg to have been terrorised for some time by the dreadful appearance every night of
the fearful form of a mooncalf roaming the streets. Long in the
legs and breathing fire from its nostrils, this creature of terror
would course the town, bellowing so menacingly that all wise
people ran home and bolted their doors. The mooncalf would then
hide around a corner, leap on the back of some unfortunate passer-
by and bring him to the ground. None dared to oppose the ap-
parition. The only safety lay in flight.

Strangely, the creature would sometimes enter houses and
drive the terrified citizens out before it helped itself to anything of
particular value, and nobody was courageous enough to intervene
until at last there was placed in charge of the municipal night-
watchmen a captain who was more courageous than most. Col-
lecting some stout fellows together and arming them with staves
he set out one night and scoured the town until, sure enough, the
mooncalf's roaring could be heard. He led his troop in pursuit

and managed to drive the monster into a cul-de-sac. Trapped, the mooncalf suddenly fell on its knees and in very proper and refined German began to beg for mercy.

The creature's head was pulled off, and there knelt revealed a pair of robber knights. Their houses were at once raided and all the stolen goods were found on the premises. Driven out of the town by the angry citizens, both fore-legs and hind-legs fled, never to be seen in Limburg again. However, they reconstituted themselves in Westphalia, where they lived successfully in their original guise for many a happy year of robberies.

Limburg has long been one of the *Thames Commodore*'s favourite halts, and not just because there is a good vertical deep-water quayside above the lock. Nor is it just a matter of incomparable steak and fried onions in the Weinhaus Schultes, with a glass of the best Assmannshäuser Rotwein to be found anywhere. It is a fascination compounded of the view down the river, the rustle of the weir where the water pours under the many-arched road-bridge, and the steep and narrow cobbled alleys which thread the old part of the town and climb toward the cathedral which over-looks them all as though determined to see that there is no secession.

> *Des Baumeisters Name ist ohnbekannt.*
> *Man findet seines Gleichen nit in dem Landt.*
>
> *The master builder's name unknown,*
> *In all the land he stands alone.*

These words refer to the craftsman who designed this gem of German romanesque, the mighty seven-towered cathedral of Limburg standing severe upon a basalt cliff which thrusts up-wards from the river bank and offers room on its flat top only for the great church and the bishop's palace. The builder is indeed unknown, but probably it is his own portrait which looks down from one side of the main portal, a little man, crouched and wear-ing a workman's cap and with his hands resting on a stick. On the other side sits – but this time on a throne of sorts to emphasise the gap in class – the figure of Konrad Kurzbold, the Duke of Nassau who earlier founded the first church upon the same rock.

Narrow streets are not unusual in German towns, but the steep Fahrgasse which leads up from the bridge into the centre of Limburg and once formed part of the main road from Cologne to Frankfurt was so beset with overhanging upper storeys that – as an inscription still reminds one – 'At Cologne on the Rhine, at the Waggoners' Inn in the Haymarket, the measurements were written up which laden waggons could not exceed if they were to be able to pass this corner, and also the arch of the bridge-gate'.

The bridge gate is still there, hard by the lock which is crossed by a final arch added to the medieval structure at a later date. It originally had a purpose quite apart from serving in the defences of the town, for the old bridge of Limburg used once to be a toll bridge and travellers were obliged to pay their dues to the collector, who lived in the archway house up in the tower of the gateway. This official is said to have been very careful that none escaped without paying, but he also overcharged whenever persons came over the bridge who had little idea of the correct rates – very much as London taxi-drivers will sometimes fleece foreigners who do not understand the peculiar English currency. Naturally, he kept the extra profit for himself.

One day, this simple system failed to pay off. The traveller whom he had selected as a victim for a little mild robbing let out a fearful curse, and turning upon the toll-collector he ordered him to be turned to stone upon the spot, and to stand there for ever. And sure enough, the man became petrified, right there upon the pavement.

The only trouble was that the collector proved an obstacle to the traffic, and later he was prised loose and incorporated in the corner of the bridge gate, where he still leers with a horrid grimace at the passers-by, waiting for the return of the man who banned him to stone. This person, it seems, is the only one who can release him at all, but I think it improbable that he will come back. If not dead long ago, he is more likely nowadays to come by motor and pass over the new by-pass bridge further downstream.

Another figure which used to adorn the bridge gate and which somehow had disappeared between our successive visits by water was a madonna. Maybe she was taken away for renovation, for

Limburg

certainly she had an endowment of indestructibility. For centuries already this wooden statue had stood in its niche when some cossacks came to be stationed in the town. At least, I was told they were cossacks, and if this were so it must have been during the Napoleonic period.

These wicked Russians noticed the veneration accorded to the statue and the fact that candles were always lit at the feet of the madonna, so one night they pulled her down and flung her into the Lahn. But behold – next morning she was back in her niche, a glazing of ice extending over her robes and down to her feet. The next night the soldiery flung her once more into the stream, no doubt farther from the shore than before. Again she made a silent but successful return.

The Russians, it seems, were no more to be trifled with then than now. They lit a bonfire and laid the Madonna upon it. This time the wooden figure did not jump back to her proper position, but instead she emitted a cloud of heavy vapour which put out the fire. Admittedly she was a little singed down the back, but that was all. Next morning the people found her lying on top of the heap of ashes and they carried her triumphantly back to the gateway. The cossacks – if they really were cossacks – gave up their attempts upon her and let her alone.

Limburg has another particular connection with that titanic struggle between France and the rest of Europe, and it is one of which the town is justifiably proud. Whether or not there is any substance in the claim, one of the more unexpected assertions of Limburg is that a single citizen of the town was responsible for the defeat of Napoleon at Waterloo – an event that we in Britain foolishly attribute in our schoolbook history to the generalship of the Duke of Wellington. It seems that the trumpeter of Blücher's army was a Limburger named Georg Kaschau, a fellow who was fond of his liquor to the extent of being muddled and sometimes incapable. During the battle the French were pressing so hard upon the Prussians and their allies that their commander decided to retreat. Kaschau was ordered to blow the signal, but as he had imbibed very freely during the course of the fighting – though only, of course, to keep his throat properly wet in case he had to sound his trumpet loud and clear – he mixed up his signals and blew the call to advance. The other trumpeters took up the message, the troops surged forward instead of back, and the wicked French were routed.

Kaschau was to have been cashiered, but as his mistake was so successful the Prussians awarded him the Iron Cross instead. It is sad to relate that half a century later he was still inclined to take just a bit too much, and one evening when he was staggering home he lurched off the towpath into the Lahn and was drowned.

The first time we drew in to Limburg there was a figure standing on the bridge parapet over one of the arches near the gate, and though he was wearing an unusual piece of ecclesiastical head-gear and a spotted cassock there was no mistaking a Nepomuk. He was a fine baroque one, too, and he had long stood there with his back to the river, gazing intently at the crucifix held in his arm. On our second visit I was carrying our refuse bags to dump them in the litter baskets in the miniature garden projecting from one of the buttresses when I noticed that the Nepomuk had gone. When I reached the baker's shop I asked the woman behind the counter what had become of him.

'Vandals,' she said, shaking her head. 'Nothing is safe these days. One night some vandals stopped on their way over the bridge and threw him into the Lahn.'

Ha, I thought. History repeats itself. Was it not nine centuries since John Nepomuk was gagged and bound and flung off the Charles Bridge in Prague? 'I suppose the statue has been dragged out, ready to put back,' I said.

'No. It was smashed to pieces. The vandals knocked off his head and attacked his body with sledge-hammers. To repair him would have been impossible. It is terrible what these people will do. Of course they were Americans.'

'Americans?' It seemed to me unlikely that United States servicemen would resort to iconoclasm. They were more likely to be busy chasing the Limburg girls than taking their gear to the bridge to attack a harmless statue. 'It doesn't sound very like Americans,' I said.

'But who else would do such a thing? They must have been Americans. Everybody knows it,' she said indignantly.

'Were they caught?'

'No,' the bakerwoman admitted. 'But that doesn't matter – though I wish they had been.'

'Look here,' I said, 'I don't believe you know anything about Americans. You occasionally see some foolish village lad from the

United States Army lurching about on half a litre of weak beer, certainly. But unless you *know* it was Americans who smashed the Nepomuk you should keep your opinion to yourself. It might just as easily have been German vandals.'

'Germans would respect a statue of a saint.'

'Hm, I wonder. But in any case I have an idea who flung the saint into the river,' I said. 'The villain was a lorry with an overhanging load. Probably the driver never even noticed – or, if he did, he just drove on.'

Whether it was vandals American or vandals German – or even English – or merely a lorry as I suspected, the Nepomuk had gone, and in a curious way Limburg was not quite the same without him.

A year later we came again up the reach to our berth by the lock, and once more I took the refuse bags to the familiar baskets by the bridge gate. Looking along the curve of the stonework toward the solid silhouette of the cathedral I saw a finely carved and brand new statue of white Diez marble standing confidently on the parapet where its predecessor had held watch over the bridge traffic. I walked over to examine the figure, then crossed the river to buy new rolls at the bakery. The woman nodded as she recognised me.

'*Schon wieder da?* Here again already? And have you seen we have a new Nepomuk, a very fine one?'

'Yes,' I said. 'I did not expect him to be replaced.'

'Somebody presented him. An unknown benefactor. Nobody knows who,' she said.

'Perhaps it was an American,' I suggested.

She smiled grudgingly. 'Perhaps.'

IX

*Voyage with Lisa – Dietkirchen and Dietrich – the alchemist
of Stolzenfels – Rhine tolls and right of staple – Rhens and
the Electors – Konrad of Boppard – bad brothers and blind
sister – St Goar and the Hansa – dancing rights for sale*

O NE of our voyages up the Lahn was undertaken for a curious
reason. I wanted to see Lisa. I knew that she was not to be
seen every day but there had already been an exchange of letters
about our proposed visit and it was only a matter of waiting. And
as there are few better places to lie for a day or two than Limburg
it was to Limburg that the *Thames Commodore* took us. We
berthed as usual above the lock, just far enough beyond the
slaughterhouse not to have fearful dreams as every morning at
first light the animals began to scream, then I walked through the
arch with its petrified toll-collector, on past the Nepomuk and up
into the old town to telephone. Of course one could not speak to
Lisa herself, but only to a pleasant individual who acted somewhat
as an equerry.

'Shall we come today?'

'*Nein, Herr Doktor*. Unfortunately today will not be suitable.
The wind, you know. It is not good for her. But kindly ring me
again tomorrow.'

And so it went on until at last we were bidden to present ourselves at Egelsbach at four o'clock precisely. Soon we were racing
across the country to Egelsbach, beyond the River Main. It was a hot,
still summer's afternoon, proper garden-party weather I thought.

I had once seen Lisa at a distance, very much as I had also seen
General de Gaulle drive over the Pont Alexandre III when we
were berthed in Paris. The general was the last survivor of the
dying race of grand, self-sufficient politicians, and I realised that
Lisa was also the sole survivor of her kind. That was why I wished
to see her, while there still was time.

'Here she comes!' The equerry seemed no less excited than myself. Sure enough, far away over the woodland there appeared a silvery carp moving slowly across the sky, descending elegantly toward the tiny airfield of Egelsbach. When she was nearly down, four young men sauntered across the grass to grab the ropes which hung like whiskers from her nose. Gently, gracefully, Lisa touched down on the wheel under her abdomen. Somebody held her by the step and told me to climb in quickly, before anyone else jumped out. Otherwise she might have taken off vertically from loss of weight. For Lisa was an airship.

She was handsome, all the 158 feet of her, and her body bore the words SCHWAB VERSAND HANAU. D-LISA. The only dirigible in Europe, her job was to keep the name of the mail order house of Schwab before the public in letters fifteen feet high, flying across the German countryside whenever the weather was favourable. The Schwab people had come to love her, and she had turned them into airship fanatics, convinced that the world had made a great mistake in discarding lighter-than-air transport. Airships could do things that airplanes could not, they argued, such as lifting bulky loads, hovering, and staying aloft when the fuel ran out. In an airship you were safe, and felt it. In a few moments I would see for myself.

The young men let go and away we went, up, up, up as steeply as a jet to the dizzy height of 1,800 feet. The two motors slung outboard made very little noise. After all, they were only thirty horsepower. They did not have to keep Lisa airborne by sheer push. They left the lifting to the hydrogen.

As the evening began to glow beyond the Rhine we were humming over the Odenwald forest, and at a mere twenty-five miles per hour we could open the windows and look down at the people in their village gardens or along the streets. They stood stock still, their faces turned up so straight that I wondered they did not fall over. They waved scarves, hay-rakes, anything. After all, it wasn't every day that one had an airship over the house.

Hens fled flapping for the hedges and horses raced in bewilderment round their fields, yet the cows hardly missed a beat in their grazing. They would munch, look up, look down, and

continue to crop the grass. Exactly, I thought, as the Jersey cattle
had done thirty years before, leaving the American poultry to
hurdle the hedges and the horses to play rodeo while we droned
over their farmsteads. That time I was aboard the *Hindenburg*,
pride of the German conquest of the air.

It is one of my few regrets about the modern age that none will
have that tremendous experience of airship riding unless they are
lucky enough to be invited aboard one of the only three dirigibles
still existing. Its attraction lies partly in the fact that one can
understand how it works, whereas only an aerodynamics expert
can see that a blunt edge and bulbous shape is the best form for
an aircraft wing.

An airship performs a continual balancing feat, even when on
the ground – a simple enough matter with the Lisa and her total
complement of one crew and five passengers, but very different
for the *Hindenburg* with sixty passengers boarding her, a crew of
forty-five, and a considerable export cargo of Munich beer for
delivery to the United States. I still recalled how, as I stepped
over the scales to the gangway, a checker called out my weight, and
eighty kilos of trimming weights were unhooked from the giant
belly. On came my bag, and off went exactly twenty-one kilos. It
was all so precise that after half a day of embarkation and loading
the *Hindenburg*, 848 feet in length, weighed only a quarter ton.

Dr Hugo Eckener leaned out of the gondola window and blew
his whistle. As the ropes fell from the nose a splash told that half
a ton of water had also been dropped. With a now slightly minus
weight the *Hindenburg* lifted slowly and in silence until a cheer
came from the crowd which had been ranged alongside her. Even
then her own four motors were not yet started. That only happened
minutes later, when we were ready for Dr Eckener to swing her
tail and head her for the Rhine.

Dr Eckener was a great man for sight-seeing. 'You must see
Cologne Cathedral,' he said briefly. I leaned out into the warm
night air and saw the suburbs and the river, then the great Dom
itself sweeping at 40 m.p.h. through the fixed circle of the searchlight beneath.

The four heavy motors devoured plenty of fuel, so the airship had to compensate by releasing gas – which then had to be bought again for the return trip – or by milking. Dr Eckener was an expert cloud-milker. He called ships by radio to find the whereabouts of a suitable cow-cloud, and when a cargo-ship told him of one about thirty miles to starboard we went off in pursuit. It was a large cloud, but it must have felt smaller when we had finished with it. The *Hindenburg* condensed two thousand gallons of it into her ballast tanks, then headed away for Newfoundland, far northward of our true destination.

Eckener knew that over Newfoundland he could find a strong wind blowing toward the States. It proved even better than he had hoped, and with 60 m.p.h. of blow behind us we raced down the Canadian coast and beat the *Queen Mary* to New York by two hours. The doctor could not resist finding and circling her in the early morning, and she floodlit her funnels in reply.

It was soon after this that I noticed the hens, for as we crossed the coast the *Hindenburg*'s improbable bulk flying at no great height over their ranges scared the White Wyandottes and drove the horses in circles. But not a single cow hiccoughed. Now, thirty years later, the Lisa seemed tiny in comparison. She had no dining saloon, no range of forty cabins, no aluminium grand piano on which to play a rhapsody above the moonlit clouds. Lisa had five seats, nothing more. One cannot have everything when the limiting factor is the difference in molecular weight between the ambient air and hydrogen.

Hydrogen? Why not the safe inert helium, I asked. The lifting power is as twelve to fifteen, but of those fifteen for hydrogen only the last four or five represent pay-load, the pilot explained. Helium was also very costly. Having no compounds it could not be made; it could only be distilled from liquid air. Besides, hydrogen was theoretically no more dangerous than was petrol or jet-fuel aboard a 'conventional 'aircraft. Of that the Schwab men were convinced.

Lisa was now more than twenty years old, but airships did not age quickly. Another twenty years and she might still be purring gently across the forests and towns of Germany, I thought, reminding people of her owners and showing that there are still some who believe in the dream of lighter-than-air voyaging. But there I was wrong. My first airship, the *Hindenburg*, had died in a fearful disaster at Lakehurst. Lisa's fate was more ordinary, more dreadfully commercial. Not so long after she had taken us skimming over the Odenwald on a summer's evening they sold her.

Limburg lock is the last which can be used by craft of even the modest dimensions of a Lahnship. Certainly the old navigation runs many miles further and simple rural locks lead up to Weilburg and the only navigation tunnel in Germany. Plans have often been put forward for enlarging the waterway to serve the industries of Wetzlar and Giessen, but the return on the expense would probably not be great enough. The upper reaches will remain a paradise for canoes and boats of the get-out-and-push class, but even such a modest vessel as the *Thames Commodore* will never be able to negotiate the stream. However, she cannot reach Limburg without running a little further, to where one of the most dramatically situated churches in all Germany is set upon an extraordinary lump of rock which rises abruptly and with no apparent reason from the gentle Thames-like countryside above the city.

The patron saint of bargees throughout Germany is usually St Nicholas of Myra, the original Santa Claus, whose statue may still be seen standing in a niche of many a cliff where once there were dangerous rocks or rapids. On the Lahn he is replaced by St Lubentius, the former colleague of St Castor of the Moselle. It was Lubentius who founded the first church on that massive rock which rises sheer above the river, a rocky eminence which must certainly have been a sacred site of the nordic pantheon.

In his old age Lubentius retired to the Moselle, and it was at Kobern that he died in the year 351. But when saints-to-be come to die strange things seem to happen, and on this occasion the Koberners found that when they tried to lift his body to take it for burial they could not move it. Somebody thought Lubentius had once said that he wanted to be buried at the scene of his labours on the Lahn, but as there was some doubt about what should be done the people adopted the usual solution of placing the corpse on an unmanned boat and pushing it out into the stream. Another version of the tale states that he was buried with considerable

ceremony at Koblenz, and as this happened well within the era of
wonders we must not be surprised to know that the grave could
not contain the bones of such a holy man. A flood invaded the
town, the water swirled over the grave, opened it, and carried the
body away to the Rhine. At Deutsches Eck the corpse of Lubentius turned to starboard and forged upstream against the full
force of the flood to Niederlahnstein, where the saint entered the
valley which had been the scene of his labours and floated up the
stream for more than forty miles (there were as yet no locks) before
running aground on the river bank at Dietkirchen, where the
delighted inhabitants rushed to the bank to load the body of their
old friend on an ox-cart to take it to the burial ground. But behold,
the worthy and obstinate beasts refused to haul anywhere but to
the top of the hill, and there Lubentius was duly buried.

The name Dietkirchen suggests that the great romanesque
basilica which so splendidly crowns the solitary cliff was actually
built by a man named Dietrich. And so it was. In a Saracen prison
the crusading knight Dietrich of Dehrn – the village a mile or
more upstream of the rock – who had had the misfortune to be
wounded and taken prisoner by the infidel Infidels, languished in
a hot cell, longing for his wife and child, and eventually he made a
vow to build a church if ever he should see once more the lovely
Lahn. With this pious resolve in mind he went to sleep upon the
hard floor of his cell, and one can imagine how surprised he must
have been to awake next morning in full sunshine under a great
oak-tree. Before him stood his familiar castle, and he was so
delighted to be home again that he leapt to his feet, rushed into
the family home and flung himself into the arms of his dear wife,
who was as astonished as he, and I hope had the sense to realise
her good fortune to be born in the middle ages, when such curious
things could happen.

Dietrich of Dehrn was very, very human, and the thrill of
being miraculously transported to the banks of the Lahn made
him forget all about building the church he had promised. However, one day when he was out hunting he narrowly escaped being
electrocuted when an oak tree beside his path was struck by
lightning, and the very next day he had the work put in hand. A

site was chosen on his own land, close by his castle, and the masons set to work.

Yet every piece of material would vanish overnight and be found next morning piled up on the top of the rock where Lubentius had founded his chapel in the fourth century. And this was of course a much better site, except from the point of view of the people of Dehrn, who had a much longer walk to church. Dietrich lived to see the work completed, and when he died he was buried in one of the transepts.

Dietkirchen or its neighbour of Dehrn had to be the *Thames Commodore*'s turning point, so putting her nose carefully against the bank between a blackberry bush and a brown cow she swung her stern slowly upstream, straightened, and began to move happily down on the gentle current. She did not race, partly because a rapid pace would have been out of keeping with such a golden-cropped countryside but also because downstream of Dietkirchen the Romans or some other early people had once built a ford which we had gently struck upon the way upstream. Soon we were bearing down upon the ugly bridge which carries a hideous motorway mercifully clear of Limburg, and then there opened out the incomparable view of the cathedral and its bishop's palace serene and safe upon its cliff. Another hour and Diez in turn stood to port, at its foot the bridge with the little toll-house corbelled out from the roadway. This view of Diez from upstream is the better, and one can only be thankful that the dreadful Swedes did not sack the place.

In fact they forced Countess Sophie of Diez to have the bridge blown up after they had crossed it, and when the ferocious northerners had gone far enough on their way a temporary bridge of wood was laboriously erected. It had only just been completed when news was received that another army was approaching, this time the Spaniards under Don Fernando. The Spaniards were notorious, and from the surrounding country the panicking peasants poured into Diez, driving their cattle before them and carrying their belongings on carts, for somehow they felt safer in proximity to their beloved ruler the countess. She, however, remained calm and dignified. When the Spaniards were actually visible

Niederlahns

across the river the people dived for cover, locking themselves in the cellars, but Countess Sophie waited at the castle gate, her ladies-in-waiting in attendance upon her.

The Spanish commander advanced. Graciously the countess welcomed him and his entourage to Diez, invited him and his senior officers to dinner, and through her own charm and personality succeeded in winning from him a promise that his army would move out of the town and the soldiery would not lay a finger upon life or property.

The commander was as good as his word. Next morning he sat erect upon his horse in the market-place of Diez as his troops filed past and out of the gate. Only when the last trooper had left did he give a gracious farewell bow to her ladyship. Then he turned and cantered along the cobbles and away.

But we must return to the Rhine. At Niederlahnstein we have to

Stolzenfels

blow three long hoots and two short ones, then put the wheel hard over and give a burst of speed to turn into the swift current. On the further side of the river the downstream traffic is clipping along at a fine speed, surging past the rather unsightly, bright yellow and Victorianized mass of the Stolzenfels.

Proudcliff Castle was erected by the Elector of Trier to protect his toll upon the Rhine below, and it was so strong a fort that when the emperor ordered all such customs-posts to be abolished the elector disregarded the order, as did the Archbishop of Mainz, who also did well from fleecing the shipping. In charge of Stolzenfels he put an official named Frundsberg who not only raised the dues but also used tracking dogs to follow any merchants who tried to dodge round through the woods at the edge of the Hunsrück forest. An unprincipled scoundrel, he diverted much of the takings to himself.

History records that one of the less warlike of the electors of
Trier installed in the Stolzenfels an alchemical laboratory where
he sought to transform metals into pure gold. 'It would not have
been time and labour cast away, had he instead sought to do the
same with his spiritual subjects,' an English visitor once wrote,
but in fact the search for the Philosopher's Stone was not always
a matter of sheer greed. In the centuries before Robert Boyle it
was believed that the physical state of affairs here on earth was a
sort of mirror or cipher of the arrangements in the spiritual realm.
If by grace base men could be made pure, so surely in the world
of chemistry the dirty, sinful metals (we still call them *base* metals
even in the most exalted scientific circles) could be transformed to
the shining purity of gold. If only one could discover the reagent
to perform this change, then automatically one would understand
more about the operation of divine grace. And if one happened to
make a fortune on the side – well, what was wrong with that?

It may have been this same alchemist, I think, who gave rise to
a curious story about Frundsberg the tax-collector at Stolzenfels.
It is said that Frundsberg's accumulating wealth soon drew the
attention of another man, an Italian adventurer named Leonardo,
who called at the Stolzenfels and found little difficulty in per-
suading Frundsberg that he was an alchemist who was within an
ace of discovering the Philosopher's Stone. If Frundsberg ploughed
his wealth back into alchemical research – which, the man pointed
out, was unfortunately rather expensive – he would not just be
rich but fabulously so.

Leonardo was soon installed in a laboratory at Stolzenfels, and
(just as he had said) the experiments proved extremely costly.
Frundsberg soon ran through his own cut of the toll-money and
had to begin falsifying the electors' account books. His daughter
Gertraud tried to dissuade him, but failed to do so. Nevertheless,
she constituted a threat to Leonardo's business, so he decided that
he would have to silence her. When it was announced that the
elector was coming to Stolzenfels to collect the toll-monies there
was considerable and very reasonable alarm, but Leonardo persuaded the poor girl that the only thing lacking to bring the
alchemical reactions to a successful conclusion was the life-blood

of a pure virgin. Moved by love for her father, and perhaps by an idea that the greasy Italian might after all be telling the truth, Gertraud agreed to offer herself.

And so at dead of night Gertraud presented herself at the laboratory. On the table was a bowl for the blood and a dagger. Leonardo told her to strip and wrap herself in a sheet before lying on the table, and the man then carried out some mumbo-jumbo, burning in a flame some wood from the Lebanon. Then he ripped the sheet from his victim, seized the dagger, and would have stabbed the maiden through the heart if his raised hand had not suddenly been gripped by a hand even stronger than his own. No, it was not that of Frundsberg, nor even of the Elector of Trier. The rescuer was young Reinhard of Westerburg, captain of the Stolzenfels guard, who had noticed Gertraud's distraught appearance and had trailed her on tip-toe as she went to the laboratory. It need hardly be added that for a long while he had loved her devotedly from a distance.

Reinhard struck the Italian such a blow on the chin that he went down unconscious. Then he stood with eyes averted while Gertraud wrapped herself in the sheet again, after which the girl told him all that had happened and Reinhard confessed his love for her. He also added that he would have Leonardo handed over to the Archbishop-Elector of Trier who was due the next day and was always accompanied by a very experienced hangman.

At this Leonardo, whose amnesia was no longer genuine but only a pretence, leapt to his feet and rushed from the laboratory, uttering horrible oaths. He fled for his life, but as it happened to be the middle of the night he unfortunately ran over the edge of the cliff and fractured his skull beyond repair. Gertraud and Reinhard helped cook the books and put the funds in order, and when the elector arrived he was delighted to find things in such excellent order. A few days later he personally conducted the wedding of Gertraud Frundsberg to Reinhard von Westerburg before returning to Trier with the takings of the Stolzenfels toll.

This story is enough to remind us that as we turn out of the

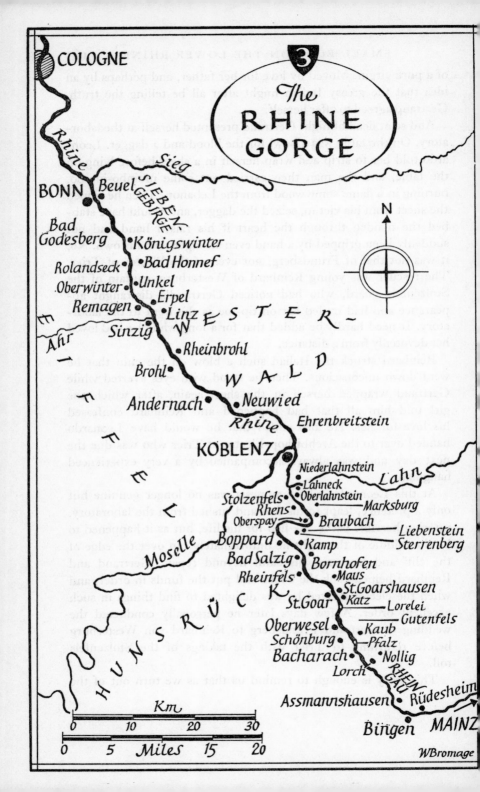

Lahn we are entering the 'Romantic Rhine' of the poets and minstrels, the *Gebirgsstrecke* or hill reach of the bargemen. I doubt if there can be any stretch of river in the world so embattled with ruins, so overhung with tales of villainy and chivalry, so beset with stories of fair maidens wooed and loved or driven to suicide. It is fortunate that the current is strong enough to cut our speed over the ground to a bare four knots, for there is plenty to be seen on either hand. Each time I have run the Rhine downstream the castles have flashed by so swiftly that I have hardly been able to check them against the map, but now that we are moving at less than one third of the pace we shall be able to take our eyes off the channel and lift up our eyes unto the hills whence, in former times, a well aimed shot might have reminded us that it was wiser to heave to and be fleeced.

The Rhine was a river where, in the middle ages, the territories of a number of feudal overlords met. There were no clearly recognized frontiers, and so every smallest patch of ground was hotly contested and, when won, defended by a fortified strongpoint. The three most important powers were the archbishops of Trier, Mainz and Cologne, but there were also the Elector of the Palatinate and the counts of Cats Elbow. Finally there were the others who came in from outside, stormed a castle belonging to one of these powers, and held on to it. This did not happen very often, and when voyaging up the Rhine it is not difficult to see why. Most of the castles are so well placed that it would have been almost impossible to bring a force up the valley to attack them. Although some castles were sacked in the thirteenth century, it was the armies of Louis XIV that first ruined most of them, and those of the French Revolution which finished the job.

In Roman times the number of ships using the Rhine ran into four figures, but the vessels were severely reduced by the waves of invasions which swept over the valley. In the fifth century the Vandals reached it, then the Huns. In the ninth it was the turn of the Vikings, who penetrated up the river as far as Worms. After them came the Hungarians. Yet the river always managed to recover, and the opening of the St Gotthard pass in 1230 gave a great impetus to the import and carriage of goods from Italy which had previously been carried by the Rhône and the Moselle or Meuse. Goods from Britain were shipped direct to Cologne for loading into river barges, and as the great monasteries and the larger cities became involved in the prosperity of trade the River Rhine gradually came to have a peaceful bustle of continual international traffic which was in great contrast to the burning and sacking which characterized most of Europe.

Such merchandise as was carried on the Rhine was very naturally attractive to brigands, and it was because of the insecurity of travellers by land in the earliest middle ages that the arch-bishops of Trier, Mainz and Cologne set about providing the elements of a water police authority, and they built toll stations at which they could take payment from the passing ships – the famous Mouse Tower lying in the river off Bingen was built as early as the ninth century for this purpose. Originally the dues levied at a few points in the Rhine valley were no more than payments for services provided in ensuring the safe transit of goods over a particular stretch of territory, but medieval arch-bishops and the rough knights to whom they entrusted for favour and later for hard cash the management of their Rhine fortresses were not very different in some respects from modern ministers of finance, and they found the temptation to increase the taxes for their own advantage irresistible. By the end of the fourteenth century a ship travelling the length of the Rhine from Strasbourg to Holland would have to heave to and pay duty on its cargo at no less than sixty-two different places. Added to these were the unofficial but sometimes even more costly duties levied by the robber lords and knights who lived in the castles on the heights along the gorge and sent their armed men out in boats to intercept the merchant ships and extract as much as they could in pay-ment.

This watery highway-robbery was to endow the Rhine with the string of castles which stand as romantic ruins today, but the system was a plague to commerce. It was Mainz and Worms which first established a league of mutual aid, and the other towns of shippers joined them to provide six hundred armed craft upon the river. This imposing force drove the raiders from the stream and even sacked the robber strongholds of Reichenstein above Bingen and Rheinfels at St Goar.

Yet the 'legal' tolls were quite enough of an obstruction, and Albrecht Dürer's diary of his travel down the river shows the way things were managed. Dürer had a free pass from no less a dignitary than the Archbishop of Bamberg, yet this made no difference to the demands of the customs men, even at the toll-posts of other church dignitaries. Furthermore, the imperial edict only permitted duties to be levied upon articles of trade, but this in no way prevented the officials in Eltville and Ehrenfels, Bacharach and Kaub, St Goar, Boppard and Oberlahnstein and elsewhere from robbing Dürer of a piece or two of silver before allowing his belongings to pass.

It was the men of Strasbourg who first protested openly about the tolls authorised by the emperor, but their complaint that the shipping was being fleeced and hindered was rejected with contempt. Infuriated, the City Council then sent out work-boats to drive oak piles into the river from shore to shore and to span the gaps between them with chains. This effectively stopped all imports – notably grain – reaching the imperial domains from upstream, and the blockade was so effective that after two or three years the emperor had to accede to the city's demands.

Even before the toll system became such a menace to the shipper on the Rhine there was another means of obstruction employed by some of the cities on its banks. Several insisted upon their *Stapelrecht* (right of staple), which meant that no goods might pass by the town, whatever their intended destination, without being landed and offered for public sale for several days on end. Of course this led to the growth of marketing, but for the shipmen it meant nothing but delay and loss of profitable trade. Strasbourg and Speyer, Mainz, Cologne and Dordrecht all succeeded in establishing their own *Stapelrecht* which survived until the Congress of Vienna in 1815, which cleared the Rhine not only of these obstacles but also of the tolls which so hindered the shipping.

One of the earliest tolls was that of Oberlahnstein, which brought in revenues for the archiepiscopal treasury of Mainz. Its surviving accounts show how greatly the shipping was affected by the political upheavals and wars which so often swept across the country, as well as by drought, floods, and winter ice. They also reveal some of the difficulties of carrying on a customs post at all. For example, a downstream ship was by no means easy to hold up when it had the flow of Father Rhine behind it, and this was one reason why some of the toll stations were inclined to tackle only the upstream craft as they crept up the river behind their teams of straining horses. Then there was the period of the War of the Spanish Succession, when French troops often penetrated to the left bank of the river. It so happened that the gravel carried down by the Lahn caused a shoal extending half-way across the Rhine from the right bank and so diverted the current sufficiently for the navigation channel to swing across to the left shore. It was impossible for laden ships to cross to the Oberlahnstein side to be milked, quite apart from the difficulty of changing sides in a ship drawn by horses on the towpath. When the customs men rowed over to tackle the craft they were sometimes captured by the French, and one can assume that the captains of the ships did not exert themselves to defend the officials. Eventually a bargain was struck with the French that the ships were to anchor until they had been cleared, but in fact the bargemen disregarded the injunction and the French had no interest in enforcing an edict which only benefited others.

Then there was the difficult matter of customs-free transit. Very properly, the archiepiscopal toll had to permit exemptions to non-commercial undertakings – which in practice meant the Order of Teutonic Knights and a number of abbeys which carried their own produce on the river. A surprising amount of goods made their way up and down the river in the guise of genuine monastically produced crops and wares, and so the Oberlahnstein customs station had a priest on call before whom the brother in charge of a shipload had to swear the origin of the goods, laying his hand on his heart if he was a priest and raising his finger if he was a lay brother. Nevertheless, a considerable tonnage of goods filtered through, hidden beneath other cargoes or under the top layer of logs on timber rafts.

The chief customs clerk at Oberlahnstein was paid mainly in wine, for by an agreement of the fifteenth century any vessel carrying more than one thousand gallons of wine had at each toll-station to give two quarts to the clerk and a further two to be shared among the guards and other minor fry. Barges bound for trade fairs paid in kind, and the officials received cakes and lemons, glass and pottery, fish, ham, fruit and butter, onions, herbs, chestnuts, sugar and coal.

So the tolls which had begun as a reasonable charge for a public service quickly developed into a mere impost. Or rather into a series of imposts, for if already in the year 1200 there were a score of tolls on the river, only a century later the number had been doubled. Most were conducted under the shadow of a great territorial strongpoint, but other forts were constructed for that purpose alone. Ehrenfels and Rheinfels, the Pfalzgrafenstein and the Marxburg were only four of the posts built specifically to hold up the shipping by force – often by chains in the river – and to demand money under the sights of a row of skilled archers or crossbowmen. It says much for the bargemen and merchants of the period that they were prepared to stay in business at all.

Pushing upstream abreast of Stolzenfels we can already see ahead and to starboard the village of Rhens. It is an insignificant but charming place, its half-timbered houses nodding with age as the river rolls past them and the wash of the barges breaks upon the shore. But behind it stands a curious erection of stone pillars which show more clearly than anything else the way in which the territories of the feudal lords jostled each other along the Rhine.

Zu Rhense stand der Königstuhl bereit,
Kur Köln zu Rhense, Pfalz zu Marksburg warten;
Nach Lahneck kam Kurmainz mit Heergeleit,
Es trägt der Stolzenfels Kurtriers Standarten.

At Rhense stands the Coronation throne.
Within the walls Cologne's Elector waits,
At Marksburg rests his brother Palatine
Whilst he of Mainz, the senior of them all,
Arrives at Lahneck with his men-at-arms.

And still one more – proud Trier – is near to hand,
His standard floating over Stolzenfels.

Wolfgang Müller von Königswinter reminds us in this verse
that four electors had castles within a mile or two of the village;
and that was why it came to be the place at which traditionally the
Holy Roman Emperors were chosen. The stone structure visible
from the river is in fact the reconstructed Königstuhl at which this
important ceremony occurred. Unfortunately, the fourteenth-
century Coronation Stone, which stood near the bank of the Rhine
on nine tall pillars and was half surrounded by a stone bench on
which sat the seven electors, was broken down by the enthusiastic
French revolutionaries. Later it was cleared away completely in
order to make room for a new road. But more than a century ago a
society was formed in Koblenz to restore it in the image of its
original simple splendour.

In fact the Königstuhl where the electors chose their emperor
was not always situated at Rhens. Earlier it was at Mainz, but when
the number of electors was only seven, of whom four had seats in
the lower part of the Rhine gorge, Rhens was obviously a good
choice. The four close at hand could foregather quickly, and if a
quarrel ensued each might retire swiftly to a well-fortified defensive
position where he could not be shot down by the others.

The Königstuhl was used mainly for the deliberations, the final
formal election being usually performed at Frankfurt and carried
out according to elaborate protocol. The Elector of Mainz had first
to address the Elector of Trier and ask him whom he wished to
nominate. Next he inquired of the Elector of Cologne, then of the
King of Bohemia 'on account of his supreme standing among the
temporal electors'. Next it was the turn of the Count Palatine of
the Rhine, who also had the duty of informing all the other
electors of the former emperor's death within one month. After
him it was the turn of the Duke of Saxony, followed by the
Margrave of Brandenburg. These electors then all in turn asked
the Elector of Mainz.

The seven electors were supposed to be able to reach a unani-
mous decision within thirty days, and should they fail to do so it

was laid down by the Golden Bull of 1356 that they were to be confined to a diet of bread and water. This was an admirable provision which might well be introduced into the proceedings of such bodies as the Security Council.

Although it was usually neither the place of actual election nor of coronation, the Königstuhl of Rhens came to be held in as great reverence as the old Stone of Scone, and in later times the newly elected Mayor of Koblenz would travel up the river in his official yacht, accompanied by the whole city council. Landing nearby, they held a mayoral banquet on the Königstuhl and then retired by water again to Koblenz, well satisfied with a good day's official duty. But the *Thames Commodore* has to move past Rhens without stopping. There is no water along the edge, no quay or harbour, and much too great a density of shipping for her to risk dropping the anchor to let her crew row ashore. The first stop will be to fuel on the tankship at Boppard more than an hour ahead, and she will turn a long double bend to pass the pretty orchard villages of Spay, Osterspai and Niederspai before the fine promenade and waterfront of Boppard opens up ahead.

Little of Boppard's castle survives, and it is preserved mainly in the tale of Konrad of Boppard, a pleasant young man but perhaps rather too easily led by others. He was engaged to a girl named Maria, but when the lads twitted him for being willing to give up his independence and become a stay-at-home newly-wed he had second thoughts about the matter and wrote Maria a note to say that he wished to break it off.

Some time later he was out hunting when he was confronted by a young knight in black armour and closed vizor who addressed him through the slits in the metal to the effect that he had better get ready to be killed. The insult he had given to Maria was now to be avenged by her own brother.

The fight did not last long, and I am sorry to say that Konrad of Boppard was the victor. However, he had the courtesy to open the helmet of his severely wounded opponent and there beheld the pale face not of Maria's brother, but of the girl herself. A few minutes later she was dying – happy, she whispered with her fading breath, to have fallen at his hand alone.

Poor Konrad was filled with remorse, as he certainly should have been. He spent all his money on building a convent (the Marienburg) in her name, and it was to become one of the richest along the Rhine valley. As for himself, at first he joined the Templars, but as his spirit could find no peace he eventually set off for the Holy Land to join the army of gallant warriors, disappointed lovers, conscience-stricken deceivers and impetuous murderers whose only fulfilment lay in cleaving Infidels in half until they themselves fell to a well-aimed spear or the slash of a heavy scimitar.

Until it was destroyed by the marauding Swedes Boppard also had a monastery, which was founded by the Franciscan Bernard of Siena. Locally it was alleged that he reached the Rhine at Kamp and asked to be carried over in the ferry. The ferryman insisted on the usual small fee, but Bernard took the rule of poverty so literally that he had no coin of any kind to offer. Too bad, said the waterman. No cash, no carriage.

But Bernard, it seems, was a resourceful man. Casting his habit on the water he stood on it, and holding up the corners to form a sail he sped across the river before a following wind. The people of Boppard streamed out to see such a sight, and no wonder, for Bernard made the crossing faster than the ferry.

Boppard to starboard, then Bornhofen to port, and high above it the twin crags with the castles of Sterrenberg and Liebenstein. Probably there is little truth in the tales of the brothers who lived in these keeps, but it would be unwise to look too far into such medieval legends in case the cold light of a reasoning and scientific age should rob them of their character. Better by far to go along with local tradition – which is not always at fault – and assert boldly that there were indeed two brothers, and a sister too. Their father left his fortune to be divided equally among the three of them, and the brothers set about distributing the money. Their sister happened unfortunately to be blind, so the two young men adopted the ruse of sharing out the rents and incomings with a shovel, carefully turning it over and using the back whenever it was their sister's turn. Poor girl, she was fleeced of most of her fortune, but even the portion allotted to her she used to found a convent in Bornhofen.

Happy in their deceit, the two brothers decided one day that on the next morning they would go hunting together. The first one up was to rouse the other. The Sterrenberg brother was first to awake, and seeing the shutters on his brother's room in the Liebenstein still closed he decided to knock him up with a bolt from his crossbow. He pulled back the string, aimed, and pulled the trigger. And just at that moment the tardier brother himself threw open the shutters and was killed instantly as the bolt struck him over the heart. The one who had fired the shot was so overcome with remorse that he went to the Holy Land, either to forget or perhaps in some hope of expiation for his unintentional fratricide. So, with both brothers gone, the blind sister came into the full inheritance from her father, which she spent upon the convent she had already begun.

Upstream the current becomes stronger, and off Bornhofen or in the roadstead of Salzig the tugs of the heavy tow-trains drop some of their barges, leaving them swinging at anchor for a day whilst the rest of the train is hauled up the gorge and anchored off Bingen so that the tug can gallop back again to retrieve the rest. The *Thames Commodore* can notice the difference too. In the Dutch reaches she was making more than twelve kilometres in the hour, above Duisburg or Düsseldorf only ten, from Koblenz perhaps nine, and now she is cut to seven. The Rhine must here be flowing as fast in the opposite direction, or possibly a little faster. But she does not mind. Ahead at St Goar there is a reasonable harbour where she can rest while the crew does the shopping. Opposite lies St Goarshausen, overlooked by the ruins of Castle Cat (of the Cat's Elbow counts) and the smaller Castle Mouse.

Opposite Burg Katz there was formerly a formidable whirlpool off the shoal known as the Bank, and according to Victor Hugo the men who piloted the rafts through the gap between the eddy and the shore would prepare a tree-stem attached to a long line. This object was known as a 'dog', and the system was to hurl the stem toward the whirlpool, which would greedily snatch it and hold it fast, and so swing the raft back into the middle of the stream again, after which the rope was cut and the dog left behind for the whirlpool to swallow whole.

When steam towage came to the Rhine the Bank was still

G

regarded with awe, and the skipper of a tug would strike three times on the bell to remind the men on the rafts that it was time to pray. All stood with bared heads, the pilot wished them a safe passage, and then it was a matter of all hands to the sweeps. The commander of the raft would bellow his orders according to whether the men were to aim for the right bank or the left, but to avoid the confusion which resulted from the fact that some of the men would be facing backwards the words right and left or port and starboard were never used. Instead, the cry for the right bank was '*Hessen!*'. Or, if it was a case of moving toward the other side of the channel, '*Frankreich! Frankreich!*' And in much the same way the two banks of the river Rhône below Lyons are even now known to the older steersmen as *Royaume* (i.e., France, the right bank) and *Empire* (the Holy Roman Empire, left bank).

To pass the Bank on a raft was an exciting experience, for the river fell through more than four feet in 150 yards. As a result the mass of timber was running at a considerable incline, and emerging from the passage its momentum would often carry it forward for some distance at the same angle, so that the men at the sweeps were sometimes up to their waists in the cold water. But like so many of the great sights of the river this has long since gone. A more practical age has regulated the river, and even if it is still a thrilling experience to navigate the gorge one can be reasonably sure that the craft will not be awash.

Up to St Goar the unregulated Rhine was sufficiently deep for English trading vessels to bring their cargoes up the river without transshipment. But ahead the reefs and shallows began, and so a transference to inland craft was essential. As a result, St Goar itself became a centre of trade, and perhaps that was how its guild or Hansa came into being.

Until little more than a century ago, when a stranger arrived in the town he was somewhat alarmed to find a metal collar being snapped round his neck so that he could be attached to a bracket on the wall of the old customs house. When he had recovered from his shock he was asked if he wished to be baptized with water or with wine. If he chose water, then a bucket from the Rhine was inverted over his head and he was released, but if he selected the wine he was taken into the nearby tavern, crowned with a tin crown, and given an enormous beaker of Rhine wine to empty. He was then told of his privileges, which included such useful ones as being permitted to fish from the Lorelei cliff and to hunt on the shoals in midstream. The stranger was next required to make a donation for the poor of the town and of course to stand drinks all round. Nor was there any escape. An edict of the Landgrave of Hesse-Darmstadt specifically forbade any merchant to trade at St Goar's Fair unless he had been 'hansed', and when we sat (voluntarily, for the edict appeared to have run out) over a glass of wine in the *Krone* I noticed a sketch made in 1668 by Edward Browne, personal physician to King Charles II. It showed a merchant having a bucket of water inverted over his head at a hansing ceremony, and a note added that Browne himself was also duly hansed. Many notables underwent this ceremony without complaint, but some of the English travellers who visited St Goar in the era of the Grand Tour did not enjoy it. They thought it just one more of those rude and asinine pieces of tomfoolery that one might expect from foreigners.

With the decline of St Goar as a trading port the Hansa eventually died, but it was resuscitated in the twentieth century in a somewhat different form as a society with an international slant (there are members from such unlikely countries as Japan) and the additional objects of encouraging interest in local antiquities, running a museum, and having a thoroughly good time at its own annual festival, wisely placed in the height of the summer holiday season. It provides a mixture of horse-play, folk-lore and serious local historical research, each annual meeting being preceded by an evening when a paper is read on some aspect of local history such as 'Sankt Goar and the Castles in Poetry', or 'Sankt Goar and the Dukes of Cats Elbow'. The festival, with plenty of wine and medieval costumes, is held in the vast ruin of the mighty Burg Rheinfels which lowers over the top of the grey-roofed little town and glares across at Burg Katz, once a fellow fortress but eventually the one which provided an artillery site from which Rheinfels, last of the Rhineland castles to fall, was bombarded.

I knew that there was a Hansenmeister. I had seen his picture on the town brochure, wearing a red and gold crown and a gown much like that of an alderman of the Corporation of London. He was holding a gold beaker in his hand and was obviously about to give the brotherly greeting of the Hansa: '*Hie Rheinfels! Hie Sankt Goar! Heil und Humpen!!*' Being myself a warden of one of the London livery companies (originally much the same as a Hansa) I thought it proper to call upon him – even if in my own company we never said anything more sensational by way of greeting than 'Hallo, George,' or possibly 'Good evening, Master.'

Hansenmeister Bogler was very pleased to receive a visit from a dignitary of another guild, and we sat over a bottle of wine at his open window while he went on with his work. His office was upstairs and looked out over the river, for Hansenmeister Bogler was a shipping agent. No doubt he had a heap of paper work to be accomplished from time to time – quite apart from chasing up the affairs of the Hansa – but his operations on that morning at least consisted in looking across the water in the direction of Castle Cat and watching the shipping. Sometimes a barge-master would step out of his wheelhouse and wave his arms like a tic-tac man and Hansenmeister Bogler would reply. Occasionally figures were shouted across the water and noted. I had no idea what it was all about, but the occupation struck me as being a pleasant one. I could see myself sitting there in the winter with the great stove stoked high with wood, a muffler round my neck and a bottle of St Goar beside me, waiting to wave a signal to the next ship which belonged to one of my clients, and wondering how many lots there would be at the auction held at the Hansa's next festival. For this auction, revived by the modern Hansa, is also a strange local custom from the days of medieval prosperity.

The St Goar auction has only one class of goods – the girls of St Goar itself. Probably it began as a sensible and practical way of preventing quarrels and fights, the Hansenmeister said. Once each year the maidens of the town were put up individually for sale and knocked down to the highest bidder, who then for twelve months had the privilege of being the only man who might dance with her. The buyer of this right was also to some extent responsible for her safety.

But a girl might not want to have the sole company of the man who had the most money, I said. He could be the biggest bore on earth.

The Hansenmeister looked through his binoculars at a heavily laden ship panting up the stream and noted a figure on a piece of paper. 'So you would think,' he said. 'But it does not work out that way. If a boy is really serious about a girl he will promise the earth for the privilege. More perhaps than he can afford. And then he will go out and work until he has got it. Don't you think a girl would prefer that?'

'But surely, in the middle ages it just meant that the robber barons came and outbid all the rest,' I objected.

'No. It was a case of local girls for local men, and usually at the end of the year they got married. If a robber baron had his eyes on some local beauty he didn't come to the auction and bid. He rushed in with a band of armed men and snatched her away. That was how it was. So perhaps our modern times are really just a little better, don't you think?'

X

The lime of Rheinfels – St Goar the hermit – a paternity case – signals for shipping – eel-fishers of the Rhine – the Lorelei – the origin of Seven Sisters Reef – murder of Werner – Oberwesel – mid-river romance – Kaub – Gutenfels and the English knight

O Rheinfels! How sad the story of your young daughter of the house who fell in love with George Brömser of Rüdesheim, but who was half-promised by her father to the wealthier if scoundrelish knight of Berg. With determination the girl announced her engagement to her beloved George and the date of the wedding was already fixed for only a short time ahead when the Emperor Albrecht summoned all good men and true to help him bring to heel the Swiss confederates, who had just broken away into a neutrality which in fact they were to keep for ever. Brömser, being indeed both good and true, obeyed the call to the colours. Not so the nasty knight of Berg.

George dug a hole in the Rheinfels garden with his sword and planted in it a lime sapling, telling his beloved that if it flourished he was safe, but if it wilted he was dead. Then he went off to fight the Swiss peasants, who trounced their attackers at the battle of Morgarten and littered the field with the corpses of Rhineland nobility.

As the months passed and a few mutilated knights came trailing home there was still no news of Brömser. However, the lime tree was healthy and in full leaf, so the young girl did not entirely give up hope. This was infuriating for Berg, so after searching the woods for a decayed lime tree of suitable size he one night crept into the garden, flung the original sapling over the cliff and put the wilted one in its place.

Next morning when the girl looked out of her window she uttered a piercing shriek. Then she wept for weeks on end, and it was only at the end of that interval that Berg could approach her and ask for her hand. She replied that she would be as faithful in death as in life, but certainly not to him; whereupon he impetuously drew his sword and rushed upon her.

Like most men who murder in a moment of fury he immediately wished that he had not done the deed, but there was no bringing the girl back to life. So Berg went off and hanged himself, and when at last poor George came limping back to Rheinfels he was met with a sorry tale of tragedy. He pulled out the dead lime tree and planted a bed of white lilies over the grave of his dearest love. He never married, nor did he take refuge, like most disappointed men, in a monastery. He became a minstrel and spent the rest of his life touring the castles of others, striking up the songs of his own composing which told of chivalry, and undying love, and of a great sorrow.

Castle Rheinfels was erected by the counts of Katzenelnbogen as a formidable strongpoint to protect the entirely unauthorised toll-collecting which they operated in the river below. It was one of the worst of these levies, and so the League of Rhine Towns decided that it must be reduced. In 1255 the twenty-six members contributed a total force of eight thousand foot soldiers, and under the protection of a thousand horsemen and fifty armed barges the battle was begun. For sixty-six weeks they invested the place and on no less than forty separate occasions they attempted to take it by storm, but Rheinfels held out until at last the forces of the League had to withdraw 'amid the derision of the defenders'. The toll still survived, and I presume the dues for the ships of the League cities were suitably increased.

As for the line of Cat's Elbow, it came to an end in the fifteenth century with the death of Count Philip at the age of seventy-seven. His life seemed dogged by misfortune, for his son and heir was stabbed in an affray at Bruges when only twenty-seven, and as the father had already separated himself from his insufferable wife he could not beget another lawful heir during her lifetime. She lived to a good age, but shortly after her death Philip, who was already seventy-one, married again – 'to please the people', as he so nicely put it. However, his relations saw in the possible fertility of his new wife a real threat to their inheritance, so they paid the old count's chaplain one thousand gulden in cash to get rid of him by giving him poison in the chalice when he next went to mass. Unfortunately the wary old man noticed the smell or taste and declined the sacrament. Instead he had his chaplain burned alive – but after all these excitements either he or his new spouse Anna of Nassau-Dillenburg was sterile and no heir was born.

Having withstood the League, Rheinfels again held out against a massive onslaught by the French forces of Louis XIV, who lost four thousand men in two weeks whilst trying to force the surrender. In the end it was captured in the most ignominious fashion, for the successors to the Cat's Elbow had become careless in keeping up the fortifications and mounting a proper guard. One night in 1758 the commandant gave a splendid ball for all the neighbourhood, and this gave the Marquis de Castries his opportunity to overpower the guard and lead a small force of French soldiers into the ballroom, where all the officers were quickly relieved of their swords. The gallant marquis requested the orchestra not to be dismayed but to continue with their repertoire, and the French – full of courtesy as was their wont on such occasions – invited the ladies to dance with them. In this pleasant way Rheinfels was taken, and during the Revolution it was blown up.

The town of St Goar is a pleasant little place of no great distinction, but it is at least unusual in that if almost every other army tried to sack it the Swedes left it undamaged. Or very nearly so, for when Gustavus Adolphus entered the protestant church and saw the damage done to it by the Spaniards he brought his mailed fist down with such a thump upon the corner of the altar that he broke it right off and it had to be repaired with iron cramps. As for St Goar himself, some historians have doubted his existence and have suggested that he is just a corruption of *Sand Gewer*, meaning the dangerous swirl by the sandbank at the upper edge of the town, but how they would then account for the early medieval biography of the man himself I am not certain. Personally I like to think he existed.

If so, then St Goar himself seems to have been a cheerful and practical monk from Aquitaine who wandered across the land of the Treveri, the people around Trier on the Moselle, and eventually reached the Rhine at the point where it broadens slightly after its constriction at the whirlpool beneath the Lorelei. At this point a trackway crossed the river by ferry, and on either bank there was a small settlement of fishers and ferrymen. Obviously this was a good place to settle as a missionary, and Goar constructed a cell on the hillside above the river and settled down. The remains of what is alleged to be the site are still there in the form of a niche known as St Goar's Bed – another difficulty if one thinks he was only a swirl in the river.

It is believed that Goar made a study of the river and took upon himself the job of Rhine pilot for the heavily laden rafts and rowed cargo-boats which swept down the stream – a very practical piece of Christianity. Certainly Goar became beloved of the local people, and after his death his fame lingered on to such an extent that Charlemagne himself would not pass through the gorge without calling at St Goar. On one occasion, however, he was in so great a hurry to voyage down toward Cologne that he decided to sail past Goar's cell without paying his usual courtesy call. As one might expect, the dead saint disapproved of such a slight and showed his displeasure by dropping a thick fog bank into the gorge immediately below the village.

The emperor's men cast anchor, but even then they had to row all day to prevent the ship dragging and being cast on a reef. At last in the evening the fog began to clear and Charlemagne had his men row over to the shore so that he could spend the night in the open, declaring his resolve never again to attempt to run past without paying his proper respects. And just to confirm his intent he made an endowment of money to St Goar's own foundation.

There is a typically medieval tale about how Bishop Rusticus of Trier heard of the hospitality which Goar gave to travellers, and himself not being a very generous man he sent two underlings to see just what went on in the cell beside the Rhine. When they arrived they found Goar taking a round meal with a party of travellers, and having denounced him as a gluttonous man and a wine-bibber they ordered him to accompany them immediately to Trier and appear before the bishop.

Rusticus asked him peremptorily what he meant by feasting

instead of fasting, and Goar mildly replied that it would hardly be Christian to turn away pilgrims from his table, and downright churlish to provide them with a meal but himself abstain as though there were something wrong about the whole business of eating and drinking.

Incensed, the Bishop of Trier was just about to have Goar shown out when the door opened and a party of local men came in who had discovered when out hunting a new-born baby abandoned to die. This gave Rusticus his chance.

'Ha!' he exclaimed. 'Now we'll see what this so-called Holy Man of the Rhine can do. You there, you who are so clever at knowing divine mysteries, whose child is this miserable brat?'

Goar was silent for a moment. Then he looked straight at the prelate. 'The mother's name is Flavia,' he pronounced. 'The father's, Rusticus.'

Or, according to the monk Wandalbert, the child (which had been discovered abandoned in the church) itself interrupted and answered the bishop's question. Though not yet three days old it announced in a clear voice that Rusticus was its father, Afflaia (or Flavia) its mother. At which great wonder the bishop flung himself grovelling upon the floor before Goar.

The result of this incident was that the hermit Goar was very speedily removed from the episcopal palace. But too many people had heard, and soon the news reached King Sigbert, who removed Rusticus from his seat and offered it to Goar. But the hermit refused, preferring to remain at his task on the shore of the Rhine.

A short way above the ferry which connects St Goar with St Goarshausen the river bends sharply to the right before the Lorelei, and there opposite the whirlpool and right by the sand from which St Goar did not take his name a little cabin is set on the roadside, with flagpoles projecting over the stream. This is one of the Rhine signal-stations, and between here and the Mouse Tower at Bingen there are several others. They are there because the bends in the stream are so sharp that up-bound traffic cannot otherwise guess what may be sweeping round the corner toward it, and though the *Thames Commodore* could dodge out of the way easily enough the captain of a tow-train may need to take action to

St Goar Signal Station

avoid a collision. Nowadays the signal-flags are being replaced by an elaborate system of flashing lights, but when I walked up to speak to the *Warschauer* in his cabin he was still busily attaching flags and running them in and out according to the traffic.

In former times it was the watchman's duty to pass on the signal to the next station by racing down the towpath on foot. Later he took to a cycle, but the same mechanical progress which brought faster ships to the Rhine also produced the telephone, so he was able to lead a less athletic existence and confine himself to visual signals for the ships.

When I knocked at the cabin door the watchman only opened it a few inches, just wide enough to ask me my business. He was obviously suspicious, probably because no stranger would be expected to call upon him at all. He still kept a foot behind the door until I had assured him that I was a skipper and just wanted to know all about his signals. Then he let me in, and little by little he unbent and explained the system.

A large red flag run out on the main staff announced that a single vessel was coming downstream, but a white flag indicated a tow. Red and white together meant a pusher-train, the lighters rigidly braced around the propelling vessel and forming a large mass for such a restricted channel. However, with so much shipping on the river it was impossible to signal every vessel, the watchman explained as he took up his glasses and studied the craft sweeping down from the Lorelei. One could only indicate the largest unit in the reach, and show where it was at the moment. That was the purpose of the smaller flags which he ran out below the others.

'The white one, that means she is now up at the Seven Sisters reef. The red will mean she is near the Goat's Back. And when she comes into view, then I run out the blue.'

'And the red blink-light you have just switched on?'

'That is to tell that there are other craft coming ahead of the one I am signalling – which of course is only the largest one in the reach, as I said.'

We sat and talked as the ships came by, sometimes two or three of them in a minute. The telephone rang frequently to bring messages of still more vessels approaching from beyond the Lorelei. All of them took the bend wide.

'You see, there is no water on this side. Look at that plastic bottle turning a slow circle here, just below. It will go round and round all day, perhaps for all the week. There is always the same eddy, and it deposits sand to make that large shoal that is almost awash. It is useless to dredge, for the current merely brings more sand to fill up the hole. Of course it's a good, safe place to bathe. At least, it used to be. Not so long ago there was a proper beach here with a fence and boom out in the river to prevent people getting caught in the main current and swept away. Yes, St Goar had a bathing instructor and all. Oh, it was pleasant enough, but nobody bathes here nowadays.'

'Why not?'

The watchman laughed. He ran out the blue flag below the red and white as a huge French pusher unit came into sight. 'Why not? Have you tasted the water?'

I had not, but I had smelt it all the way from Rotterdam. Yet there seemed to be fish right enough, I said.

'Ah yes. And the fish are very good, too. They have survived well on the whole, though not the salmon. You can eat them, provided you catch them in the flood-time. But not at low water as it is now. Then they taste of diesel oil, and grease, and tar. Lower down they smack of phenol too.'

In fact there is one particular fishery which survives commercially on the river and is responsible for the nostalgically beautiful fishing-vessels which hang in the stream in the most unexpected places, not only in the gorge but below Düsseldorf, above Bonn, and here and there along all the course of the German river. Usually a long net hangs idle from the top of the stout mast, but sometimes it is set out in the stream, slung from a boom. That is a sure sign that the eel run has begun, that the strange sinuous creatures are on their way down the Rhine on the freshwater part of a journey that will take them to their spawning grounds in the remotest depths of the Atlantic.

Forty feet across is the mouth of the funnel of netting, and the gear which can hold such a trap in the current must be stout and strong. Only on completely dark nights is the net put out, because the eels only travel either at that time or when the Rhine is in flood – a state of affairs which makes netting impossible because of the number of branches and tree trunks driving down the river to wreck the nets. The dark nights bring the eels in their hundreds, their writhing forms filling the trap at the end of the net and mingling with the other and less prized fish which swell the haul.

Eel-fishing is still a profitable occupation, but none can guess how long it will continue. Every year the chemical pollution increases, and a Rhine pike may already taste more of laboratories than of fish. Once, the French court was regularly supplied with salmon caught at Duisburg, of all unlikely places, but – as the watchman pointed out – it would be a brave salmon nowadays that attempted to risk its gills in the effluvia of the Ruhr. And sometimes there are major disasters, such as the one in 1969 when a comparatively small quantity of a chemical poured into the water poisoned all the fish down to Holland and the sea, causing irreparable damage to the ecology of the Rhine.

It is only six kilometres from St Goar to Oberwesel, but there are five signal-stations even in that distance, the next one being

Lorelei and eel Boats

opposite the Lorelei cliff. Here the passenger steamers of earlier
years would always stop in order to toot with the siren and fire
guns to awaken the echo, and when Rev. W. Phelps, AB, FSA,
author of *A Mirror of the Duchy of Nassau*, passed along the river in
1841 he noticed that in a small grotto on the right was stationed 'a
person with a gun and a French horn; who on the approach of a
steamer first fires his piece, and then sounds his bugle to show the

effect of the echo. In some particular states of the atmosphere the sound has been repeated ten times.' In fact there is still a professional echo-tooter at St Goar, and such a post is yet another of the curious jobs I have noticed along rivers which would prove a genial if perhaps rather repetitive occupation during retirement.

Ich weiss nicht was soll es bedeuten – there can be no German legend better known abroad and in Germany itself than the tale of the siren girl who sits high on the cliff and lures incautious bargemen to their doom. As the big white ships of the Köln–Düsseldorfer line steam round the bend the familiar song rings out from their loudspeakers, the words of Heine echoing over the reach. Yet curiously enough the story, although it may well have its roots far back in pagan times, is in its present form not very old at all. Clemens Brentano first wrote a poem on the Lorelei in 1802. Heine followed. The lovely lady was soon established as a Venusberg model, and yet she was not much more than the deliberate invention of a couple of poets. At least, that is what Baring-Gould had to say of the matter, but I am not so sure that he was right. As we came forging up the reach to swing on the water of the whirlpool I looked up, and four hundred feet above us was the figure of a girl in a bikini. That I saw the bikini shows that I was sufficiently lured to take a quick glance through the ship's binoculars.

She was slim and had long hair which might have passed for golden. She was not combing it, but then endless combing is not good for the hair. I waved, and so did the crew, and the girl waved back. Then I kept my eyes fixed very firmly indeed upon the swirling water, for I knew the danger. *Er schaut nicht die Felsenriffe, er schaut nur hinauf in die Höh.* Yes, he had disregarded the reef and only looked up to the heights above, and that was the end of barge and bargemaster. A good thing we had had to learn the poem by heart at Rugby, I thought. Otherwise Lore might have had another victim.

In fact the real lure of Lore was supposed to lie not in her blonde hair but in her eyes, a sure sign that she was one of those naughty spirits which inhabit the German countryside. With a glance she could bewitch men, and for this offence she was sentenced to be confined in a convent. Such a fate was so distasteful to the poor girl, who much preferred bargees to nuns, that she hurled herself from the cliff top (where the Rhine happens to be twenty fathoms deep), and it is of course from there that she emerges as a spirit, bikini and all.

Thick and fast come the sights of the Rhine above St Goar, and not only the sights but the rocks and reefs also. The last time I passed that way a fleet of work-boats was anchored in the river and steam chisels were attacking such famous dangers as the Goat's Back and the Seven Sisters. I am old-fashioned enough to regret that the ever larger ships of the Common Market trading make such sacrilege necessary, and I do not like to think that I shall have to tell my growing grandchildren that over there, some way out from the bank, there used to be seven rocks, and that they were originally seven beautiful but haughty maidens. If they disbelieve me it will be the fault of the Rhine Navigation authority.

However, it seems that there were indeed seven sisters of great beauty who lived at Oberwesel, and between them they amassed a very considerable number of gallant and noble suitors. Many girls would have been pleased at such an achievement, and for all I know the Oberwesel sisters were flattered by these attentions, yet every one of them rejected the advances of their admirers. A good time with plenty of parties and troubadours sent to sing songs of eternal devotion to them – why, certainly. But anything as serious and binding as becoming tied for life to one man was not on the programme as far as they were concerned, and they said so.

Gradually the eligible young men of the Rhineland grew impatient. They were not to be held for ever on the strings of these hard-hearted girls. At one of the parties given in honour of the sisters they became very insistent, and nothing would satisfy them but a solemn assurance given by the girls that on the very next morning they would collectively and severally announce whom each one would choose.

Next day the gallants reassembled at Oberwesel. The seven noble maidens were there as they had promised. The girls climbed aboard a Rhineship which happened to be lying near the bank, and from its hatches they delivered their judgement. There was not one of them, they said, who would demean herself so far as to select a husband from such a brainless, swaggering, misshapen, unattractive, detestable and ill-bred collection. Rather than be touched by any of them they would leave home and seek their fortune among the better choice that must surely exist elsewhere.

With that, they cast off the anchor and let the ship drift out from the shore. Unfortunately, she was only half turned round when a sudden squall whipped up the waves just as it can do today, and the boat was overset. I doubt if any of the young lordlings standing on the shore considered diving in to save them. Frigid and virginal to the end, the seven heartless maidens were turned to stone where they were drowned, and in their day they have broken as many backs of ships as hearts of Rhineland knights.

The *Thames Commodore* was just passing the virgins when a black cloud dropped into the gorge, burst open, and released such a torrent of thunderous rain and hail that the signal lights on Oberwesel's Ochsenturm vanished from sight. But she plugged ahead, keeping her distance from the shore, and after a few minutes more she was sliding past the dredger which was scooping the mud from the entrance to Oberwesel harbour, the best port in all the gorge because it has a proper quay wall and is right in the town itself.

Undoubtedly Oberwesel is one of the most impressive sights of the Rhine gorge. Fourteen towers can still be counted along its line of walls whilst the Schönburg looks down upon the whole from its rocky shoulder as though to make certain that Castle Gutenfels on the further shore is not up to any mischief. Inside the town the cathedral stands up fearlessly, and so does the Wernerkirche.

If I here recount the story of young Werner the orphan, that is because he began his short working life as an apprentice glass-blower. Glassmakers and glass-sellers are usually among the most pleasant of men, but it seems that the master glassman for whom Werner worked in a glasshouse near Bacharach was an exception. He maltreated the boy so ferociously that Werner fled to Oberwesel, where he found a job in service with a 'Jewish merchant'. He was then fourteen years old.

Now, before we go any further we should look back in history and recall that St Hugh of Lincoln was supposed to have been murdered by Jews, that at the time of the Black Death the Jews were charged with poisoning the wells and were burned alive even in such enlightened cities as Strasbourg. Later along the time base of history there was Adolf Hitler. For one reason or another the Jews have always been a favourite target for blame, and so we should not be too surprised that when Werner came to a sad and violent end his death was laid at the door of the Jews. And with that we can take up the tale again and repeat the once popular but unfounded story that when at the time of the Jewish passover the good little Christian Werner had dutifully gone to church in Oberwesel and had taken part in the Communion, he was promptly seized by a band of Jews, hung up by his heels in a cellar and belaboured so that he would vomit up the hated wafer.

It would be hard to invent a more rousing anti-Semitic story, yet even the inverted hanging was not enough. The boy did not eject the Communion wafer, so the Jews gagged him and then slit open his veins. Unfortunately, the story says, they were seen at their wicked work by the other servant, a maid who happened to be spying through the hinge of the cellar door, and she ran to the magistrate. But when this dignitary arrived the Jews quickly fixed him with a handsome bribe and he told Werner – who by this time should long have been dead – that he was extremely sorry about it but he could not really interfere.

'Whereupon Werner commended himself to God, and upon the third day he died, his blood having all issued forth.' The wicked Jews were alarmed – though it is difficult to imagine that they could really have expected anything else to happen – and as they wished to conceal the murder they took a boat and rowed the corpse by night up the river until they came near to Bacharach, where they carried the body ashore and flung it into a bramble thicket. Then they departed.

But, wonder of wonders, around the thicket there now appeared a strange luminous glow which so startled Bacharach's night-watchman that he went to investigate. It was not every day that a murdered boy was surrounded by a mysterious light, so with proper ceremony Werner was buried in the chapel on the hill above the town. The news spread to Oberwesel, the serving girl hurried to Bacharach and revealed how she had seen the boy hanged and how the Oberwesel magistrate had had his mouth shut with a suitable gift of money.

In a second version of the tale the Jews threw the body in the Rhine and on the following day the captain of a passing barge was astonished to see an arm raised from the water to attract his attention. He pulled the body on board, and the hand then raised itself again and pointed to the shore, to which the man obediently rowed it. The corpse was placed in the church at Oberwesel and all the members of the Jewish community were led in to pass before it one by one. If the wounds oozed blood, this was a sure sign that the person in question had taken part in the murder, and he was seized. What became of him is not stated, but it is not difficult to guess. If by any chance he were a money-lender or merchant there would have been plenty who welcomed the opportunity to have their debts simply expunged. A third account says that the corpse, thrown in at Oberwesel, voyaged upstream to Bacharach under its own saintly power. The distance is only seven kilometres, so the voyage can hardly compare with that of Lubentius, but it would nevertheless have been a considerable achievement.

I have never been one for entering a cathedral with guide-book in hand, dutifully to observe the apses and pyxes, stoups and crypts, tabernacles and tympana and aumbries. For one thing, I am not quite sure which is which, but more than that I have an obstinate objection to churches becoming artistic show-places. Curiously, I share this dislike with minor atheists – the major ones in Russia like not just to turn churches into curiosities but actually convert them into museums – although our reasons are rather different. The atheist cannot abide the thought that the soaring and unequalled beauty of romanesque and gothic or the exuberance of mid-European baroque such as Bavaria's Wieskirche were inspired by a belief which he thinks childish. I on the other hand would rather the guide-books concentrated on what the church has done, or is doing, than merely harp on the brilliant works of art within the once practical buildings put up for worship. Neverthe-less, I frequently stray into churches from curiosity, or to spend a

few minutes in quiet and very ordinary meditation, or to see in
what direction the interest of the local community is slanted, or
perhaps just because it is cooler inside. But what led me into
Oberwesel's not very notable cathedral was the sound of
singing.

Standing at the front of the nave was a group of two busloads of
what looked like Women's Institute and was in fact something very
similar, a Catholic Mothers' Club from some village tucked away
in the Westerwald. The women had their priest with them, and he
was standing on the chancel steps conducting with his hand. Apart
from myself there were no other visitors but this large and solid
group of women on a summer outing, and I had only just entered
when they came to the end of what I supposed must have been a
chorale of some sort. The priest raised his hand for the final note,
drew out the sound, then cut it off with a flourish. The singing
stopped, and sixty heads turned to look at me.

I hoped I was not intruding, and conscious of so many solid
stares I thought I should at least say something.

'That was nice. Very nice indeed.'

'You think so?' The priest smiled. 'We are not the Oberwesel
choir, you know.'

'No, but I still think it was well sung.'

'Good! Ladies, we shall sing it once again, for the benefit of our
audience. First and last verses. Ready?'

He raised his hand and away they went, the rather medieval
strain soaring up to the dimness of the gothic vaulting and echoing
back. At the end the women turned and inclined their heads ever
so slightly in my direction. I stood up and bowed as deep as I
could.

No voyage up the Rhine is complete without a visit to a vintner's,
and I discovered that there was indeed one vintner in Oberwesel
who occasionally allowed visitors to behold something of the
mysteries underground. Herr Daubenspeck only did so when
parties came by arrangement, but he added that we were in good
luck because a Dutch party was expected that same evening,
coming up the Rhine on their own ship, the *Arnhem*. If the *Arnhem*
was in the harbour by seven o'clock the visit would take place, and

he would be delighted to let the *Thames Commodore*'s crew come along with the Hollanders.

I had expected Herr Daubenspeck to treat us to a learned and somewhat agricultural lecture about Riesling and Sylvaner grapes, the various blights and pests, the effect of rainfall and sunshine, and the complex matter of maturing wine in casks or tanks made of different metals, but the vintner was by nature more of a poet and philosopher than a chemist. We sat on benches down either side of a long underground vault lit by a row of candles at each end, and as the yellow light flickered on the profiles of the audience it was as though some weird cult were to take place. And so it was, for soon Herr Daubenspeck had closed his eyes. He began to quote Goethe and Heine, Shakespeare, and indeed anyone who had spoken or written in the tenor of the Rhinelander's theme that wine is the medium of goodness and well-being, of relaxation and friendliness, indeed of all the higher virtues.

As each point was made the vintner focused it upon the quality of some particular vintage of his own production. Then his wife and daughter would silently advance from the end of the vault and fill us each a glass. To drink, certainly, but not like schoolchildren putting away pop. We had to taste the wine, to close our eyes and smell it, then take a sip and hold it right in the front of our mouths, drawing in the breath through our teeth so that the aroma was carried effectively – if a trifle noisily when thirty tasters were performing at the same time – to the taste buds around the tongue and the nerve-endings up at the back of the nasal passage. They were good wines, and they lost nothing from their surroundings. Goethe, Heine and the rest slipped overnight as easily from my memory as they had dropped from Herr Daubenspeck's lips, but the savour of the Oberweseler Bienenberg Spätlese remained.

Barely a mile above Oberwesel the ships sweep past Kaub and round the Pfalzgrafenstein, the massive toll station that stands like some great ship in the very middle of the river. So compact, so neat does it stand there with its direct gravity lavatory apertures hanging over the water that one would hardly suspect that within the eight-foot thick walls of this sturdy fort there used to be a

Pfalzgrafenstein

pleasant courtyard with trees. For although it was a toll station it was also something of a medieval maternity home, and it became so as a result of a particular Rhineland romance.

Agnes, daughter and only child of the Count Palatine, fell in love with Prince Henry of Brunswick, but unfortunately the romance enraged the Emperor Henry VI, who saw that thereby the Palatinate would become Brunswick territory instead of being a dependency of his own. Agnes's father so feared the wrath of the emperor that he decided to stop the match by confining his own daughter in the mid-stream castle. He locked up her mother in the same place, and therein lay his error. When Henry of Brunswick arrived disguised as a pilgrim and rowed out to the Pfalzgrafenstein to beg a night's lodging, Agnes had the full support of her mother in the romantic events which followed. A priest was obtained, the wedding was conducted in private and after a proper time Henry departed.

After some months the Count Palatine was astonished to receive the news that out in her midstream prison Agnes was soon going to give birth to a child. I am happy to report that instead of beheading her or throwing her out of the window he was delighted that she

had found her true love. So too was the emperor. Romance had
turned away his wrath also, and the young couple received the
imperial blessing on their future happiness. In due time Agnes's
child was born, and ever afterwards it was the custom for the
wives of the electors to be rowed out before the onset of labour that
they also might have their babes delivered in the room which had
such romantic associations. Another and more practical explanation
of this curious custom is that the princesses of the Palatinate had to
be delivered in the midstream strongpoint to prevent the substi-
tution of spurious offspring of ignoble blood, who thus might take
over the sovereignty of the Palatinate itself.

Kaub itself was long defended by a stout fortified tower, which
still stands dark and forbidding, a little way back from the left
bank of the river. During the Thirty Years War it was besieged by
the invading forces not of villainous Swedes but in this case of
equally or even more villainous Spaniards. After the capture of the
town itself the strongpoint held out, and after weeks of siege it still
remained defiant. At last the troops were ordered to storm the
tower, but when scaling ladders were raised toward the loopholes
which provided the only entry every Spaniard rash enough to climb
the rungs was neatly picked off by a sniper's shot. Cannon would
have made short work of the tower, but the Spanish command
happened to have none available at Kaub, and so a truce was offered.

But the offer was ignored. The Spaniards tried again to storm
the place, and once again they retired leaving some of their men
dead below the walls. Withdrawing to a prudent distance they sat
down to wait. It was four weeks before a white flag fluttered from
an upper loophole-slit and a trumpet call announced that the
garrison would surrender. Then, after the door had been opened
and a ladder let down, the entire force of defenders came down.
First, lowered on a rope, was a goat, which had lived upon the
herbage on top of the tower and until this was finally exhausted had
provided the only sustenance of the fighting force, which consisted
of an elderly retired trooper and his wife.

At the sight of the tiny troop which had held them so long at bay
the Spanish soldiers at first felt injured – particularly as the people
of Kaub could not entirely disguise their amusement. But I am

glad to say that their commander stood by his word and gave the gallant defenders all the rights of an honourable and unmolested withdrawal.

Even now, some of the town wall of Kaub remains, its top carrying a path called the *Notgang* which once connected with a second and upper-floor front door of every house built against the inside of the defences. *Notgang* means Emergency Way; and that is precisely what it was – not to provide escape from the murderous French or Spaniards or Swedes but from the waters of old Father Rhine himself. Often when the ice broke up in the spring – for winters were colder in times gone by – the floes would jam in the narrows at the Lorelei and quickly form such a dam that the water would back up and flood through the houses of the little towns upstream. Over the banks and into the town the water would rise, but already the people had made their swift preparations. The cattle were driven to higher ground away from the river, the valuable barrels of wine were lashed or wedged in place in the cellars, the ground floors of the houses were cleared. The *Notgang* was then the only thoroughfare unless one went by boat.

When the ice dam at last collapsed, the water would race away toward Koblenz, leaving behind it driftwood and mud. It was a messy business that then confronted the householders as they began to shovel the slime from their parlours and bale out the cellars. But there must have been compensations, just as there were in the Fenland floods in England. I once went into a house near Hermitage Lock at Earith and noticed that for several feet from the floor the wall-paper had disappeared.

'The floods took it,' the woman said. 'And floods make a pile of mess. But it's not all that bad in some ways. The carp that got itself stuck behind the strings of the piano was the biggest I've seen all my days.'

It was at Kaub that the allied troops chose to cross the Rhine as the French retreated westwards in 1813. Other crossings were made at Mannheim and Lahnstein, but General York chose Kaub with its midstream fort as a suitable place for a third. The French were ranged along the opposite shore, so to cross the stream would have appeared a formidable and risky undertaking, but York hit upon

an ingenious ruse. He ordered all the village bands to play dance
music in the inns on Old Year's night, and as the sound of these
pleasant tunes drifted across the river the French soldiery retired
to the inns also to enjoy some *Wein* and maybe *Weib und Gesang*
also. Meanwhile, the shippers and fishermen of Kaub had been
busy preparing pontoons of wooden framework covered with
tarred cloth, and at two o'clock in the morning they began to ferry
the allied soldiers over the Rhine.

Almost opposite the Pfalzgrafenstein stands Castle Gutenfels,
one of the many strung out along the edge of the gorge. It has a
particular connection with England, and if we overlook a few
minor details of discrepancies of dates we can believe that at a
tournament in Cologne there appeared a beautiful girl whose
father was Dietrich of Falkenstein. Her name was Jutta. So lovely
was she to behold that one of the knights who had come to joust in
the lists bowed before her and asked that he might have one of her
dainty gloves to wear on his helmet, so that he could then tilt for
her, and her alone. Graciously the fair Jutta consented, and with
the piece of millinery on his helm the unknown knight charged
upon one adversary after another in the friendly fight of chivalry,
and knocked every one of them from their horses. Jutta congratulated him and asked his name, but this he declined to give. He
merely stated that he had pressing business elsewhere, but he
would see her before long. I am not sure whether he kept her glove
or gave it back, but as he was so chivalrous he must certainly have
done the right thing by the accepted standards of etiquette.

So the knight left Cologne. Sure enough, he soon afterwards
arrived at Kaub to call upon Jutta. She fell in love with him and
promised to marry him. Yet still the knight would not tell his name.
Perhaps she knew from his accent that he was a foreigner, but he
would tell her no more than that he was an Englishman, and that
he loved her deeply. He unfortunately had to go home to see to his
business affairs but she need have no worries. He would be back at
Kaub as quick as he could, and then they would get married. I
presume he had asked Jutta's father, for there seems to have been
no objection from that quarter.

When the suitor returned he was no longer incognito but the

newly chosen Emperor of the Holy Roman Empire, Richard of
Cornwall, the second son of King John. Richard was the only
Englishman ever to have been chosen by the German barons as a
candidate for this supreme position in Europe, and though in fact
he was elected he never managed to make the journey to Rome for
his coronation. So he remained uncrowned, a sort of emperor in
name rather than in fact, and his title of Richard of Almain
(Allemagne, that is) was almost the only glory he derived from the
appointment. But I am glad to say that he married the daughter of
Dietrich of Falkenstein and brought her back to Berkhamsted. Her
name, however, was Beatrix, and as he was sixty years old at the
time I suspect he was too old to enter the lists and emerge as victor
over all the tough young warriors of the Rhineland.

The name Gutenfels really meant Good Cliff, and the castle
became endowed with that name because its site made it so difficult
to take during the wars of religion. In fact, when it was occupied
by the Spaniards it was only captured with the help of a local girl
named Elslein, who disguised herself as a male servant and
volunteered to pilot the leader of the investing forces under the
Landgrave of Hesse through the reefs and rocks of the Wildes
Gefährt to where he could attack it from the flank. Later in
history it was not Goethe but Napoleon who stayed a night at
Castle Gutenfels. That was in 1802, and as a mark of his gratitude
he ordered it to be pulled down. Thereafter it was used as a stone
quarry until the final defeat of Napoleon, when such as was left of
it reverted to its owner.

Nevertheless, the name of Gutenfels was sufficiently like that of
Dietrich's lovely daughter of a few centuries earlier for the two to
have become confused, and if the Kaubers still like to think it was
named after Jutta, what harm is there in that? Besides, if she won
the heart of Richard of Almain, that in itself is a reasonable
matter for local pride, and almost demands that the *Thames
Commodore* dip her flag in salute as she passes on her way up the
river.

At this point, with Castle Gutenfels on the port beam, our good
ship has come far up the river. The next number-board on the
bank is close by the Pfalzgrafenstein, and even without his glass

her captain can make out the number 546, this being the distance in kilometres from the town bridge in Konstanz, where the Rhine races out of that immense lake which laps the shores of three countries. Not that the course is navigable right up to the figure o. The Rhine fall at Schaffhausen is only one of the barriers which keeps the upper reaches for the fish and the birds, the anglers, and the few enterprising young people who come to camp beside the swift and clean grey water. In fact Rhineships can push up the stream to Km. 149, but there at the shallows by the old bridge of Rheinfelden their voyage must end.

The *Thames Commodore* is going to make Rheinfelden too, but not in this volume. At Rotterdam she noted in her log the number 1,002. Passing Osterspai, just upstream of Rhens, she was only half way up the navigable course. Many days of summer sun and even of winter snow lay ahead of her before she would finish her voyage up Europe's most splendid river. There would be ancient cities to explore with curious waterways to thread, and quiet harbours hidden away from all but the shipmen of the river. She would sail past the foothills of Alsace with their proud and ruined castles, and skirt the hauntingly beautiful hills of the Black Forest before the shallows at last brought her to a halt.

All up the river there would be so much to experience, to discover, to love and to set down in her journal, that she could fill another volume with her journeyings from Oberwesel harbour to the riverside villages far ahead in Switzerland. And that is why she is closing the first volume of her Rhine voyage with Oberwesel still in sight astern as she puts out her blue flag to starboard to tell the fat Swiss barges that for a while she is going to hug the bank to port on her way up the river toward their own country.

INDEX OF NAMES

(For ease of reference people and legendary creatures or beings are printed in italics.)

Aachen, 51, 64
Adenauer, Konrad, 55
Agnes, 198, 199
Agrippina, 119
Ahl, 106, 121
Ahr, River, 56, 84
Albert of Coburg-Gotha, 57
Albrecht, Emperor, 182
Alken, 120
Amsterdam, 34
Andernach, 71, 88–90
Anna of Cleves, 16–17
Annecke, 57
Anno, Archbishop, 49–50
Antwerp, 28
Apollinaris, 83–4
Ardennes, 43
Arnhem, 8, 34
Arnstein, 128 ,135–6
Arnstein Fathers, 136
Ascham, Roger, 43, 45
Attila the Hun, 46
Aymon, 43, 73,

Bacharach, 85, 171, 193, 194, 195
Bad Ems, 102,103 ,107–14, 115–22, 143
Bad Godesberg, 55–7, 60, 69
Bad Neuenahr, 84
Bad Salzig, 177
Balduin, Archbishop, 144
Balduinstein, 139, 144, 145
Bank, 177, 178
Barbara, Lake, 31
Barbarossa, Emperor, 45, 127
Baring-Gould, Sabine, 50, 88, 191
Batavia, 8
Bayard, 43
Beatrix, 13–14, 16
Beatrix of Falkenstein, 202
Beethoven, Ludwig van, 54, 57
Benedetti, Count Vincent, 119
Benedict VIII, Pope, 88
Benz, Carl, 69
Berg ,182, 183
Berlin, 28, 58
Bertha, Lake, 31
Bessemer, Sir Henry, 52
Bijlandsche Kanaal, 8

Bingen, 137, 170, 171, 177, 186
Bismarck, Otto von, 119
Black Forest, 69, 92, 203
Blücher, Gebhard von, 124,154
Bodensee, 2, 62
Bohnenfeld, 82
Bonn, 54, 57, 60, 62, 83, 189,
Boppard, 120, 171, 175, 176
Boppard, Konrad of, 175–6
Bornhofen, 176, 177
Brentano, Clemens, 191
Brewster, Elder, 3
Brienen, 10–12, 16, 18
Brohl, 86–7
Brömser, George, 182, 183
Browne, Edward, 179
Brunhilde, 23
Bullwer-Lytton, Edward, 4

Caligula, 119
Canal du Nord, *see* Erft Canal
Castle Mouse, 177
Castries, Marquis de, 184
Cat's Elbow, 169 ,183, 184
Chalampé bridge, 3
Chamberlain, Neville, 55
Chardin, Teilhard de, 64
Charlemagne, 43, 51, 64, 73, 123, 185
Charles II, 179
Charles V, 17
Charles the Bold, 40
Christine of Denmark, 17
Churchill, Sir Winston, 24
Clement V, Pope, 98
Clementia, 148–9
Cleves, *see* Kleve
Cologne, 29, 40–1, 43–54, 62, 71, 75, 84, 93, 102, 103, 152, 171, 173, 185, 201
Cologne, Ruprecht, Archbishop of, 40
Conan, 46
Cotta, 109
Cramberg, 138, 144
Cromwell, Thomas, 17

Darwin, Charles, 38, 47
Datteln, 25
Dausenau, 122–5, 137
Dehrn, 162–3

Delft, 3
Deutsches Eck, 91, 93, 162
Dietkirchen, 162, 163
Dietrich of Dehrn, 162–3
Dietrich of Falkenstein, 201, 202
Dietrich of Teisterbart, Count, 13
Diez, 106, 142, 146, 147, 148, 163, 164
Diez, Jutta, Countess of, 148
Diez, Sophie, Countess of, 163, 164
Dirstein convent, 147–9
Dordrecht, 4, 71, 171
Döring, Dr, 108
Dortmund, 44, 45
Dortmund-Ems Canal, 28
Drachenberg, 69, 71, 74
Drachenfels, 61, 63, 65–6, 67, 72, 73
Dückenward-Schneckenschanz ferry, 10
Duisburg, 25, 27–34, 37, 43, 177, 189
Dürer, Albrecht, 19, 171
Düssel brook, 36–7
Düsseldorf, 34, 35, 36–40, 41, 177, 189

Echternach, 20
Eckener, Dr Hugo, 159–60
Edward III, 75
Egelsbach, 157, 158
Eginhard, 123
Ehrenbreitstein, 90–1, 93
Ehrenfels, 171, 173
Eifel, 69
Elberfeld, 37, 57
Elisabeth, 100–1
Elsa, Widow, 13–15
Elslein, 202
Eltville, 171
Emmerich, 19–21, 22
Engelbert, Archbishop, 51
Erft Canal, 40, 65
Erpel, 82–3
Essen, 28

Fachingen, 145–6
Ferdinand II, Emperor, 60
Fernando, Don, 163
Flavia, 186
Forschegrund, Brother Petrus, 63, 64, 72
Fossa Eugenia, 28–9
Frankfurt, 41, 152, 174
Frederick William III, Emperor, 63, 126
Freiligrath, 75
Freyr, 11
Friedrich Ebert bridge, 35
Frundeberg, 164–7
Frundeberg, Gertraud, 166–7
Fuhlrott, J. C., 37

Gabelstein, 138, 139, 140, 141, 143
Geilnau, 144
Gel brook, 129
Gelderland, 28
Gelsenkirchen, 129, 137
Gerard, 43, 47
Gerlach of Limburg, 148
Germanicus, 119
Gertrud, Sister, 75–6
Giessen, 104, 161
Goethe, J. W. von, 12, 54, 84, 88, 96–7, 104, 124
Gorinchem, 5
Gottfried, 53
Gottfried, Abbot, 136
Graalsburg, 15
Grafenwerth, 61
Grotius, Hugo, 5–7
Gryn, Bürgomeister, 51
Guda of Arnstein, 135–6
Gustavus Adolphus, 184
Gutenfels, 193, 201, 202

Hamburg, 59
Hammerstein, 87–8
Hannoversch Münden, 55
Heine, Heinrich, 191
Heinrich III, Landgrave, 40–1
Heisterbach, 63, 64, 65, 72, 134
Helena, 22
Helyas, 13–15
Henry VI, Emperor, 198
Henry VIII, 17
Henry of Brunswick, Prince, 198
Hess, Rudolf, 58
Heuss, President, 126
Hildegund, 73, 74, 75,
Himmerode, 65
Hitler, Adolf, 55, 194
Hochstaden, Konrad von, 50–1
Holbein, Hans, 17
Hollar, Wenceslas, 60
Hollerich, 128
Honnef, 61, 82
Horsrik, 66–7
Hugo, Victor, 177
Humboldt, Alexander von, 55
Hunsrück forest, 164

Irlich, 70
Irmingard, 87–8
Isabella Clara Eugenia, 28, 29

John, King, 51, 202
Jülich, Captain Jonas, 51
Jutta, 201

Kaiserwerth, 35, 36, 40
Kalkofen, 137, 140

Kamp, 176
Kaschau, George, 154–5
Katherine of Aragon, 17
Katz, 177, 179, 180
Katzenelnbogen, 183
Kaub, 171, 197, 199, 200
Kinkel, Gottfried, 57–9
Kleve, 8–16
Knights Templar, 97–9, 176
Kobern, 161
Koblenz, 52, 69, 83, 90, 91, 93, 103,
    132, 162, 174, 175, 177, 200
Koch, 34
Königstuhl, 174, 175
Königswinter, 65, 67, 71, 73, 81
Königswinter, Wolfgang Müller von,
    103, 174
Konstantz, 203
Krefeld, 35
Kremer, Gerhard, 32–3
Kripp, 59
Kursaal, 120

Lahn, River, 93, 95–107, 115–32,
    136–55, 157–69, 172
Lahneck, 95, 97–101, 173
Lahngeist, 132–4
Lahnstein, 102, 103, 104, 200
Lahnteufel, 139–41
Langenau, 129–34, 135
Laurenburg, 137–8
Lek, 8
Leopold of Hohenzollern-Sigmaringen,
    Prince, 119
Leverkusen, 41–2
Leiden, 1, 2, 3
Leonardo, 165–7
Liebenstein, 176, 177
Liechtenstein, 2
Liège, 43
Limburg, 102, 121, 148, 149–56, 157,
    161, 163
Lind, Jenny, 120
Linz, 86, 88–9
Liszt, Franz, 76, 77, 120
Lobith, 16, 18, 19, 34, 42
Loevenstein, 6–7
Lohengrin, 13–15, 18
Lorelei, 179, 185, 186, 188, 190
Lorelei, 1, 191, 192
Louis XIV, 169, 184
Louis the Bavarian, 75
Ludwig II, 15
Ludwig of Arnstein, 135–6
Lyons, 178

Main, River, 34, 69, 145, 157
Maintz, 60, 98, 171, 173, 174
Maintz, Johann, Archbishop of, 96

Malberg, 115, 120
Mannheim, 103, 200
Marburg, 104, 124
Margarete, Lake, 31
Maria, 175–6
Maria Theresa, 56
Marie, 140
Marienburg, 176
Marioth, Frau, 130–1
Marksburg, 173
Martel, Charles, 87
Martinskapelle, 84
Maternus, 66
Max Franz, Elector, 56
Maximilian, Emperor, 19
Mecklenburg, 59
Megingoz, Duke, 52–3
Mehlem, 67
Mercator, see Kremer, Gebhard
Merwede, 4, 5
Meuse, River, 25, 28, 29, 40, 43, 170
Mimer, 23
Mönchen-Gladbach, 40
Montgomery, General, 24
Moselle, River, 22, 34, 65, 90, 93, 120,
    145, 161, 170, 184
Mouse Tower, 1, 170, 186
Mülheim, 33

Nachtingallental, 65, 72
Napoleon III, 119, 202
Napoleon Bonaparte, 29, 40, 54, 65,
    124, 126, 136, 154, 202
Nassau, 103, 106, 125, 126, 127, 128,
    137, 143, 148
Nassau, Konrad Kurzbold, Duke of,
    151
Nassau-Dillenburg, Anna of, 184
Neander, Joachim, 36–7, 38, 39
Neanderthal, 37
Neckar, River, 34, 145
Neuschwanstein, 15
Neuss, 40
Neuwied, 60, 70, 90
Niederlahnstein, 93, 95, 97, 101, 102,
    104, 105, 111, 162, 164
Niederspai, 175
Niederwalluf, 109
Nieuwe Maas, 4, 5
Nievern, 102, 106, 107, 121
Nijmegen, 7–8, 13, 34
Nonnenwerth, 69, 73, 75, 76, 77, 78
Noord, 4, 5

Oberlahnstein, 95–7, 99, 101, 102,
    103, 139, 171, 172, 173
Obernhof, 136–7
Oberwesel, 189, 192, 193, 194, 195,
    196, 197, 203

Oberwinter, 60, 65, 69, 78, 81–2
Odenwald, 69, 158, 161
Offenbach, Jaques, 120
Oise, River, 45
Orange, 146
Osterspai, 175, 203
Otto III, Emperor, 53
Otto of Hammerstein, 87
Oude Rijn, 1, 2

Pestinsel, 149
Pfalzgrafenstein, 173, 197, 198, 201, 202
Philip, Count, 183
Philip of Spain, 28
Philip the Fair, 98
Pilgrim Fathers, 3–4
Pipin the Short, 35
Plittersdorf, 57, 59, 60
Priest, Degory, 3

Rastatt, 57–8
Rees, 22
Reichenstein, 171
Reinhard of Westerburg, 167
Remagen, 59, 69, 82–5, 86,
Reynaud, 43–5
Rheinauhafen, 49
Rheinberg, 29
Rheinbrohl, 86–7
Rheinfelden, 203
Rheinfels, 171, 173, 179, 182, 183, 184
Rhein-Herne Canal, 28
Rhens, 96, 173, 174, 175, 203
Rhône, River, 170, 178
Richard of Almain, 51, 202
Richard of Cornwall, see Richard of Almain
Rijn, 1
Rinbold, 66–7
Robinson, John, 3
Roland, 73, 74, 75
Rolandsbogen, 72, 75
Rostock, 59
Rotterdam, 3, 4, 35, 69–70, 95, 103, 127, 181, 203
Rüdesheim, 182
Ruhr, 32, 33, 34, 52, 78, 132, 144, 189
Ruhr, River, 28, 31, 33
Ruhrort, 28, 31, 34
Ruland, Dr Wilhelm, 24, 66–7
Ruprecht, Emperor, 96
Rusticus, Bishop, 185–6

St Adelheid, 52–4
St Bernard of Clairvaux, 65, 72
St Bernard of Siena, 176
St Castor, 161
St Gereon's Church, 50

St Goar, 41, 171, 177, 178, 180, 184, 188, 189, 191, 192
St Goar, 184–6
St Goarhausen, 177, 186
St Goar's Bed, 185
St Gotthard, 2, 169
St Hugh of Lincoln, 194
St John Nepomuk, 107, 155
St John's Church, 93, 95
St Lubentius, 161–2, 195
St Martin, 84
St Nicholas of Myra, 161
St Peter, 66, 83
St Reinhold, see Reynaud
St Severin bridge, 49
St Ursula, 46
St Victor, 22, 23
Schaffhausen, 2, 203
Schaumburg, 139, 144
Scheidt, 137, 140, 142, 143, 144
Scheldt, River, 28, 40, 45
Schenkendorf, Max von, 92
Schloss Balmoral, 120
Schönburg, 193
Schumann, Robert, 1
Schuren, Gerd von, 13
Schurz, Karl, 57–9
Schwanenberg, 15, 16
Sebus, Johanna, 11–12, 16, 27
Siebengebirge, 23, 56, 61, 62–77
Siegburg, 50
Sieglinde, 23
Siegmund, 23
Siegfried, 23–4, 65
Sigbert, King, 186
Silberberg, 131, 132
Sinzig, 69
Skaw, the, 59
Smetana, Friedrich, 120
Spandau, 57, 58
Spay, 175
Speyer, 88, 171
Spinola, Marquis, 28–9
Spoy Canal, 8–16
Stein, Freiherr von und zu, 125–7
Sterrenberg, 176, 177
Stevenson, R. L., 45
Stinnes, Hugo, 33–4
Stinnes, Matthias, 33, 52, 60
Stolzenfels, 93, 95, 99, 164–7, 173, 174
Strasbourg, 84, 119, 170, 171, 194
Streicher, Julius, 85
Stuben, 65
Suitbert, 35–6

Taillefer, 73
Taunus, 69
Telramund, 13–14

Thyrsus, 22
Tiel, 7
Trier, 22, 66, 93, 164, 174, 184

Unkel, 57, 65, 69, 82, 140
Unkelstein, 82

Vallendar, 91
Venlo, 29
Victoria, Queen, 57
Vienna, 90
Viersen, 40
Villich convent, 53, 54
Virchow, Rudolf, 37
Vosges, 3

Waal, 4, 5, 8
Wagner, Richard, 1, 13, 76, 120
Waldecks, 145
Walsum, 26
Waldalbert, 186
Wardmann, Deichgraf Gerd, 26–7
Watt, James, 52
Weber, Carl von, 120
Weilburg, 102, 161

Weinähr, 131
Weissenmühle, 100
Wenceslas of Bohemia, 96
Werner, 193–4
Wernerkirche, 193
Wesel, 24–6, 29, 34
Weser, River, 55
Wesseling, 59
Westerwald, 89, 196
Wetzlar, 161
Wieskirche, 195
Wildes Gefährt, 202
Willem, Jan, 39
Willemstad, 93
William the Silent, 146–7
Willibrord, 19–20
Worms, 169, 170

Xanten, 22–4

York, General, 200

Zalt-bommel, 7
Zeeland, 28, 93